A Pastor's Biblical Formula
For Preaching The Word Of God

A Pastor's Biblical Formula For Preaching The Word Of God

✝

Book Of Powerful Sermons

Pastor Kenneth W. Rucker

iUniverse, Inc.
Bloomington

A Pastor's Biblical Formula For Preaching The Word Of God Book Of Powerful Sermons

iUniverse books may be ordered through booksellers or by contacting:

iUniverse
1663 Liberty Drive
Bloomington, IN 47403
www.iuniverse.com
1-800-Authors (1-800-288-4677)

ISBN: 978-1-4502-7140-0 (sc)
ISBN: 978-1-4502-7141-7 (ebk)

Printed in the United States of America

iUniverse rev. date: 01/03/2011

Dedicated to:

Pastor Thomas R. Walker, who first gave me the opportunity to memorize Biblical Scriptures and also preach the Word of God.

2 Timothy 4:2–5

Preach the Word; be prepared in season and out of season; correct, rebuke and encourage-with great patience and careful instruction. For the time will come when men will not put up with sound doctrine. Instead, to suit their own desires, they will gather around them a great number of teachers to say what their itching ears want them to hear. They will turn their ears away from the truth and turn aside to myths. But you, keep your head in all situations, endure hardship, do the work of an evangelist, discharge all the duties of your ministry.

Introduction

When my wife and I bought my son Kevin his first two-wheel bike, he was about six years old. The bicycle came with training wheels to teach him how to ride it. After Kevin had gotten used to riding the bike with training wheels, he no longer needed them. Kevin was then able to enjoy riding his bicycle without the training wheels. *A Pastor's Biblical Formula For Preaching The Word Of God* is designed the very same way. Many pastors, and ministers, and teachers, and lay leaders are always looking for ways to effectively present the Word of God to others. In this book, there is a biblical formula for preaching and also teaching the Word of God to others. It all has to do with how well you can memorize biblical Scripture. If you can memorize Scriptures, you can preach and teach the Word of God. We are told in 2 Timothy 4:2, "Preach the Word; be prepared in season and out of season; correct, rebuke and, encourage—with great patience and careful instruction." The question is, how are you going to preach the Word if you do not know how?

In this book, there are many Scriptures referenced, and you can learn how to memorize them. Wherever you see a Scripture citation (e.g., John 3:16–17) followed by the word "quote," this tells you where to find the Scripture you need to memorize. All throughout this book, the quoted Scriptures are used over and over again so that you can be familiar with and memorize the Scriptures. You will find that each sermon is introduced by a Sermon Message. Next you have the body of the sermon. Finally, you will see a Conclusion, which allows you to wrap up the sermon in each chapter.

If you write your sermons on a computer, you can use different colored text for different sections. For example, you can use dark red for your sermon titles. Keep all of your sermon titles the same color. Keep the body of your sermons the same color. You could use blue for narrating your sermons. Whenever you are commenting on the Scriptures of the Word of God, use a darker blue. Whenever you present a Scripture and the word "quote," you can use the color green. Red can be used for all of the Scriptures that you type out. Purple can be used for illustrations outside of your message. Brown can be used for illustrations that are centered around you and your family in your personal life.

So there you have it. *A Pastor's Biblical Formula For Preaching The Word Of God.* This book is designed the same way training wheels operate on a bicycle; you use it as long as you need it. Once you are done, you will be able to move on to the very next level of your destiny. This is just Volume 1.

Contents

1

Avoid All Distractions that Can Bring Temptation

1 Corinthians 10:13. No temptation has seized you except what is common to man. And God is faithful; he will not let you be tempted beyond what you can bear. But when you are tempted, he will also provide a way out so that you can stand up under it.

SERMON MESSAGE:

Right at the very beginning of Jesus' earthly ministry after His baptism, he was led into the wilderness, where he fasted forty days and forty nights. While Jesus was fasting in the wilderness, He was tempted by the devil. The Books of Matthew, Mark, and Luke recorded only three temptations that Jesus did not yield to. While Jesus was fasting in the wildness, we can assume that He was tempted off and on by the devil all throughout those forty days and forty nights during His wilderness experience. Jesus was not being tempted for His very own benefit. And the reason was, Jesus was God in the flesh.

John 1:14 quote: The Word became flesh and made his dwelling among us. We have seen his glory, the glory of the One and Only, who came from the Father, full of grace and truth.

When the Virgin Mary gave birth to Jesus, we are told in Matthew 1:23 quote: "The virgin will be with child and will give birth to a son, they will call him Immanuel-which means, "God with us."

There is enough evidence in the Word of God to actually prove that God existed in human form. And when you look at it, only God and God alone could have redeemed the human race. Jesus' wilderness experience would not be the only time that Jesus would deal with temptation without yielding. Jesus was tempted throughout His earthly ministry. After the Lord Jesus withstood the temptation that was directed at Him by the devil, the Scripture tells us in Luke 4:13, "When the devil had finished all this tempting, he left Him until an opportune time." There were many opportunities when the devil tried to get Jesus to sin. But Jesus would not give in to the tempter. Listen to what the Scripture says about Jesus in Hebrews 4:15: "For we do not have a High Priest who is unable to sympathize with our weakness, but we have one who has been tempted in every way just as we are—yet without sin." The only difference between Jesus and every human being, except for Adam and Eve, is that Jesus had no sinful nature. Jesus could have easily given into temptation, but He chose not to. And there was a very good reason why Jesus chose not to sin. The Lord Jesus Christ had made it a choice to do His Father's divine will.

This is why Jesus was able to say in John 5:19, quote: Jesus gave them this answer: "I tell you the truth, the Son can do nothing by himself; he can do only what he sees his father doing, because whatever the Father does the Son also does.

Church, the very reason why Jesus could not have sinned was because of where His focus and His aim were: pointed directly at doing His Father's divine will. Jesus knew the very reason why He had come to earth.

In Matthew 5:17, quote: "Do not think that I have come to abolish the Law or the Prophets; I have not come to abolish them but to fulfill them.

Jesus was the only one who could fulfill God's moral standards. Fulfilling God's moral standards had to do with keeping the moral law that was given through Moses, which we all know today as the Ten Commandments. This is what Jesus came to fulfill. And while fulfilling the law and the prophets, Jesus also laid down His life as a ransom for many.

John 8:34–36 quote: Jesus replied, "I tell you the truth, everyone who sins is a slave to sin. Now a slave has not permanent place in the family, but the son belongs to it forever. So if the Son sets you free, you will be free indeed.

Jesus came to set the captive free from the jaws of sin and death. If you are a believer in Christ today, the very reason why you have been saved is because Jesus set you free from the bondage of sin by laying down His life on the cross for you.

John 10:17–18 quote: The reason my Father loves me is that I lay down my life-only to take it up again. No one takes it from me, but I lay it down on my own accord. I have the authority to lay it down and authority to take it up again. This command I receive from my Father.

Church, if Jesus had sinned, could He have laid down His life for us? The answer is no. He couldn't have. All Jesus had to do was yield just one time, and one time only, to sin. Because that's all it takes: just one time.

James 2:10 quote: For whoever keeps the whole law and yet stumbles at just one point is guilty of breaking all of it.

This very same principle was also given to Adam and Eve. The very moment that they disobeyed God's one and only commandment, it opened up the very first door to disobedience. This is the reason why someone had to pay. The Lord Jesus Christ was that someone.

Romans 6:23 quote: For the wages of sin is death, but the gift of God is eternal life in Christ Jesus our Lord.

Just imagine what would have happened if every one of us had to pay for our very own sins. We would all be spending eternity in hell and in the lakes of fires. God knows that we cannot pay for all of our sins. This is why God gives us mercy. What is mercy? God not giving us what we deserve. But instead, God gives us His grace.

Ephesians 2:8–9 quote: For it is by grace you have been saved, through faith-and this is not from yourselves, it is a gift from God-not by works, so that no one can boast.

What is grace? God giving us what we do not deserve. Have there ever been times when you have blown it, and you just gave up and threw in the towel? Instead of someone just throwing you underneath the bus, they gave you another chance. Church, this is what God has done for us by giving us His unfailing grace. When it to comes down to grace, we have nothing to boast about before God. Grace is "God's Righteousness At Christ's Expense." Again, someone had to pay. The Lord Jesus Christ became that someone.

2 Corinthians 5:21 quote: God made him who had no sin to be sin for us, so that in him we might become the righteousness of God.

When God sees you, He sees the righteousness that has been placed inside of you. All of this is because of what the Lord Jesus Christ has done for us. Therefore, since we all have been declared as the righteousness of God, we now begin to live like God says we are. It starts out by the way we ought to live as believers in Christ.

Ephesians 5:15–17 quote: Be very careful, then, how you live-not as unwise but wise, making the most of every opportunity, because the days are evil. Therefore do not be foolish, but understand what the Lord's will is.

Church, the only way that we are going to know the Lord's will is by getting connected into the Word of God. The Word of God is going to connect us to the very will of God. So, how can we know the will of God? By getting ourselves into God's Word. As we begin to read the Word of God, it is going to allow us to mature in the Christian faith.

We are told in 1 Peter 2:2–3, quote: Like newborn babies, crave pure spiritual milk, so that by it you will grow up in your salvation, now that you have tasted that the Lord is good.

Whenever you taste the goodness of the Word of God, it allows you to grow up in your salvation. This is called spiritual growth. While you are maturing in the Christian faith, you will be *avoiding all distractions that can bring temptation.*

1 Corinthians 10:13 quote: No temptation has seized you except what is common to man. And God is faithful; he will not let you be tempted beyond what we can bear. But when tempted, he will also provide a way out so that you can stand up under it.

Whenever we discuss the subject of yielding to temptation, there are so many temptations that we encounter, which come in so many packages. For example, an unsaved person will always yield to temptation because he is operating out of his sinful nature, which represents his flesh.

Romans 8:8 quote: Those controlled by the sinful nature cannot please God.

The unsaved person doesn't have a choice, because it is his nature to continue to yield into temptation by sin. And the majority of the time, he is going to yield to it. The only way that an unsaved person can overcome temptation is to be born again.

John 3:1–3 quote: Now there was a man of the Pharisees named Nicodemus, a member of the Jewish ruling council. He came to Jesus at night and said, "Rabbi, we know you are a teacher who has come from God. For no one could perform the miraculous signs you are doing if God was not with him. In reply Jesus declared, "I tell you the truth, no one can see the kingdom of God unless he is born again.

Once the individual has accepted Jesus Christ as Lord, they will now have the opportunity to avoid yielding to temptation of all kinds. Before we were saved, it didn't really bother us whenever we yielded to temptation. This was because there were no convictions to convict us of sin. But now that we are saved, we are getting into the Word of God.

Philippians 4:8 quote: Finally, brothers, whatever is true, whatever is noble, whatever is right, whatever is pure, whatever is lovely, whatever admirable-if anything is excellent or praiseworthy-think about such things.

What is the opposite of what is right? What is wrong. As believers, our goal is to do what is right, and not what is wrong. We need to focus on thinking about doing the right things, and not the wrong things. How do we think on these things? Always look at what the outcome is going to be. You may get caught in doing what you have no business doing. You may bring shame upon yourself. You may place yourself in a very difficult situation, which will wind up exposing you.

In Galatians 6:7–8, quote: Do not be deceived: God cannot be mocked. A man reaps what he sows. The one who sows to please his sinful nature, from that nature will reap destruction; the one who sows to please the Spirit, from the Spirit will reap eternal life.

As believers in Christ, we need to be sowing seeds to please the Spirit. Because whenever we are sowing to do good, we are sowing seeds that will allow us to reap a spiritual harvest.

7

Galatians 6:9 quote: Let us not become weary in doing good, for at the proper time we will reap a harvest if we do not give up.

There are going to be times when you think that your breakthrough is long overdue, but instead of you remaining faithful and committed in the very things of God, you let your guard down. This is when the tempter steps in to get you to yield to temptation's sin.

1 Peter 5:8 quote: Be self-controlled and alert. Your enemy the devil prowls around like a roaring lion looking for someone to devour.

The devil wants to destroy your testimony. He wants to take advantage of you by any means necessary. There is a lot of work that you have done for the Kingdom of God. Stand firm and do not give up.

2 Corinthians 10:3–6 quote: For though we live in the world, we do not wage war as the world does. The weapons we fight with are not the weapons of the world. On the contrary, they have divine powers to demolish strongholds. We demolish arguments and every pretension that sets itself up against the knowledge of God, and we take captive every thought to make it obedient to Christ. And we will be ready to punish every act of disobedience, once your obedience is complete.

We have spiritual weapons that we need to fight with. These spiritual weapons are not to be abused or misused. In the world we live in, there are guns that are designed for our protection. If you use the gun to rob someone or a business establishment, then the weapon itself is being abused and misused. One of the weapons that we have is the sword of the Spirit. This weapon is known as the Word of God. With the Word of God placed in our lives, we will learn how to *avoid all distractions that can bring temptation.*

1 Corinthians 10:13 quote: No temptation has seized you except what is common to man. And God is faithful; he will not let you be tempted beyond what you can bear. But when you are tempted, he will also provide away out so that you can stand up under it.

Because we live in a sinful and wicked world, it is quite obvious we can expect to be tempted. Every one of us has a weakness. And this is where Satan attacks us the most. One moment you think you are doing real good. You say to yourself, *I'm going to beat this thing.* Then here it comes again, when you least expect it.

This is why we are told in Galatians 5:16–18 quote: So I say, live by the Spirit, and you will not gratify the desires of the sinful nature. For the sinful nature desires what is contrary to the Spirit, and the Spirit what is contrary to the sinful nature. They are in conflict with each other, so that you do not do what you want, but if you are led by the Spirit, you are not under law.

Church, the Spirit of God, which is the Holy Spirit, doesn't want you to give in to temptation, or the devil's schemes and tactics. This is when we must submit ourselves to God.

James 4:7 quote: Submit yourselves, then, to God. Resist the devil, and he will flee from you.

Church, your Heavenly Father is going to be the one who will give us an escape route.

For example, if you are dealing with sexual lust, we are told in 1 Corinthians 6:18–20, quote: Flee from sexual immorality. All other sins a man commits are outside his body, but he who sins sexually sins against his own body. Do you not know that your body is a temple of the Holy Spirit, who is in you, whom you have received from God? You are not your own; you were brought at a price. Therefore honor God with your body.

God's Word is telling you to run. You are not to sit there and entertain and fantasize what you are lusting after. God's people have to flee from sexual immorality of all kinds. When King David saw Bathsheba bathing, he should have taken off running. But instead, King David became obsessed with her, which led to adultery and having her husband Uriah killed. King David yielded to temptation.

Romans 15:4 quote: For everything that was written in the past was written to teach us, so that through endurance and the encouragement of the Scriptures we might have hope.

However, Potiphar's wife tried to seduce Joseph but from day to day, he refused her offer. But when Potiphar's wife couldn't take it any longer, she grabbed Joseph by his coat, and Joseph took off running, leaving behind his coat. Here's the point: When Joseph took off running; he did the right thing. And the Scripture says in Genesis 39:23: "because the Lord was with Joseph and gave him success in whatever he did." The same can be said about every believer, providing that they do the right thing. Listen to what the Lord God said to Cain, before Cain killed his brother Abel: Genesis 4:6-7: Then the Lord said to Cain, "Why are you angry? Why is your face downcast? If you do what is right, will you not be accepted? But if you do not do what is right, sin is crouching at your door; it desires to have you, but you must master it."

All Cain needed to do was to do what was right, then he would have been accepted by the Lord. But instead, through Cain's jealous anger, he went out and took his brother's life. Because of Cain's anger, he yielded to temptation. Your weakness may not be sexual lust, but it can be something else.

1 John 2:15–16 quote: Do not love the world or anything in the world. If anyone loves the world, the love of the Father is not in him. For everything in the world-the cravings of sinful man, the lust of the eyes and the boasting of what he has and does-comes not from the Father but from the world.

There are so many things that the people of this world lust after. Christians also lust after these things as well.

But the antidote is found in 1 John 2:17 quote: The world and its desires pass away, but the man who does the will of God lives forever.

As we focus on doing the will of God for our lives, we will *avoid all distractions that can bring temptation.*

1 Corinthians 10:13 quote: No temptation has seized you except what is common to man. And God is faithful; he will not let you be tempted beyond what you can bear. But when you are tempted, he will also provide a way out so that you can stand up under it.

There are so many distractions that we face from day to day. This is where our five senses come into play. They were not designed so that they can control us, but we have them so that we can control them. Our five senses are there for our benefit.

Apostle Paul was able to say in 1 Corinthians 9:26–27 quote: Therefore I do not run like a man running aimlessly; I do not fight like a man beating the air. No, I beat my body and make it my slave so after I preached to others, I myself will not be disqualified for the prize.

After an individual becomes converted to faith in Christ, they no longer can allow their sinful flesh to control them anymore.

This is why the Lord Jesus Christ said in Luke 9:23 quote: "If anyone would come after me, he must deny himself and take up his cross daily and follow me.

Church, this is something that we have to do every day until we are called home to glory. Our flesh is one of the enemies that we have to deal with.

This is why we are told in Galatians 5:19–21 quote: The acts of the sinful nature is obvious: sexual immorality, impurity, and debauchery; idolatry and witchcraft; hatred, discord, jealousy, fits of rage, selfish ambition, dissensions, factions and envy; drunkenness, orgies, and the like. I warn you, as I did before, that those who live like this will not inherit the kingdom of God.

If you are struggling, trying to get the Kingdom of God to work for you, then this might be the very reason why you have been unable to seek after it. You are practicing a sinful lifestyle that you need to get rid of.

1 Timothy 4:7 quote: Have nothing to do with godless myths and old wives' tales; rather, train yourselves to be godly.

To become a godly person doesn't just happen overnight. This is why we've got to train ourselves to be godly. It is very exciting to know that people everywhere are getting saved by accepting Jesus Christ as Savior and Lord. But as long as we remain on this earth, we must learn how to be godly.

Matthew 5:14–16 quote: "You are the light of the world. A city on a hill cannot be hidden. Neither do people light a lamp and put it under a bowl. Instead they put it on its stand, and it gives light to everyone in the house. In the same way, let your light shine before men, that they may see your good deeds and praise your Father in heaven.

If we constantly yield to temptation all the time, no one is going to see our goodness and praise our Father in heaven. If we deal with a habitual sin, then we need to bring it before the Lord. Let the Lord know that you are ashamed of what you have done by yielding to this type of temptation. Then confess it.

1 John 1:9 quote: If we confess our sins, he is faithful and just and will forgive us our sins and purify us from all unrighteousness.

Why do we need to confess our sins? Whenever we confess our sins, it keeps us under God's umbrella of protection. When Jesus gave the Lord's Prayer to His disciples, He designed the prayer to be a model prayer.

It says in Matthew 6:13 quote: And lead us not into temptation, but deliver us from the evil one.

Our Heavenly Father has given the believers in Christ a way out so that we can escape temptation's stronghold. As long as we are reading the Word of God, we can grow into spiritual maturity. And we will able to say, "I've been there, and I've done that." As we learn to overcome temptation, we can also help others to overcome temptation.

Hebrews 10:24 quote: And let us consider how we may spur one another on toward love and good deeds.

We must not yield to temptation's stronghold. When Apostle Paul came to the very end of his life, this is what Paul said in 2 Timothy 4:6–8 quote: For I am already being poured out like a drink offering, and the time has come from my departure. I have fought a good fight, I have finished the race, I have kept the faith. Now there is in store for me a crown of righteousness, which the Lord, the righteous Judge, will reward me on that day-and not only me, but also to all who have longed for his appearing.

Paul said he fought a good fight. Did Paul win every fight? No. Paul didn't say he won every fight. But Paul said, "I have fought a good fight, I have finished the race, I have kept the faith." In each of these areas, Paul never gave up or quit. Church, there are going to be times when you are going to be dealt some heavy blows in your Christian experience. You are going to get knocked down and beaten up. But when temptation comes knocking at your door, be ready to stand your ground by fighting the good fight of faith. Remember this: You are laboring in the Lord.

1 Corinthians 15:58 quote: Therefore, my dear brothers, stand firm. Let nothing move you. Always give yourselves fully to the work of the Lord, because you know that your labor in the Lord is not in vain.

CONCLUSION

Whenever temptation strikes, have a plan for resisting temptation. To flee temptation, (1) ask God in earnest prayer to help you stay away from people, places, and situations that may tempt you. (2) Memorize and meditate on Scriptures that combat your specific weaknesses. At the root of most temptation is a real need or desire that only God can fill, but we must trust His timing. (3) Find another believer with whom you can openly share your struggles, and call this person for help when temptation strikes. As you are doing this, you will *avoid all distractions that can bring temptation.*

1 Corinthians 10:13 quote: No temptation has seized you except what is common unto man. And God is faithful; he will not let you be tempted beyond what you can bear. But when you are tempted, he will provide a way out so that you can stand up under it.

My time is up, and I thank you for yours. Amen!

2

Be the Person that God Really Wants You To Be

Jeremiah 29:11. For I know the plans I have for you, "declare the Lord, "plans to prosper you and not to harm you, plans to give you hope and a future.

SERMON MESSAGE:

When our Heavenly Father created each and every one of us in His image and in His likeness, He didn't do this just because He was just doing it. God created us for a purpose and a reason. Seeing that we are living in the Grace Period, instead the Period of Law, the purpose that God created each of us for first of all is to become Born Again.

John 3:3 quote: In reply Jesus declared, "I tell you the truth, no one can enter the kingdom of God unless he is born again.

Why do we have to be Born Again if we are already born? In the Grace Period, every one of us is born spiritually dead. We have all inherited Adam's sinful nature because of the fall. But right at the very moment when an individual receives the Lord Jesus Christ as Savior Lord, their dead spirit comes to life.

2 Corinthians 5:17 quote: Therefore, if anyone is in Christ, he is a new creation; the old has gone, the new has come.

No longer are we to allow our flesh to control us. Once we are in Christ, we have the opportunity to take control over our sinful nature and its desires. This doesn't happen automatically. As believers we have to be taught how to accomplish this task. We have to be trained in the very things of God. We start out by getting into the Word of God.

This is why we are told in 2 Timothy 3:16–17 quote: All Scripture is God-breathed and is useful for teaching, rebuking, correcting and training in righteousness, so that the man of God may be thoroughly equipped for every good work.

All of the ingredients that are mentioned in these verses of Scriptures are designed to help train us in the area of living a life of righteousness.

2 Timothy 2:15 quote: Do your best to present yourself to God as one approved, a workman who does not need to be ashamed and who correctly handles the word of truth.

Notice where all of this biblical information is coming from? It's not coming in from second-hand information or hearsay. Or something that someone has made up. Or something that is not based on fact. Or something that has to do with a fantasy, that isn't real. But the training in righteousness is coming from the Word of God. Again, the Word of God is like no other book.

We are told in Hebrews 4:12–13 quote: For the word of God is living and active. Sharper than any double-edged sword, it penetrates even to dividing soul and spirit, joints and marrow; it judges the thoughts and attitudes of the heart. Nothing in all creation is hidden from God's sight. Everything is uncovered and laid bare before the eyes of him to whom we must give account.

Whenever we read God's Holy Word, it's going to touch each of us in a different way; reading exactly what God's Word says to our hearts has a different impact on each of us." God's Word is going to touch you much differently than it will touch me.

For example, Jesus tells us in Matthew 6:32–33 quote: For the pagans run after all these things, and your heavenly Father knows that you need them. But seek first his kingdom and his righteousness, and all these things will be given to you as well.

Jesus doesn't tell us to seek first the Kingdom of God without showing us how to seek it. The people of this world are running after money, fame, success, power, materials, and recognition. Christians today are attending their local churches for all the wrong reasons. I attended a nice-size church after I became saved. I became a member. I committed to attending the services whenever I could because of my job (I worked swing shifts). And the thing that bothered me the most was, I was never used. Other members were being used, but they would only attend the services on Sundays. When I attended services on Mondays, Wednesday, and Fridays, I never saw the ones who were being used attending these services. This bothered me, so I left the church.

18

Hebrews 10:24–25 quote: And let us consider how we may spur one another on toward love and good deeds. Let us not give up meeting together, as some are in a habit of doing, but let us encourage one another-and all the more as you see the Day approaching.

If we are going to spur others on, shouldn't we give them something to do in the local church? This will encourage them to want to get involved in church attendance in the local church. You have to start somewhere.

Ephesians 2:10 quote: For we are God's workmanship, created in Christ Jesus to do good works, which God prepared for us in advance for us to do.

If you have accepted the Lord Jesus as your Savior, and you are very serious with your decision, then you can expect the Lord to use you. If your local church won't use you, then God will. When Jesse sent David to take food to his brothers when they were fighting the Philistine army, even though David's brothers assumed that David was just being nosey, the Lord was getting ready to use David for battle. And the reason why the Lord was getting ready to use David was because David was already trained for battle. This was why David was able to defeat Goliath the giant. This is why church attendance is so very important to every believer. We are believers in training.

As pastors in the local churches, we are told in 2 Timothy 4:2–4 quote: Preach the Word; be prepared in season and out of season; correct, rebuke and encourage-with great patience and careful instructions. For a time will come when men will not put with sound doctrine. Instead, to suit their own desires, they will gather around them a great number of teachers to say what their itching ears want to hear. They will turn their ears away from the truth and turn aside to myths.

You can really tell who the worldly Christians are. These are the ones who like to have their ears tickled. Every time you see them, they want to listen to feel-good sermons all the time. If you are a parent, and all you do is give your children sweets all the time, eventually they are going to get sick and wind up dying. The same is true if all you do is give your children everything that they want; you are spoiling them. They are going to wind up in prison or dead. Living the Christian life is the same way. Church folks need to hear what they do not want to hear. This is going to allow them to have the opportunity to change. If you say something that is offensive to people, they look for ways to retaliate in order to look good or keep from getting embarrassed.

1 Corinthians 10:23 quote: "Everything is permissible"- but not everything is beneficial. Everything is permissible"-but not everything is constructive.

What is in your best interest when you are attending your local church? Are you looking to be entertained? Then you are in the wrong place. Are you looking to be fed the Word of God in your life? Then this is where you need to be. As a pastor, I'm not here to give you what you want. But I'm here to give each and every one what they need. After the resurrection Jesus gave these instructions to Apostle Peter. Jesus told Peter to feed His sheep, and to feed His lambs. And Peter passed this same information on to the local shepherds in the local churches.

1 Peter 5:2–3 quote: Be shepherds of God's flock that is under your care, serving as overseers-not because you must, but because you are willing, as God wants you to be; not greedy for money, but eager to serve; not lording it over those entrusted to you, but being examples to the flock.

The very reason why we have pastors today is because these are the roles in which the Lord has placed us. The same is true with you as a believer. *Being the person that God really wants you to be.* Jeremiah 29:11 says, "For I know the plans I have for you, declares the Lord, plans to prosper you and not to harm you, plans to give you hope and a future." When the Lord mentions this prophesy to the Prophet Jeremiah, the Lord was speaking to the Jews who were in captivity, or went into exile, and their future descendants. But notice, now, every believer is connected to this verse of Scripture.

Galatians 3:29 quote: If you belong to Christ, then you are Abraham's seed, and heirs according to the promise.

Church, this passage of Scripture can be applied to you also. This is only if you belong to Christ. The point to knowing God's plan is getting into reading or listening to His Word. Because once you get into understanding what God's Word is for you, you are going to want to put it into practice for your life.

James 1:22–24 quote: Do not merely listen to the word, and so deceive yourselves. Do what it says. Anyone who listens to the word but do not do what it says is like a man who looks at his face in a mirror and after looking at himself, goes away and immediately forgets what he looks like.

21

It would amaze you how many preachers and teachers know the Word of God. But how many of them put the Word of God in practice? When Jesus was ministering to His disciples, He always told them what to look out for when it came down to the Pharisees and the teachers of the law.

Jesus told His disciples in Matthew 23:2–3 quote: "The teachers of the law and the Pharisees sit in Moses' seat. So you must obey them and do everything they tell you. But do not do what they do, for they do not practice what they preach.

The main point in practicing what we preach in the local church as pastors is so that we can pass this teaching along to you.

Philippians 4:9 quote: Whatever you have learned or received or heard from me, or seen in me-put it into practice. And the God of peace will be with you.

You can tell when a pastor is not doing what he is supposed to be doing: when it doesn't line up with the Word of God. To live the Christian life is going to cost you. It cost Jesus His life for us.

John 3:16–17 quote: For God so loved the world that he gave his one and only Son, that whoever believes in him shall not perish but have eternal life. For God did not send his Son into the world to condemn the world, but to saved the world through him.

Jesus had become our sin offering. John the Baptist understood this. This is why when he saw Jesus, he told his disciples: "Behold the Lamb of God who takes away the sins of the whole world." What does this mean?

2 Corinthians 5:21 quote: God made him who had no sin to be sin for us, so that in him we might become the righteousness of God.

Church, we are the righteousness of God. Whenever our Heavenly Father sees us, He sees the righteousness of Christ that has been placed in every one of us who have been saved. The next step is to live like God's Word says we should: *being the person that God really wants you to be.*

Romans 8:28 quote: And we know that in all things God works for the good of those who love him, who have been called according to his purpose.

This verse of Scripture is letting the believer know that God is working it out for us. You may not like what you are going through at this very moment. Some of you are going through storms and trials and crises. You are going to get through them.

James 1:2–4 quote: Consider it pure joy, my brothers, whenever you face trails of many kinds, because you know that the testing of your faith develops perseverance. Perseverance must finish its work so that you may be mature and complete, not lacking anything.

But once we get to the other side, our storms and trials will all be over. But until then, the Lord has plans to prosper you and not to harm you. The very reason why we have so many conflicts in our Christian upbringing is because we like to rebel.

James 4:1–3 quote: What causes fight and quarrels among you? Don't they come from the battle within you? You want something but don't get it. You kill and you covet, but you cannot have what you want. You quarrel and fight. You do not have, because you do not ask God. When you ask, you do not receive, because you ask with wrong motives, that you may spend what you get on your pleasures.

Others can have high respect for you, but you still can rebel against the Lord, while the Lord is working it all out for your good. Such was the case of Moses. Moses had taken matters in his own hands, when he took the life of an Egyptian soldier after Moses saw him beating an Israelite slave. When the word got back to the pharaoh as to what Moses did, Moses ran for his life. Moses was forty years old when this took place. Forty years later, Moses was eighty years old and a shepherd for his father-in-law's sheep. The Lord had got Moses' attention at the burning bush. All the time that Moses was attending Jethro's flock, the Lord was preparing Moses for the leadership position. The same is true with each one of us; as believers, our Heavenly Father is preparing us for a position. Remember what Jesus said to His disciples and what He says to us today. John 9:4 says, "As long as it is day, we must do the work of Him who sent me. Night time is coming, when no one can work. While I am in the world, I am the light of the world." Jesus has passed His light on to every believer. What are we supposed to be doing with this light?

Matthew 5:14–16 quote: You are the light of the world. A city on a hill that cannot be hidden. Neither do people light a lamp and put it under a bowl. Instead they put it on its stand, and it gives light to everyone in the house. In the same way, let your light shine before men, that they may see your good deeds and praise your Father in heaven.

The good work that we are to do is to bring glory to our Heavenly Father in everything that we do.

This is why we are told in Galatians 6:9 quote: Let us not become weary in doing good, for at the proper time we will reap a harvest if we do not give up.

Whenever we are doing good, we are investing in the Kingdom of God for our lives. All throughout the Scriptures, we will find that as long as we continue to do good, we will already be able to reap a harvest.

Philippians 1:6 quote: Being confident of this, that he who began a good work in you will carry it on to completion until the day of Christ Jesus.

The very day that you gave your life to Christ was the very moment that your Heavenly Father began a good work in you. And the Lord is not done with you yet. The Lord wants to change you right where you are. You must be willing to let the Lord change you Himself.

John 15:1–5 quote: I am the true vine, and my Father is the gardener. He cuts off every branch in me that bears no fruit, while every branch that does bear fruit he prunes so that it will be even more fruitful. You are already clean because of the word I have spoken to you. "Remain in me, and I will remain in you. No branch can bear fruit by itself; it must remain in the vine. Neither can you bear fruit unless you remain in me." I am the vine; you are the branches. If a man remains in me and I in him, he will bear much fruit; apart from me you can do nothing.

So many Christians are so busy doing their own thing that they have no time for God. When they begin to wonder why they are not being used, it is because they are out of the will of God for their lives. You cannot expect the Lord to use you when you have chosen to disobey Him. Such was the case with the call of Jonah.

The Lord wanted Jonah to go and preach to the city of Nineveh. It was because of the wickedness in that city that had come up before the Lord. But instead of obeying the Lord's command, Jonah ran from the Lord. But the Lord had to get Jonah's attention where he had to obey. When it comes down to the believer in Christ, the Lord will do whatever it is that He has to do get our attention. By any means necessary. *Being the person that God really wants you to be.*

Jeremiah 29:11 says, "For I know the plans I have for you, declares the Lord, plans to prosper you and not to harm you, plans to give you hope and a future." Our future is not just here on earth, but our future is also in heaven.

John 14:1–3 quote: "Do not let your heart be troubled. Trust in God; trust also in me. In my Father's house are many rooms; if it were not so, I would have told you, I am going there to prepare a place for you. And if I go and prepare a place for you, I will come back and take you to be with me that you also may be where I am."

We also know that in heaven there will also be rewards to be given out. The things that we do for Christ will be the only things that matter when we get to heaven.

2 Corinthians 5:10 quote: For we all must appear before the judgment seat of Christ, that each one may receive what is due him for the things done while in the body, whether good or bad.

As long as we stay committed to the very things of God, the Lord will always direct our pathways straight.

We are told in Proverbs 3:3–7 quote: Let love and faithfulness never leave you; bind them around your neck, write them on the tablet of your heart. Then you will win favor and a good name in the sight of God and man. Trust in the Lord with all of your heart and lean not on your own understanding; in all of your ways acknowledge him and he will make your paths straight. Do not be wise in your own eyes; fear the Lord and shun evil.

As long as the believers stay in the Word of God and continue to apply the Word of God to their everyday life, they can expect to prosper. Listen to what the Lord said to Joshua: Joshua 1:8 quote: Do not let this Book of the Law depart from your mouth; meditate on it day and night, so that you may be careful to do everything written in it. Then you will be prosperous and successful.

The same encouragement that the Lord gives to Joshua is also given to every believer today as well. If we truly want to know how we can learn how to live a godly life, then we have to get the Word of God inside of our hearts so that we can meditate on it every day. The Bible explains to us how to be saved, but it just doesn't stop there. The Lord left us on earth for a purpose and a reason: to help touch the lives of others with the Gospel of Jesus Christ.

John 15:16 quote: You did not choose me, but I chose you and appointed you to bear fruit-fruit that will last. Then the Father will give you whatever you ask in my name.

The very reason why the Israelites went into captivity was because they didn't keep most of the Lord's commands. The very reason why so many Christians are living defeated lives all of time is because they are not grounded in the very things of God.

John 10:10 quote: The thief comes only to steal and to kill and destroy; I have come that you may have life, and have it to the full.

The devil is a thief, and he doesn't want any of God's children to succeed. But if we as believers do what we are supposed to do, then we do not have to fall to the enemy's schemes.

In the story of the blessed man, we are told in Psalm 1:1–3 quote: Blessed is the man who does not walk in the counsel of the wicked or stand in the way of sinners or sit in the seat of mockers. But his delight is in the law of the Lord. And on his law he meditates day and night. He is like a tree planted by the streams of water, which yields its fruit in season and whose leaf does not wither. Whatever he does prospers.

The more that we get into the Word of God, the more we are going to enjoy it. This is what it means to delight ourselves in the Lord. Whenever we are desiring and enjoying Him, the Lord is going to desire us. It will allow us to remain connected to the true vine, which is the Lord Jesus Christ.

Ephesians 5:15–17 quote: Be very careful, then, how you live-not as unwise but as wise, making the most of every opportunity, because the days are evil. Therefore do not be foolish, but understand what the Lord's will is.

Beloved, our Heavenly Father wants us to know His will for our lives. If the Lord didn't want us to know His will, He would never have allowed it to be written down in His Word.

The Word of God is God's plan for our lives. This is why it is called the Bible: "Basic Instructions Before Leaving Earth." The spiritual guidelines to being exactly what God wants us to be are found in the Word of God.

Romans 12:1 quote: Therefore, I urge you, brothers, in view of God's mercy, to offer your bodies as living sacrifices, holy and pleasing unto to God-this is your spiritual act of worship.

Church, this is what God wants us to be. Living sacrifices, holy and pleasing to God. When others see it, God will also see it.

This is why Peter tells us in 1 Peter 2:12 quote: Live such good lives among the pagans that, though they accuse you of doing wrong, they may see your good deeds and glorify God on the day he visit us.

CONCLUSION

When you ask the younger generation exactly what they want to be when they grow up, you never hear them say they want to be anything negative: "I want to be a criminal when I grow up. I want to be a prostitute or a pimp when I grow up, or I want to be homosexual, I want to be a murderer, because I want to kill people." The very reason why you do not hear this among young people is because it is not in their nature to do these things. When God created the human race in His image, God created us with hope. And this hope has to do with *being the person that God really wants you to be.* Jeremiah 29:11 says, "For I know the plans that I have for you, declares the Lord, plans to prosper you and not to harm you, plans to give you hope and a future." As believers, we can choose to obey, or we can choose to disobey. The choice is ours.

Galatians 6:7–10 quote: Do not be deceived: God cannot be mocked. A man reaps what he sows. The one who sows to please his sinful nature, from that nature will reap destruction; the one who sows to please the Spirit, from that Spirit will reap eternal life. Let us not grow weary in doing good, for at the proper time we will reap a harvest if we do not give up. Therefore, as we have the opportunity, let us do good to all people, especially to those who belong to the family of believers.

Amen!

3

How to Receive Favor in the Sight of God and Man

Proverbs 3:1–10 My son, do not forget my teaching, but keep my commands in your heart, for they will prolong your life many years and bring you prosperity. Let love and faithfulness never leave you; bind them around your neck, write them on the tablet of your heart. Then you will win favor and a good name in the sight of God and man. Trust in the Lord with all your heart and lean not on your own understanding; in all your ways acknowledge him, and he will make your paths straight. Do not be wise in your own eyes; fear the Lord and shun evil. This will bring health to body and nourishment to your bones. Honor the Lord with your wealth, with the firstfruits of all your crops; then your barns will be filled to overflowing, and your vats will brim over with new wine.

SERMON MESSAGE:

Do the words *good luck* means anything to you? Whenever you see people gambling, one of the things that they like to do is carry around with them a good luck charm or some type of relic. These things are nothing within themselves. But when you look at it, people put their faith in just about anything. Everything, except God.

For this reason, we are told in 1 Timothy 6:6–10 quote: But godliness with contentment is great gain. For we brought nothing into the world, and we can take nothing out of it. But if we have food and clothing, we will content with that. "People who want to get rich fall into temptation and a trap and into many foolish harmful desires that plunge men into ruin and destruction." For the love of money is a root of all kinds of evil. Some people, eager for money, have wandered from the faith and pierced themselves with many griefs.

What does it mean that people have wandered from the faith? Christians has taken their eyes off of the Lord and have placed them on the things and the stuff of this world's system. One of the worst things that a Christian can do is take their focus off of the Lord and place it where it does not belong. Church, you have already been there, there's nothing out there for you.

1 John 2:15–17 quote: Do not love the world or anything in the world. If anyone loves the world, the love of the Father is not in him. For everything in the world –the cravings of sinful man, the lust of his eyes and the boasting of what he has and does-comes not from the Father but from the world. The world and its desires pass away, but the man who does the will of God lives forever.

As believers in Christ, we have an alternative to what this world's system has to offer. People today are looking for fame, fortune, power, recognition, and wealth. And yet, none of these things can satisfy.

Jesus said in John 10:10 quote: The thief comes only to steal and kill and destroy; I have come that they may have life, and have it to the full.

What is Satan doing to the people of this world today? The devil is known as a thief. He is giving the people of this world's system fifteen minutes of fame, fortune, power, recognition, and wealth. The devil wants to steal, kill, destroy, and take as many lost souls as he can to hell with him.

Matthew 6:32–33 quote: For the pagans run after all these things, and your heavenly Father knows that you need them. But seek first his kingdom and his righteousness, and all these things will be given to you as well.

Instead of seeking after the world's system, the believers in Christ need to seek first the Kingdom of God and His righteousness in their lives. Because for the unsaved, after it is all gone, it's gone. But on the other hand, Jesus wants them to have life more abundantly. In order for this to happen, the unsaved people of the world have to be saved. This is the very first step in seeking first the Kingdom of God.

John 3:1–3 quote: Now there was a man of the Pharisees named Nicodemus, a member of the Jewish ruling council. He came to Jesus at night and said, "Rabbi, we know you are a teacher who has come from God. For no one could perform the miraculous signs you are doing if God were not with him. In reply Jesus declared, "I tell you the truth, no one can see the kingdom of God unless he is born again.

This is why every believer need not to fall prey to the devil's tactics and schemes.

1 Peter 5:8 quote: Be self-controlled and alert. Your enemy the devil prowls around like a roaring lion looking for someone to devour.

If you are a Christian and you have not been trained in the Word of God when it comes down to being self-control and alert, the devil is going try to devour you. This is the reason why so many Christians today are living defeated lives, when they do not have to. There are so many distractions in our world today. They are there to take our focus off of the Lord Jesus Christ.

This is why we are told in Hebrews 12:1-2 quote: Therefore, since we are surrounded by such great clouds of witnesses, let us throw off everything that hinders and the sin that so easily entangles, and let us run with perseverance the race marked out for us. Let us fix our eyes on Jesus, the author and perfecter of our faith, who for the joy set before him endured the cross, scorning its shame, and sat down at the right hand of the throne of God.

If you know someone who is a godly person, who's been grounded in biblical Scriptures by the very life that they live, these are the ones you need to be connected with. Constantly living in sin can hinder and entangle us if we let it. The believer is told to throw off everything that hinders.

For example, we are told in 1 Corinthians 10:13 quote: No temptation has seized you except what is common to man. And God is faithful; he will not let you be tempted beyond what you can bear. But when you are tempted, he will also provide a way out so that you can stand up under it.

Church, God is not the one who is tempting us, but the devil is. But what the Lord is doing, is pointing to you the way out to escape, so that you do not have to give in to it. Temptation can come in so many packages. This is where we have to be alert as believers in Christ.

34

This is why we are told in Galatians 5:16–18 quote: So I say, live by the Spirit, and you will not gratify the desires of the sinful nature. For the sinful nature desires what is contrary to the Spirit, and the Spirit what is contrary to the sinful nature. They are in conflict with each other, so that you do not do what you want. But if you are led by the Spirit, you are not under law.

Notice who these Scriptures are directed to? These passages are directed to every believer who wants to live a godly life. We are given a choice to walk by the Spirit, which is the Spirit of God, who is the Holy Spirit. All believers have the Holy Spirit dwelling inside each of them.

Ephesians 1:13 quote: And you also were included in Christ when you heard the word of truth, the gospel of your salvation. Having believe, you were marked in him with a seal, the promised Holy Spirit.

Now if the Holy Spirit doesn't dwell inside of you, then it is no question; you need to be saved.

Because we are told in Romans 8:8 quote: Those controlled by the sinful nature cannot please God.

The very first step in pleasing God is that you have to be saved so that you can receive the promise of the Holy Spirit. Why is it so very important to receive the promise of the Holy Spirit? It is so that we can follow the Spirit's lead in our lives and become connected to Him. Whenever we follow the Spirit's lead in our lives, we take on the characteristics of the Holy Spirit, which is the fruit of the Spirit.

Galatians 5:22–23 quote: But the fruit of the Spirit is love, joy, peace, patience, kindness, goodness, faithfulness, gentleness, and self-control. Against such things there is no law.

The first three virtues are directed toward God. The second three virtues are directed toward others. And the last three virtues are directed toward ourselves. Faithfulness, gentleness, and self-control are characteristics that we need to have in our Christian walk. So whenever Satan brings on his attack against us as believers, we need to be in control and alert at all times. Now where can we go to learn how to walk in the Spirit? You can't go into the world's system, because this world's system doesn't believe and accept exactly what the believer in Christ is promoting and doing. So you go to reading and the study of the Word of God.

2 Timothy 3:16–17 quote: All Scripture is God-breathe and is useful for teaching, rebuking, correcting and training in righteousness, so that the man of God may be thoroughly equipped for every good work.

Now when God's Holy Word speaks of all the Scriptures, it is speaking about the Scriptures that are listed in the Word of God. From Genesis to Revelation, what we have today in the Bible is considered as the inspired Word of God. As believers, if we really want to know anything about living the Christian life, we have to get into the Word of God, because this is where we receive our training in the area of righteousness. Because whenever we are living a godly life, and in the will of God, we learn *how to receive favor in the sight of God and man.* Proverbs 3:1–2 says, "My son, do not forget my teaching, but keep my commands in your heart, for they will prolong your life many years and bring you prosperity."

36

Church, as believers, we are to take God's Words and place His commands into our heart. So how do we do this? By getting into reading and studying of the Word of God. We discipline ourselves so that it can become a habit. All throughout our day, there are so many things that we do that have become a habit. For example, we get up at a certain time in the morning. We go to bed at a certain time. We eat at a certain time. There are a lot of good things that we do, and there are a lot of bad things that we have chosen not to do. We have made it a habit to do and not do these things. When it comes down to reading the Word of God, we have to make it a habit to study.

2 Timothy 2:15 quote: Do your best to present yourself to God as one approved, a workman who does not need to be ashamed and who correctly handles the word of truth.

It is all well and good that you bring the Word of God with you whenever you attend your local church, but do not let attending your local church be the only time that you allow yourselves to study God's Word.

David asked a question in Psalm 119:9–11 quote: How can a young man keep his way pure? By living according to your word. I seek you with all my heart; do not let me stray from your commands. I have hidden your word in my heart that I might not sin against you.

Church, if you possess a Bible at this very moment, then you are without excuse. Every time you read and understand exactly what you are reading, you are being held accountable. Whenever we do something that is completely out of the will of God, we can expect the Word of God to bring us under conviction. And here's the reason why:

Hebrews 4:12–13 quote: For the word of God is living and active. Sharper than any double-edge sword, it penetrates even the dividing soul and spirit, joints and marrow; it judges the thoughts and attitudes of the heart. Nothing in all creation is hidden from God's sight. Everything is uncover and laid bear before the eyes of him to whom we must give account.

If we truly want to obey God's will in our lives, and prolong our lives many years so that we can be blessed with prosperity, then we have to stay in the Word of God.

We are told in James 1:22–24 quote: Do not merely listen to the word, and so deceive yourselves. Do what it says. Anyone who listens to the word but does not do what it says is like a man who looks at his face in a mirror and, after looking at himself, goes away and immediately forgets what he looks like.

Reading the Word of God is not all there is to it; we also have to apply God's Word to our everyday lives. It's called following biblical instructions. Whenever we pick up medicine from the pharmacy, we follow the instructions on the bottle. We do not just place the bottle in the medicine cabinet without reading the instructions. If we expect to be cured of whatever is ailing us, we do what it says. The same is true when it comes down to reading and applying the Word of God to our lives.

Luke 11:28 quote: "Blessed rather are those who hear the word of God and obey it.

In order to live the Christian life, we must not come up with our own rules and then turn them into man-made church traditions.

Jesus said this in Matthew 15:8–9: quote: 'These people honor me with their lips, but their hearts are far from me. They worship me in vain; their teachings are but rules taught by men.

Church, we must practice what we preach by the very way that we live our lives each day. If we remember to do this, then we will learn *how to receive favor in the sight of God and man.*

Proverbs 3:3–4 quote: Let love and faithfulness never leave you; bind them around your neck, write them on the tablet of your heart. Then you will win favor and a good name in the sight of God and man.

The two things that believers need to connect with in their lives are love and faithfulness. Love and faithfulness are also included in the fruit of the Spirit. Every believer needs to have love. The love that is mentioned here is the agape kind of love, which is the God kind of love.

Romans 5:8 quote: But God demonstrates his own love for us in this: While we were still sinners, Christ died for us.

If God the Father didn't love us, He would have never given up His very best. The Lord Jesus Christ is God's very best.

Listen to what Jesus said about His Father's love: John 10:17–18 quote: The reason my Father loves me is that I lay down my life-only to take it up again. No one takes it from me, but I lay it down on my own accord. I have authority to lay it down and the authority to take it up again. This command I received from my Father."

Church, this was all done because of love. This is the same exact love that we need to have for one another. The very reason why people are hurting one another, and lying to one another, and killing one another, and so on is because they do not love one another.

As believers, we are told in Galatians 6:10 quote: Therefore, as we have the opportunity, let us do good to all people, especially to those who belong to the family of believers.

"All people"; this includes everybody. This has nothing to do with how bad they are treating you. As believers in Christ, we have to be the very first ones to break the ice. How serious do you want to see a lost soul saved? Then it starts with you. This is one of the ways that we get our foot into the door.

1 Peter 3:15 quote: But in your hearts set apart Christ as Lord. Always to be prepared to give a answer to everyone who asks you to give the reason for the hope that you have. But do this in gentleness and respect.

Church, you cannot expect to do this if you do not possess love. Next, we are to have faithfulness. Whenever you start to do something for the glory of God, you do not quit, no matter what. God planted that in us the very moment we were saved.

Ephesians 2:10 quote: For we are God's workmanship, created in Christ Jesus to do good works, which God prepared in advance for us to do.

So if God has programmed us to do good work, then why are we quitting and giving up? Many Christians today are abandoning the Christian faith. And the reason is, they have taken their eyes off of the Lord and placed them on someone or something else. When Jesus gave Peter the okay to walk on the water, as long as he kept his eyes on Jesus, Peter did all right. But when Peter saw the wind and the waves, he had taken his eyes off of Jesus and placed them on the circumstances. It was Peter's lack of faith that made him sink.

Hebrews 11:6 quote: And without faith it is impossible to please God, because anyone that comes to him must believe that he exists and that he rewards those who earnestly seek him.

In order for believers to have faithfulness in their Christian lives, they have to have faith in the very things of God. As believers, we are going to come up against storms and trials in our Christian walk. We do not throw in the spiritual towel.

Listen to what James 1:2–4 says, quote: Consider it pure joy, my brothers, whenever you face trials of many kinds, because the testing of your faith develops perseverance. Perseverance must finish its work so that you may be mature and complete, not lacking anything.

Whenever you go through trials of any kind, expect for your faith to be tested. When Jesus spent the forty days and forty nights in the wilderness being tested by the tempter, He wasn't being tested for His benefit. Jesus already knew exactly what He was going to do. Jesus was God in human flesh. Whenever you are walking in love and faithfulness, it's going to give you a good name in the sight of God and man.

41

When Jesus saw Nathaniel approaching, he said of him in John 1:47 quote: "Here is a true Israelite, in whom there is nothing false." With a good name in place, others will be able to see how well you have held up under pressure.

This is why we are told in 1 Peter 2:21 quote: To this you were called, because Christ suffered for you, leaving you an example, that you should follow in his steps.

Church, whenever you are following in the steps of Jesus, you learn *how to receive favor in the sight of God and man.*

Proverbs 3:5–6 quote: Trust in the Lord with all of your heart and lean not on your own understanding; in all your ways acknowledge him, and he will make your path straight.

What does it mean to trust in the Lord with all of your heart? It is to place your trust in God's Holy Word. How would we know how to trust God, if there were nothing or no one to tell us? This is where God's Word comes in. How do you know that God's Holy Word is God's Word? It is written down in God's Word.

2 Peter 1:20–21 quote: Above all, you must understand that no prophecy of Scripture came about by the prophet's own interpretation. For prophecy never had its origin in the will of man, but men spoke from God as they were carried along by the Holy Spirit.

This is how we got God's Word. God said it, and I believe it, and that's settles it. If God's Word tells us to trust in Him, then we should do it; we should trust in the Lord with all of our heart. The Lord knows us better than we know ourselves.

This is why we are told in Romans 8:28 quote: And we know that all things God works for the good of those who love him, who have been called according to his purpose.

If you are saved and have accepted the Lord Jesus Christ as Lord and Savior, your Heavenly Father has a plan for your life.

Jeremiah 29:11 quote: For I know the plans I have for you, "declares the LORD, "plans to prosper you and not to harm you, plans to give you hope and a future.

God's plans for our lives are all lined up in the Word of God. Each time we read and study the Word of God, our Heavenly Father will hold us accountable.

James 4:17 quote: Anyone, then, who knows the good he ought to do and doesn't do it, sins.

We are told to trust in the Lord with all of our hearts; if we do not, then we are sinning. Every decision that we make needs to be lined up in light of Scripture.

For example, we are told in Philippians 4:8, quote: Finally, brothers, whatever is true, whatever is noble, whatever is right, whatever is pure, whatever is lovely, whatever is admirable-if anything is excellent or praiseworthy-think on such things.

God's Word shows us how we can trust in the Lord with all of our hearts and still live a godly life, whenever we do not lean on our own understandings, but use our knowledge of God in all of our ways. By getting into the Word of God, the Lord is going to make our pathway straight.

Listen to what Psalm 1:1–3 says: quote: Blessed is the man who does not walk in the counsel of the wicked or stand in the way of sinners or sit in the seat of mockers. But his delight is in the law of the LORD, and on his law he meditates day and night. He is like a tree planted by the streams of water, which yields it fruit in season and whose leaf does not wither. Whatever he does prospers.

When we delight in the Lord, we are delighting ourselves in the Word of God, we are delighting ourselves in the Lord.

Psalm 37:4–5 quote: Delight yourself in the Lord and he will give you the desires of your heart. Commit your way to the LORD; trust in him and he will do this:

Many of you have desires that you would like to see the Lord bring to pass. It could be job promotions, career changes, your health, your families, having your financial needs met, strengthening your marriage, and so on.

Joshua 1:8 quote: Do not let this Book of the Law depart from your mouth; meditate on it day and night, so that you maybe careful to do everything written in it. Then you will prosperous and successful.

Everything that we seek outside of trusting in the Lord is secondary. Whenever we seek first the Kingdom of God and His righteousness, we are trusting in the Lord with all of our hearts. In everything that we do, God needs to be first.

Colossians 3:17 quote: And whatever you do, whether in word or deed, do it all in the name of the Lord Jesus, giving thanks to God the Father through him.

What are we doing? Looking out for who's number one: God. Whenever this is happening, we've learned *how to receive favor in the sight of God and man.*

Proverbs 3:7 quote: Do not be wise in your own eyes; fear the Lord and shun evil.

You have to be very careful who you listen to. A believer in Christ must use biblical discernment. In order to do this, you have to be matured in the Word of God.

Hebrews 5:14 quote: But solid food is for the mature, who by constant use have trained themselves to distinguish good from evil.

To fear the Lord is to reverence the Lord at all times.

We are told in Ephesians 5:15–17 quote: Be very careful, then, how you live-not as unwise but wise, making the most of every opportunity, because the days are evil. Therefore do not be foolish, but understand what the Lord's will is.

Doing God's will gives us favor.

CONCLUSION

In the life of Joseph, Scripture said, "The Lord was with Joseph." In everything Joseph did, the Lord God gave Joseph favor. And the reason was because Joseph trusted in the Lord his God with all of his heart. When we have an important decision to make, we sometimes feel that we can't trust anyone—not even God. But God knows what is best for us. We must trust God completely in every choice we make. Bring your decisions to God in prayer, use the Bible as your guide, and follow God's leading. He will make your paths straight by both guiding and protecting you. By doing this, you will learn *how to receive favor in the sight of God and man.*

Proverbs 3:1–2 says, "My son, do not forget my teaching, but keep my commands in your heart, for they will prolong your life many years and bring you prosperity." Amen!

4

How to Avoid Becoming a Borderline Christian

Revelation 3:15–16. I know your deeds, that you are neither cold nor hot. I wish you were either one or the other! So, because you are lukewarm-neither hot nor cold-I am about to spit you out of my mouth.

SERMON MESSAGE:

There is something going on among the Christians today that is being very easily ignored. Christians are being lied to and deceived. They are getting saved, and they are still doing the very same things that they were doing before they became saved. The Lord Jesus did not save us so that we could continue to live in sin. The very reason why we are here as believers in Christ is so that we can become fruitful and touch the lives of others with the Christian lives that we live.

Matthew 5:16 quote: In the same way, let your light shine before men, that they may see your good deeds and praise your Father in heaven.

What is the purpose of glorifying our Heavenly Father? It is so that we are able to witness to others with the very lives that we are living. We are the only Jesus that the people in our world will ever see. When Jesus selected His twelve disciples, He was preparing for them to become fishers of men. In order for this task to be accomplished, they had to become followers of Christ.

Luke 9:23 quote: "If anyone would come after me, he must deny himself and take up his cross daily and follow me.

Church, you cannot become a follower of the Lord Jesus Christ when you have your own agenda in mind. Expect for someone to expose you. Many so-called preachers are being exposed today because they are not preaching and teaching the Word of God. The Lord Jesus Christ tells us to watch out for them because they are wolves in sheep's clothing. By their fruit you will recognize them. This is the reason why many Christians today are being deceived. They are not doing their spiritual homework. All throughout grade school, junior high, and senior high, our teachers would give us homework assignments and have us turn them in the very next day. The teachers themselves could tell whether we had done our homework by giving us a passing or failing grade. For this reason, the Lord has given the Church pastors today. All of them have been given a duty and a purpose in the local church.

Ephesians 4:12-13 quote: To prepare God's people for works of service, so that the body of Christ maybe built up until we all reach the unity in the faith and in the knowledge of the Son of God and become mature, attaining to the whole measure of the fullness of Christ.

You have Christians who have been members in their church for twenty years or more who are still acting like spiritual infants.

Another word for this is spiritual babies. Apostle Paul understood this. This was going on in the church at Corinth.

Paul told them in 1 Corinthians 3:1–2 quote: Brothers, I could not address you as spiritual but worldly-mere infants in Christ. I gave you milk, not solid food, for you were not yet ready for it. Indeed, you are still not ready.

These Christians had their own agendas while they were making their own rules along the way. They needed godly counsel and spiritual leadership and guidelines to follow through. But instead they brought about divisions in the Church. Apostle Paul was writing to them to see if this problem could be corrected among them. How many of you know that this problem needs to still be corrected in the local churches today as well? You have places where the churches are calling the shots instead of the pastors. This is not biblical.

Hebrews 13:17 quote: Obey your leaders and submit to their authority. They keep watch over you as men who must give account. Obey them so that their work will be a joy, not a burden, for that will be no advantage to you.

How can the Lord hold the pastors accountable if they are not in charge of running the local church? When the local shepherds are not in charge in running the local churches, this can easily open up the church doors to all types of false doctrines. The pastor's authority is coming from the Word of God, not from within the walls of the local church.

1 Peter 5:2–3 quote: Be shepherds of God's flock that is under your care, serving as overseers-not because you must, but because

you are willing, as God wants you to be; not greedy for money, but eager to serve; not lording it over those entrusted to you, but being examples to the flock.

Nowhere in God's Word are the congregations told to keep watch over themselves. That calling has been left up to the local shepherds in the local churches. During Jesus' ministry on earth. He used many examples and illustrations. Jesus even refers to His followers as sheep. Why sheep? Because a sheep is a helpless and defenseless animal. When it comes up against a wild animal, it can't defend itself. So the enemy devours its prey. The shepherd watches over the sheep and protects them from the ferocious wolves. Jesus refers to Himself as the Good Shepherd. The Good Shepherd lays down His life for His sheep.

John 10:17–18 quote: The reason my Father loves me is that I lay down my life-only to take it up again. No one takes it from me, but I lay it down on my own accord. I have the authority to lay it down and authority to take it up again. This command I receive from my Father.

Jesus never did have to lay down His life for Himself. If Jesus wanted to, He could have kept on living in His physical body as long as He wanted to. Jesus didn't have a problem with sin, but every human being does. This was why Jesus came. He came to set the captives free. Jesus is the Son of God.

John 8:34–36 quote: Jesus replied, "I tell you the truth, everyone who sins is a slave to sin. Now a slave has no permanent place in the family, but the son belongs to it forever. So if the Son set you free, you will be free indeed.

Once we accept Jesus Christ as our Savior and Lord, we become His sheep. On the very night that Jesus was to be betrayed, He reminded His disciples of this prophecy: Zechariah 13:7 says, "I will strike the Shepherd, and the sheep of the flock will be scattered." Here Jesus refers to His disciples as sheep. Also, Jesus speaks about bringing in other sheep that are not of this sheep pen.

John 10:16 says, "I have other sheep that are not of this sheep pen. I must bring them also. They too will listen to my voice, and there shall be one flock and Shepherd." Church, when Jesus started out with sheep, He started out with the Jews. And after Jesus gave His disciples the Great Commission, this included the Gentiles as well. Jesus is speaking about us as His believers. The local shepherds in the local churches are also sheep, while they are doing the pastoral duties. Even though Jesus gave gifts to some sheep to be pastors, they also became labeled as local shepherds in the local churches.

This is why Apostle Paul tells the shepherds of the church of God in Acts 20:28–31 quote: Keep watch over yourselves and all the flock of which the Holy Spirit has made you overseers. Be shepherds of the church of God, which he bought with his own blood. I know that after I leave salvage wolves will come in among you and will not spare the flock. Even from your own number men will arise and distort the truth in order to draw away disciples after them. So be on your guard! Remember that for three years I never stop warning each of you night and day with tears.

Church, these verses of Scriptures are still in effect today. Pastors have to keep watch over their local flocks. The savage wolves are the false teachers who try to come into the local churches with their own agendas, only to deceive those who are not grounded in the Word of God or the Christian faith. *How to avoid becoming a borderline Christian?* Avoid becoming lukewarm Christians. Revelation 3:15–16 says, "I know your deeds, that you are neither cold nor hot. I wish you were either one or the other! So, because you are lukewarm—neither hot nor cold—I am about to spit you out of my mouth." During the years in grade school and junior high school, along with senior high school, some teachers were unable to give their students a grade at all. And it was because their assignments were considered incomplete. When it comes down to carrying out our spiritual assignments, what type of report card are we going to receive? There are times when our aim and focus may be set on the wrong things. Such was the case among the church of Laodicea. They were all wrapped up in the systems of their world. These people had money, nice clothes, overflowing bank accounts, and luxurious homes; everything that they wanted, they could easily afford. But they didn't have Jesus. And the reason why, was these people had pushed Jesus out of their hearts. Jesus was knocking on the door to get in.

Revelation 3:20 quote: Here I stand at the door and knock. If anyone hears my voice and opens the door, I will come in and eat with him, and he with me.

How many of you know that Jesus is saying the same thing to our church today? Our Church Age represents the Laodicea Church Age. As you look around among the local churches today, the Gospel of the Lord Jesus Christ is not being preached. What is the most important Gospel that is being presented today? The Gospel of prosperity, which is centered around money, materials, mansions, cars, and stuff. A lot of Christians today are flocking to mega churches where these sermons can be preached. But the question that needs to be asked is this: are Christians being fed spiritually and properly? The answer is no, they are not.

Matthew 4:4 quote: "It is written: 'Man does not live by bread alone, but on every word that comes from the mouth of God.

Every true believer needs to be living by the Word of God. The only time some church members read their Bibles is when they come to church on Sundays. Notice what the Lord God said to Joshua as he was getting ready to lead the people of Israel into the Promised Land: Joshua 1:8 quote: Do not let this Book of the Law depart from your mouth; meditate on it day and night, so that you may careful to do everything written in it. Then you will be prosperous and successful.

The Book of the Law is known to us today as the Word of God.

Hosea 4:6 quote: My people are destroyed from lack of knowledge.

Christians today would rather listen to second-hand information than get the information for themselves. *How to avoid becoming a borderline Christian?* By getting into the Word of God and doing what it says. If you are not reading and studying the Word of God, then you are a candidate of becoming a borderline Christian.

2 Timothy 2:15 quote: Do your best to present yourself to God as one approved, a workman who does not need to be ashamed and who correctly handles the word of truth.

So many Christians today are being deceived, because they are not paying attention to who they listen to. When you are studying the Word of God, God's Word will keep you informed so that you do not become tripped up by the false doctrines of the false teachers.

In Matthew 7:21 quote: Not everyone who says to me 'Lord 'Lord, will enter the kingdom of heaven, but only he who does the will of my Father who is in heaven.

You can recognize false teachers by their fruit. If what they are teaching you doesn't line up with the Word of God, then you need to back away from them. Those who are not able to recognize them are considered borderline Christians. They have been taught about these false teachers, but it goes in one ear and out the other. Borderline Christians are those who want to just barely make it. These are the ones who have one foot in the world's system and the other foot in the local church.

This is why the pastors who are the local shepherds in the local church are told in 2 Timothy 4:2–4, quote: Preach the Word; be prepared in season and out of season; correct, rebuke and encourage-with great patience and careful instructions. For a time will come when men will not put up with sound doctrine. Instead, to suit their own desires, they will gather around them a great number of teachers to say what their itching ears want to hear. They will turn their ears away from the truth and turn aside to myths.

The pastors have to remain true to preaching the Word of God, regardless. Not everyone is going to listen and hear the Word of God preach. As the pastors are preaching and teaching the Word of God, it's going to bring rebukes, corrections, and encouragement.

Everybody likes to receive encouragement at all times. But no one wants to be rebuked, and no one wants to be corrected. This is the reason why church members are acting like revolving doors. They are leaving one local church and going to another. This is why mega churches are so full and packed today. They have taken in excess baggage. These excess baggage are called borderline Christians.

Hebrews 5:11–13 quote: We have much to say about this, but it is hard to explain because you are slow to learn. In fact, though by this time you ought to be teachers, you need someone to teach you the elementary truths of God words all over again. You need milk, not solid food. Anyone who lives on milk, still being infant, is not acquainted with the teaching about righteousness.

The very reason why borderline Christians need to receive the elementary truths of God's Word over again is because they were not paying attention to God's Word in the first place. We have so many so-called preachers, and so many so-called reverends, that can't even teach the Word of God. *How to avoid becoming a borderline Christian?* By getting into the solid spiritual food of the Word of God.

Hebrews 5:14 quote: But solid food is for the mature, who by constant use have trained themselves to distinguish good from evil.

Believers are not going to keep on practicing and keep on living in their evil ways. They are going to become mature in the faith. They are going to concentrate on becoming trained in the Word of God.

2 Timothy 3:16–17 quote: All Scripture is God-breathe and is useful for teaching, rebuking, correcting and training in righteousness, so that the man of God may be thoroughly equipped for every good work.

I don't know about you, but I have had the Word of God put me in check many times. Whether I'm reading it on my own, or listening to someone preach it to me, the Word of God allows me to examine myself to make sure that I'm still in the faith.

2 Corinthians 13:5 quote: Examine yourselves to see whether you are in the faith; test yourselves. Do you not realize that Christ Jesus is in you-unless, of course, you fail the test.

This is why the church needs to be taught, rebuked, and corrected. This is where God's Word comes in. Church, do not let man-made traditions rebuke you if they do not line up with the Scriptures. But let the Word of God do it.

Hebrews 4:12–13 quote: For the word of God is alive and active. Sharper than any double-edged sword, it penetrates even to dividing soul and spirit, joints, and marrow; it judges the thoughts and the attitudes of the heart. Nothing in all creation is hidden from God's sight. Everything is uncover and laid bear before the eyes of him to whom we must give account.

If you believe that you have done all that you can to teach someone, or rebuke someone, or even correct someone, and you have done all of this in love, then you have to leave the rest up to the Word of God. Let the Word of God do the rebuking and the correcting for you. *How to avoid becoming a borderline Christian?* Continue to live a changed life. Be careful who you are hanging around with. 1 Corinthians 15:33 says, "Do not be misled: Bad company corrupts good character." The Lord has left us on earth for a specific reason. And this is so that we can influence the unsaved and involve them in faith in Christ. We are not to let the people of this world's system influence us any longer. Church, we have been there, and we have done that. There's no reason why we should go back to living the sinful past all over again.

Psalm 1:1–3 quote: Blessed is the man who does not walk in the counsel of the wicked or stand in the way of sinners or sit in the seat of mockers. But his delight is in the law of the LORD, and on his law he meditates day and night. He is like a tree planted by streams of water, which yields its fruit in season and who leaf does not wither. Whatever he does prospers.

Whenever we involve ourselves with the wicked, the sinners, and the mockers, all that we are doing is straddling the fence. These are the ones who are partying on the weekend and wind up in church on Sunday morning. These are ones who are cheating on their spouse and are back in church on Sunday morning. These are the ones who live a hellish life throughout the week and are back in church on Sunday morning. If we call ourselves Christians, then we cannot live like this.

2 Corinthians 5:21 quote: God made him who had no sin to be sin for us, so that in him we might become the righteousness of God.

If we are the righteousness of God, then we need to act like God's Word says we are. When our Heavenly Father sees you, He needs to see Jesus in you. Sin separates us from God, because God cannot look at sin. If you are a borderline Christian, it is time for you to turn all of this around in your life. You can begin again.

1 John 1:9 quote: If we confess our sins, he is faithful and just and will forgive us of our sins and purify us from all unrighteousness.

If you are saved, as you say you are, you no longer have to continue on living in your sins. You no longer have to allow your sinful flesh to control you. The day that you became Born Again was the day that the Lord placed you in control of your flesh.

Galatians 5:16–21 quote: So I say, live by the Spirit, and you will not gratify the desires of the sinful nature. For the sinful nature desires what is contrary to the Spirit, and the Spirit what is contrary to the sinful nature. They are in conflict with each other, so that you do not do what you want. But if you are led by the Spirit you are not under law. The acts of the sinful nature are obvious: sexual immorality, impurity and debauchery; idolatry and witchcraft; hatred, discord, jealousy, fits of rage, selfish ambition, dissensions, factions, and envy; drunkenness, orgies, and the like. I warn you, as I did before, that those who live like this will not inherit the kingdom of God.

Many borderline Christians are missing out on the blessing of the Kingdom of God for their lives. It is because they have made a choice to live the way that they want to live.

Proverbs 16:25 quote: There is a way that seems right to a man, but in the end it leads to death.

The last thing that I want to be is a stumbling block to those who are unsaved. I want to see them come to know Lord Jesus Christ and begin to live changed lives. We are the only Jesus that the unsaved people of our world will ever see. If we are living like borderline Christians, then how will they know?

CONCLUSION

How to avoid becoming a borderline Christian? Begin to operate in the Spirit, so that you can grab a hold of the fruit of the Spirit.

Galatians 5:22–23 quote: But the fruit of the Spirit is love, joy, peace, patience, kindness, goodness, faithfulness, gentleness and self-control. Against such things there is no law.

Love, joy, and peace are centered around God. Patience, kindness, and goodness are centered around others. Faithfulness, gentleness, and self-control are centered around ourselves. The very reason why the word "Christian" is used loosely is because every religion known today wants to use the word. But they do not want to live up to what Christian really means. Christian: A person declaring faith in Jesus as the Christ, or in the religion based upon His teachings.

Jesus said in Luke 11:28 quote: "Blessed rather are those who hear the word of God and obey it."

This is how you can *avoid becoming a borderline Christian.* Amen

5

Be the Teacher that God Wants You to Become

Hebrews 5:11–14. We have much to say about this, but it is hard to explain because you are slow to learn. In fact, though by this time you ought to be teachers, you need someone to teach you the elementary truths of God's words all over gain. You need milk, not solid food! Anyone who lives on milk, being still infant, is not acquainted with the teaching about righteousness. But solid food is for the mature, who by constant use have trained themselves to distinguish good from evil.

SERMON MESSAGE:

Before an individual can be used by God, it is a must that they first become Born Again.

John 1:12–13 quote: Yet to all who receive him, to those who believed in his named, he gave the right to become children of God-children born not of natural decent, nor of human decision or a husband will, but born of God.

This is what it means to be Born Again, because this is the only way you can be taught when it comes to the teaching of the Word of God.

Before Jesus was ascended on high, He commissioned His remaining disciples with these final instructions: Matthew 28:18–20 quote: "All authority in heaven and on earth has been given to me. Therefore go and make disciples of all nations, baptizing them in the name of the Father and of the Son and of the Holy Spirit, and teaching them to obey everything I have commanded you. And surly I am with you always, to the end of the age."

The disciples who Jesus was talking to went on to be with the Lord in glory. So while each and every believer is living today, this message in the Word of God is still speaking to us. If the Lord didn't want us to know this, He would never have allowed it to be written down.

In fact, we are told in John 20:30 quote: Jesus did many other miraculous signs in the presence of his disciples, which are not recorded in this book. But these are written that you may believe that Jesus is the Christ, the Son of God, and that by believing you may have life in his name.

The four Gospels are designed to show exactly what the Lord Jesus Christ was doing throughout His ministry, while He was ministering here on this earth those three years. Jesus was teaching His disciples so that they in turn could teach us as believers. How are Jesus' disciples able to teach us as believers in Christ? By teaching us through His Word.

Hebrews 1:1–3 quote: In the past God spoke to our forefathers through the prophets at many times and in various ways, but in these last days he has spoken to us by his Son, whom he has appointed heir of all things, and through whom he made the universe. The Son is the radiance of God's glory and the exact representation of his being, sustaining all things by his powerful word. After he provided purification for sins, he sat down at the right hand of the Majesty in heaven.

Every time you pick up the Word of God and read it, and study it, you are going to learn how to apply it to your life. Because until you do, the Word of God is going to bring you under conviction until you get that Word in you.

Hebrew 4:12–13 quote: For the word of God is living and active. Sharper than any double-edged sword, it penetrates even the dividing soul and spirit, joints and marrow; it judges the thoughts and attitudes of the heart. Nothing in all creation is hidden from God's sight. Everything is uncover and laid bare before the eyes of him to whom we must give account.

Many of you have been very used to me as your pastor giving you the Word of God in this format. This is basically the only local church where you can come to hear the Word of God presented to you like this. Years ago, I noticed that some of my members had difficulty turning from page to page, and they were struggling, trying to keep up. This was the reason I came up with this spiritual technique. I'm only doing what I believe the Scripture is telling me to do.

2 Timothy 4:2–4 quote: Preach the word; be prepare in season and out of season; correct, rebuke and encourage-with great

patience and careful instruction. For a time will come when men will not put up with sound doctrine. Instead, to suit their own desires, they will gather around them a great number of teachers to say what their itching ears want to hear. They will turn their ears away from the truth and aside to myths.

The pastors today do not have time to play silly games, while the world is in the mess that it is in; the world is sending lost souls on their way straight to hell, only to die in their sins.

Proverbs 16:25 quote: There is a way that seems right to a man, but in the end it leads to death.

Christians do not need to be lied to today, they need to be told the truth. Whenever Christians are being lied to, it takes their focus off of leading people to Christ.

We are told in 1 Peter 3:15 quote: But in your heart set apart Christ as Lord. Always be prepared to give an answer to everyone who ask you to give the reason and the hope you have. But do this with gentleness and respect.

By doing this, you will be able to teach others about your faith in the Lord Jesus Christ. But you cannot do this if you haven't studied.

When Paul wrote to Timothy, he told him in 2 Timothy 2:15 quote: Do your best to present yourself to God as one approved, a workmen who does not need to be ashamed and who correctly handles the word of truth.

There is a difference whenever you study the Word of God, and when you study from someone else. If there is a teacher who has it in for you, and has refused to recognize you, they may not give you the recognition or the grade that you deserve. But when it comes down to studying the Word of God for yourself, the Lord is the one who is going to promote you to the very next level of your destiny.

Remember what David said in Psalm 119:9-11: quote. How can a young man keep his way pure? By living according to your word. I seek you with all my heart; do not let me stray from your commands. I have hidden your word in my heart that I might not sin against you.

God's Holy Word can keep us from living in sin. Whenever we are studying the Word of God, we are going to learn how to do what God's Word says. When someone tries to get you to do something different from the Word of God, you are going to feel very uncomfortable about it. So you are going to take a stand for what you believe is right.

1 Corinthians 15:58 quote: Therefore my dear brothers, stand firm. Let nothing move you. Always give yourselves fully to the work of the Lord, because you know that your labor in the Lord is not in vain.

The more that we as believers spend time in studying and applying God's Word to our lives, it's going to pay off for us. There are a lot of Christians who want to be teachers, ministers, and pastors, but they do not want to do whatever it takes to become one.

Jesus said to His disciples in Matthew 23:2–3 quote:" The teachers of the law and the Pharisees sit in Moses' seat. So you must obey them and do everything they tell you. But do not do what they do, for they do not practice what they preach.

The Pharisees and the teachers of the law were filled with hypocrisy and deceit. And the reason was they didn't practice what they preached.

But on the other hand, we are told as pastors in 1 Peter 5:2–3 quote: Be shepherds of God's flock that is under your care, serving as overseers-not because you must, but because you are willing, as God wants you to be; not greedy for money but eager to serve; not lording it over those entrusted to you, but being examples to the flock.

In everything that we do and say as pastors, it is a must that we set biblical examples for the believers to follow. We are not to be greedy for money, but eager to serve. When I first became pastor of this church, money was the furthest thing from my mind. My number one priority at that time was what was in the best interest of the people in the church. As far as money was concerned, the Lord was meeting my every need, because I had become faithful and committed in my tithes and offerings to the Lord's work.

Luke 16:10–12 quote: "Whoever can be trusted with very little can also be trusted with much, and whoever is dishonest with very little will also be dishonest with much. So if you have not been trustworthy in handling worldly wealth, who will trust you with true riches? And if you have not been trustworthy with someone else's property, who will give you property of your own?

Whenever the pastor is experiencing this type of blessing, then it needs to rub off on the local church members as well. What the pastor is experiencing is what the whole church needs to be experiencing as well.

Philippians 4:8–9 quote: Finally, brothers, whatever is true, whatever is noble whatever is right, whatever is pure, whatever is lovely, whatever is admirable-if anything is excellent or praiseworthy-think about such things. Whatever you have learned or received or heard from me, or seen in me-put it into practice. And the God of peace will be with you.

If the God of Peace is with your pastor, then the God of Peace is going to be with you too. And this is providing that you are following the very same examples that your pastor is following.

Peter tells us in 1 Peter 2:21 quote: To this you were called, because Christ suffered for you, leaving you an example, that you should follow in his steps.

One of the reasons why the Lord Jesus Christ ministered on this earth was to show us how to live; Jesus did this by setting the example for us to follow and to live by.

Jesus tells us in Matthew 5:16 quote: In the same way, let your light shine before men, that they may see your good deeds and praise your Father in heaven.

Whenever we let our light shine as believers, we will have the opportunity to connect others to the same light that we have. But it has got to start with us first. *Being the teacher that God wants you to become.*

Hebrews 5:11–14 quote: We have much to say about this, but it is hard to explain because you are slow to learn. In fact though by this time you ought to be teachers, you need someone to teach you the elementary truths of God's word all over again. You need milk, not solid food! Anyone who lives on milk, being still an infant, is not acquainted with the teaching about righteousness. But solid food is for the mature, who by constant use have trained themselves to distinguish from good and evil.

While the Israelite community was in the wilderness, the Lord God had Moses get ready to move the people into the Promised Land. But the people refused to move on, and because of this, they were forced to wander in the wilderness for a period of forty years. They missed out on their blessings. Many Christians are like that today, because they have refused to move on to spiritual maturity.

1 Corinthians 3:1–2 quote: Brothers, I could not address you as spiritual but as worldly-mere infants in Christ. I gave you milk, not solid food, for you were not yet ready for it. Indeed, you are still not ready.

What was the reason Paul called these Christians worldly? These Christians still indulged in the very things that they were doing before they were saved. As we continue to allow ourselves to mature in the Word of God as we are being taught, there are going to be certain things we learn not to do any longer.

In fact, we are told in 2 Corinthians 5:17 quote: Therefore, if anyone is in Christ, he is a new creation; the old has gone, the new has come.

Every one of us who has been Born Again has a brand new spiritual nature living inside of us. This new nature that is living inside of us has been programmed not to sin. Any time there is a sin that is committed in our lives, we are sowing to the sinful nature. The very reason why Christians are not maturing in the Word of God is because they are operating in their sinful flesh.

Galatians 5:16–21 quote: So I say live by the Spirit, and you will not gratify the desires of the sinful nature. For the sinful nature desires what is contrary to the Spirit, and the Spirit what is contrary to the sinful nature. They are in conflict with each other, so that you do not do what you want. But if you are led by the Spirit you are not under law. The acts of the sinful nature are obvious: sexual immorality, impurity and debauchery; idolatry and witchcraft; hatred discord, jealousy, fits of rage, selfish ambition, dissensions, factions and envy; drunkenness, orgies, and the like. I warn you, as I did before, that those who live like this will not inherit the kingdom of God.

Church, no one is going to twist your arm and force you to do anything that you do not want to do. Whenever you look at life as a whole, everything that we do is done by choice. Whenever we make wrong choices, we have to be ready to accept the consequences as well. This can either work for you or against you.

Galatians 6:7–8 quote: Do not be deceived: God cannot be mocked. A man reaps what he sows. The one who sows to please his sinful nature, from that nature will reap destruction; the one who sows to please the Spirit, from the Spirit will reap eternal life.

The very life that you live as a believer is going to help you to teach others who are in the Christian faith.

Listen to what we are told to do in Hebrews 10:24–25 quote: And let us consider how we may spur one another on toward love and good deeds. Let us not give up meeting together, as some are in a habit of doing, but let us encourage one another-and all the more as you see the Day approaching.

Whenever you are spurring others on, and encouraging them in the faith, you are teaching and training them. This is what the Word of God has been designed to do for every believer who is in Christ.

2 Timothy 3:16–17 quote: All Scripture is God-breathed and is useful for teaching, rebuking, correcting and training in righteousness, so that the man of God may be thoroughly equipped for every good work.

Christians today do not like to be put in their place, or be rebuked, or be corrected; this is why you have to let the Word of God do it for you. What the Church needs to understand is this: it doesn't matter how long you have been saved. But it does matter that you get the Word of God placed inside of you. You have to start somewhere.

1 Peter 2:2–3 quote: Like newborn babies, crave pure spiritual milk, so that by it you may grow up in your salvation, now that you have tasted that the Lord is good.

For you to taste and see that the Lord is good, you need God's Word inside you. In order to help get God's Word inside of your heart, you need to find a Bible-believing Christ-centered local church. We are out here, you just need to look prayerfully. *Being the teacher that God wants you to become* is going to lead you to a very good teacher.

And you yourself may become a very good teacher also; Luke 6:40 quote: A student is not above his teacher, but everyone who is fully trained will be like his teacher.

You are not going to learn the things from the Word of God that you want to learn on your own. This is why the Lord has given us pastors and teachers. This is why you need to find a pastor who is grounded in the Scriptures and understands exactly what he is talking about. The pastor is going to be backed up with the Word of God, so that he can teach it.

Ephesians 4:12–14 quote: To prepare God people for the works of service, so that the body of Christ may be built up until we all reach the unity in the faith and in the knowledge of the Son of God and become mature, attaining to the whole measure of fullness of Christ. Then we will no longer be infants, toss back and forth by the waves, and blown here and there by every wind of teaching and by the cunning and craftiness of men in their deceitful scheming.

The very reason why some of the local church members have the wool pulled over their eyes is because they have not become grounded in the Scriptures of the Word of God. They are falling for anything and anybody. A mature believer in Christ can see right through their false teachings. People get offended by me when I expose the phony preachers and the prosperity message they are preaching. Whenever a person goes through a financial crisis, they begin turning to feel-good sermons, only to leave them in worse shape than they were before.

1 Timothy 6:6–10 quote: But godliness with contentment is great gain. For we brought nothing into this world, and we can take nothing out of it. But if we have food and clothing, we will be content with that. People who want to get rich fall into temptation and a trap and into many foolish and harmful desires that plunge men into ruin and destruction. For the love of money is a root of all kinds of evil. Some people, who eager for money, have wandered from the faith and pierced themselves with many griefs.

This why the writer of Hebrews said it this way: Hebrews 5:11–14 quote: We have much to say about this, but it is hard to explain because you are slow to learn. In fact, though by this time you ought to be teachers, you need someone to teach you the elementary truths of God's word all over again. You need milk, not solid food! Anyone who lives on milk, being still an infant, is not acquainted with the teaching about righteousness. But solid food is for the mature, who by constant use have trained themselves to distinguish good from evil.

The Lord is not interested in Christians just feeding only on the spiritual milk of the Word. But as you mature in the spiritual meat of the Word, others are going to be able to see results. A spiritually mature person is going to be able to tell whether a new babe in Christ is growing. They are going to see spiritual fruit in their lives.

John 15:1–3 quote: "I am the true vine, and my Father is the gardener. He cuts off every branch in me that bears no fruit, while every branch that does bear fruit, he prunes so that it will be more fruitful. You are already clean because of the word I have spoken to you.

While we are bearing good fruit as believers, the Word of God is also cleaning us up. Believers in Christ learn to discipline themselves by getting the spiritual nourishment that they need by getting into the reading and studying and applying the Word of God to their everyday life. So how do we go about disciplining ourselves in the Word of God?

Paul tells us in 1 Corinthians 9:24–27, quote: Do you not know that in a race all the runners run, but only one gets the prize. Run is such a way as to get the prize. Everyone who competes in the games goes into strict training. They do it to get a crown that will not last; but we do it to get a crown that will last forever. Therefore I do not run a like a man running aimlessly; I do not fight like a man beating the air. No, I beat my body and make it my slave so after I have preached to others, I myself will not be disqualified for the prize.

Whenever we are preaching to others, we are also teaching them as well.

1 Peter 4:11 quote: If anyone speaks, he should do it as one speaking the very words of God. If anyone serves, he should do it with the strength God provides, so that in all things God may be praised through Jesus Christ. To him be the glory and the power for ever and ever. Amen.

The only place where we know that we can speak the very Words of God is by getting into His Word. How do we know for certain that the Bible is the Word of God?

2 Peter 1:20–21 quote: Above all, you must understand that no prophecy of Scripture came about by the prophet's own interpretation. For prophecy never had its origin in the will of man, but men spoke from God as they were being carried along by the Holy Spirit.

Church, this is how we got the Word of God in its fullness. God said it, we believe it, and that settles it. As you begin to teach the Word of God, the Word of God can defend itself. All you need is someone who knows it well enough to teach it. This is the very reason why we have biblical Bible-believing teachers who are the local pastors in the local churches. Their duties are to train you and prepare you for spiritual maturity. *Being the teacher that God wants you to become* so that you can touch the lives of others with the Gospel of Jesus Christ.

And here's the reason why: 1 Timothy 5:17–18 quote: The elders who direct the affairs of the church well are worthy of double honor, especially those who work is preaching and teaching. For the Scripture says, "Do not muzzle the ox while it is treading out the grain, and "The worker deserves his wages.

The Word of God has put so much emphasis on the elders who preach and teach the Word of God. This is also why they need to be paid well as they carry out their duties in the local church. When Paul made a statement about pastors being paid, he did not take the responsibility for it, but the Lord did.

1 Corinthians 9:14 quote: In the same way, the Lord has commanded that those who preach the gospel should receive their living from the gospel.

This is why we are told in Malachi 3:10 quote: Bring the whole tithes in the storehouse, that there may be food in my house. Test me in this, "says the LORD Almighty, "and see if I will not throw open the floodgates of heaven and pour out so much blessing that you will not have room enough for it.

The food in the storehouse is now referred to as the Word of God. Whenever you come to a Sunday school, weekly Bible study, or Sunday worship service, you are being fed the Word of God. You have the opportunity to *be the teacher that God wants you to become.*

Hebrews 5:11–14 quote: We have much to say about this, but it is hard to explain because you are slow to learn. In fact, though by this time ought to be teachers, you need someone to teach you the elementary truths of God's Word all over again. You need milk, not solid food! Anyone who lives on milk, being still an infant, is not acquainted with the teaching about righteousness. But solid food is for the mature, who by constant use have trained themselves to distinguish good from evil.

The writer of the Book of Hebrews was informing the church members what they ought to have been. They needed to be teachers, because there was a great need for teachers. But they were still feeding off of the spiritual milk of the Word of God.

Notice how Jesus said we should live: Matthew 4:4 quote: Jesus answered, "It is written: 'Man does not live on bread alone, but on every word that comes from the mouth of God.

When it comes down to the Word of God, every believer needs to be jumping to get themselves in the knowledge of the Word of God. The Word of God is a valuable tool and a very powerful spiritual weapon.

2 Corinthians 10:3–6 quote: For though we live in the world, we do not wage war as the world does. The weapons we fight with are not the weapons of the world. On the contrary, they have diving powers to demolish strongholds. We demolish arguments and every pretension that sets itself up against the knowledge of God, and we take captive every thought to make it obedient to Christ. And we will be ready to punish every act of disobedience, once your obedience is complete.

Church, if it wasn't for the Word of God, we wouldn't have a clue to how we could live the Christian life. And the saddest part of it all; Christians today do not know how to really use the Word of God in their lives. They have one foot in the system of this world, and the other foot in the church.

1 John 2:15–17 quote: Do not love the world or anything in the world. If anyone loves the world, the love of the Father is not in him. For everything in the world-the craving of sinful man, the lust of his eyes and the boasting of what he has and does-come not from the Father but from the world. The world and its desires pass away, but the man who does the will of God lives forever.

You cannot live the Christian life apart from the Word of God. Because all you will be doing is making up your own rules along the way. The Word of God will point you in the direction of doing God's will. God's will is that you obey His Word.

Jesus said it this way in Luke 11:28: quote: "Blessed rather are those who hear the word of God and obey it.

Most of the preaching that you are hearing today is not preaching. All it really is, is entertainment. Today's preaching is designed to tickle your ears. It is not feeding you. When Apostle Paul told Timothy to preach the Word, he didn't tell Timothy to preach the application. But to preach the Word. Church, from the time I preach this message, and all the way to the very end of this message, I will be preaching to you God's Word. I have been called to preach.

Hebrews 5:14 quote: Solid food is for the mature, who by constant use have trained themselves to distinguish good from evil.

The ones who are labeled as mature are the ones you will find as qualified teachers, who have disciplined themselves to become grounded in the Word of God. The same is true with you; as long as you are fully rooted and committed to the Word of God, you will be able to see though all the hypocrisy and deceit of the ones who are teaching false doctrine that doesn't line up with the Word of God.

Acts 20:28–31 quote: Keep watch over yourselves and all the flock of which the Holy Spirit has made you overseers. Be shepherds of the church of God, which he bought with his own blood. I know that after I leave, savage wolves will come in among you and not spare the flock. Even from your own number men will arise and distort the truth in order to draw away disciples after them. So be on your guard! Remember that for three years I never stopped warning each of you night and day with tears.

CONCLUSION

Hebrews 5:11–14 quote: We have much to say about this, but it is hard to explain because you are slow to learn. In fact, though by this time you ought to be teachers, you need someone to teach you the elementary truths of God's word all over again. You need milk not solid food! Anyone who lives on milk, being still infant, is not acquainted with the teaching about righteousness. But solid food is for the mature, who by constant use have trained themselves to distinguish good from evil.

These Jewish Christians were immature. Some of them should have been teaching others, but they had not even applied the basics to their lives. They were unwilling to move beyond age-old traditions, established doctrines, and discussion of the basics. Commitment to Christ moves people out of their comfort zones. The mature Christians are hungry for the Word of God to be preached and taught to them, so that they can have the opportunity to present it to others. I believe that the Lord is sending pastors out in the local churches to give the people not what they want, but what they really need to hear. They may not like it. That's just too bad. This is the very reason why the Lord has given the Church leaders.

We are told in Hebrews 13:17 quote: Obey your leaders and submit to their authority. They keep watch over you as men who must give account, Obey them so that their work will be a joy, not a burden, for that would be of no advantage to you.

Being the teacher that God wants you to become has to do with you getting the milk of the Word and the food of the Word inside your spirit.

Philippians 1:6 quote: Being confident of this, that he who begin a good work in you will carry it on to completion until the day of Christ Jesus.

Amen!

6

Are You Representing Christ or Representing Yourself?

Philippians 2:3–5. Do nothing out of selfish ambition or vain conceit, but in humility consider others better than yourselves. Each of you should look not only to your own interests, but also to the interest of others. Your attitude should be the same as that of Christ Jesus.

SERMON MESSAGE:

Many of you were told in the past that we are the only Jesus that the people in our world will ever see. The only way that a believer in Christ can accomplish this task is that they first have to remove self out of the way.

Matthew 22:39 quote: Love your neighbor as yourself.

How would you like others to treat you? You would like them to treat you with the utmost respect. Well, this is how you ought to treat others. You being the believer in Christ that you are, you need to be setting biblical examples by the very life that you live around those who are unsaved. When Jesus was speaking to His disciples, the Lord was not just speaking to them alone. Jesus had recorded the most important teachings of His earthly ministry in the Word of God.

This is why Jesus told His disciples, along with us, in Matthew 28:18–20 quote: "All authority in heaven and on earth has been given to me. Therefore and go and make disciples of all nations, baptizing them in the name of the Father and the Son and the Holy Spirit, and teaching them to obey everything I have commanded you. And surely I am with you always, to the very end of the age."

Jesus' disciples are not with us today in the physical sense. So how are they teaching us? Jesus' disciples are teaching us through His Word. The Lord Jesus Christ's disciples represent the early Church.

Hebrews 1:1–3 quote: In the past God spoke to our forefathers through the prophets at many times and in varies ways, but in these last days he has spoken to us by his Son, whom he appointed heir of all things, and through whom he made the universe. The Son is the radiance of God's glory and the exact representation of his being, sustaining all things by his powerful word. After he had provided purification for sins, he sat down at the right hand of the Majesty in heaven.

In order for believers to learn how to live the Christian life, they must be willing to accept change.

This is why Jesus tells us in Luke 9:23 quote: "If anyone would come after me, he must deny himself and take up his cross daily and follow me.

You first have to remove self out of the way by denying yourself. Church, this is not a one-shot deal. This is something that we have to do every day for the rest of our lives. While we were unsaved, we were unable to control ourselves, because we did whatever we felt like doing. But the very moment that we became saved, something took place in our lives.

2 Corinthians 5:17 quote: Therefore, if anyone is in Christ, he is a new creation; the old has gone, the new has come.

Our Heavenly Father has programmed each and every one of us. Every time that you sin for now on, you are going to be aware of it. The sin that you commit for now on is going to bring about conviction. That sin is going to bother you until you confess it.

1 John 1:9 quote: If we confess our sins, he is faithful and just and will forgive us our sins and purify us from all unrighteousness.

As we stay in the Word of God, God's Holy Word is going to help us to clean up our lives and help us to remove self out of the way. Why is this so true? It is because you cannot live the Christian life apart from the Word of God.

David asked a question in Psalm 119:9–11 quote: How can a young man keep his way pure? By living according to your word. I seek you with all of my heart; do not let me stray from your commands. I have hidden your word in my heart that I might not sin against you.

Many Christians today believe that all they have to do is pray the sinner's prayer, and they automatically become a Christian. Church, there is more to that.

2 Corinthians 5:21 quote: God made him who had no sin to be sin for us, so that in him we might become the righteousness of God.

We begin at that moment to learn to live righteously. Because we have already been declared the righteousness of God, this is where the Word of God comes in.

2 Timothy 3:16–17 quote: All Scripture is God-breathed and is useful for teaching, rebuking, correcting and training in righteousness, so that the man of God may be thoroughly equipped for every good work.

The key words in these verses of Scripture are "training in righteousness." Every time you read and study the Word of God, you have the opportunity to receive the training that you really need in the area of righteousness. But the choice is up to you to see how badly you really want it.

This is why we are told in 2 Timothy 2:15 quote: Do your best to present yourself to God as one approved, a workman who does not need to be ashamed and who correctly handles the word of truth.

God is the One that will be gifting you in the area of your gift. But you need to get the Word of God in you so that you can excel in your gifts. Now why is the Word of God so very important to you? Again, the Word of God is going to help you to remove self out of the way, so that you can learn how to clean up your life.

Hebrews 4:12–13 quote: For the word of God is living and active. Sharper than any double-edged sword, it penetrates even to dividing soul and spirit, joints and marrow; it judges thoughts and the attitudes of the heart. Nothing in all creation is hidden from God's sight. Everything is uncovered and laid bare before the eyes of him to whom we must give account.

Every time you seriously read and study the Word of God, you are being held accountable.

This is why we are told in James 4:17, quote: Anyone, then, who knows the good he ought to do and doesn't do it, sins.

God's Word is going to reveal to the believer some things that they are supposed to do and some things that they are not supposed to do.

For example, we are told in Ephesians 5:15–17 quote: Be very careful, then, how you live-not as unwise but wise, making the most of every opportunity, because the days are evil. Therefore do not be foolish, but understand what the Lord's will is.

Church, it is God's will that we use godly wisdom when it comes to being very careful how we live as believers in Christ. If you call yourselves Christians, then you can't just live any ol' type of way. To do so, you will be setting a very bad example, and you will wind up becoming a stumbling block to those who are not saved.

This why we are told in Romans 12:1–2 quote: Therefore, I urge you, brothers, in the view of God mercy to offer your bodies as living sacrifices, holy and pleasing to God-this is your spiritual act of worship. Do not conform any longer to the pattern of this world, but be transformed by the renewing of your mind. Then you will be able to test and approve what God's will is-his good, pleasing and perfect will.

In order to present our bodies as living sacrifices, holy and pleasing unto God, we have to be trained. This is where the teaching and the learning that we need to receive the Word of God comes in. How do you expect to have your minds renewed? We have to be transformed through the Word of God. The Word of God is like no other teaching aid that you can compare it to. God's Holy Word is in a class all by itself. The Word of God touches you like no other book.

This is why we are told in Ephesians 4:11–13 quote: It was he who gave some to be apostles, some to be prophets, some to be evangelists, and some to be pastors and teachers, to prepare God's people for works of service, so that the body of Christ may be built up until we all reach unity in the faith and in the knowledge of the Son of God and become mature, attaining to the whole measure of fullness of Christ.

The Lord Jesus Christ has given pastors to the Church for our day. Every one of us as pastors must have the ability to preach and teach the Word of God. Church, if we did not have these God-given abilities, we wouldn't be pastors. This is why you can tell the phonies from the ones who are the real pastors in the local churches.

1 Peter 4:11 quote: If anyone should speak, he should do it as one speaking the very words of God. If anyone serves, he should do it with the strength God provides, so that in all things God may be praised through Jesus Christ. To him be the glory and the power for ever and ever. Amen.

Church, in order to speak the very Word of God, you have to know the Word of God. You have to move self out of the way. It is not about you, it's all about the Lord Jesus Christ, and what the Lord has done for you.

This is why we are told in Ephesians 2:8–9, quote: For it is by grace you have been saved, through faith-and this not from yourselves, it is the gift of God-not by works, so that no one can boast.

As believers in Christ, we have nothing to boast about before God. This is why we have to remove self out of the way. The question stands as follows: *Are you representing Christ or representing yourself?*

Philippians 2:3–5 quote: Do nothing out of selfish ambition or vain conceit, but in humility consider others better than yourselves. Each of you should look not only to your own interests, but also the interests of others. Your attitudes should be the same as that of Christ Jesus.

The people of this wicked world are representing themselves. And for this reason, we have to be very careful who we listen to. As believers in the Lord Jesus Christ, it is a must that we use biblical and spiritual discernment.

We are told in 1 Corinthians 2:14, quote: The man without the Spirit does not accept the things that comes from the Spirit of God, for they are foolishness to him, and he cannot understand them, because they are spiritually discerned.

Aquila and Priscilla came into contact with Apollos, who was a very eloquent speaker, but he was in complete ignorance, because all he knew was the ministry of John the Baptist. Apollos' message was not a complete message. When Aquila and Priscilla heard him, they invited him to their home and explained to him the way of God more adequately. This is what we need to do as believers as we move self out of the way.

1 Peter 3:15 quote: But in your heart set apart Christ as Lord. Always be prepared to give an answer to everyone who ask you to give the reason for the hope that you have. But do this in gentleness and respect.

Whenever we put self in the way, it opens up the doors to making unwise, ungodly decisions.

Proverbs 3:5–7 quote: Trust in the Lord with all your heart and lean not on your own understanding; in all your ways acknowledge him, and he will make your paths straight. Do not be wise in your own eyes; fear the Lord and shun evil.

Its possible at times some Christians can become so conceited and self-centered that all that they see is themselves. This is why we have to avoid becoming self-centered and become Christ-centered. The things that you do for Christ will be the only things that matter as you live the Christian life. Living the Christian life has to do with the Heavenly rewards, which we will receive when we get to Heaven.

2 Corinthians 5:10 quote: For we must all appear before the judgment seat of Christ, that each one may receive what is due him for the things done while in the body, whether good or bad.

Your Heavenly Father knows if what you are doing is genuine, or is being done for show.

When the Lord Jesus Christ opposed the Pharisees and the teachers of the law, He called them hypocrites and said to them in Matthew 15:8–9 quote: " 'These people honor me with their lips, but their hearts are far from me. They worship me in vain; their teachings are but rules taught by men.

Jesus wants us to avoid becoming like the hypocrites. To avoid doing things out of selfish ambition and vain conceit, there needs to be seen humility in the lives of every believer.

Philippians 2:3 quote. Do nothing out of self ambition or vain conceit, but in humility consider others better than yourselves.

There are people in your own world who think that they are better than you. So who cares? If you humble yourself just to reach out to them, it shows that you are the better person.

1 Peter 5:6 quote: Humble yourselves, therefore, under God's mighty hand, that he may lift you up in due time.

Whenever we humble ourselves under God's mighty hand, it's going to open up doors for us. I can remember when I went to high school, you had to walk a certain way to keep the other guys from picking a fight with you. I didn't want any trouble, but if it came down to it, I would fight to defend myself. When living the Christian life, don't stoop down to anyone's level. Just be ready to show humility.

Ephesians 6:10 quote: Finally, be strong in the Lord and in his mighty power.

It is not your power that you need to be strong in, because you have no power whatsoever; accept what is given to you from the Lord. The Roman governor, Pilate, got into a verbal confrontation with Jesus when He was arrested and on trial. John 19:10-11, "Do you refuse to speak to me?" Pilate said. "Don't you realize I have power to either to free you or to crucify you?" Jesus answered, "You would have no power over me if it were not given to you from above. Therefore the one who handed me over to you is guilty of greater sin."

From whom do we receive the power today? Church, we are receiving power from the Holy Spirit.

Acts 1:8 quote: But you will receive power when the Holy Spirit comes on you; and you will be my witnesses in Jerusalem, and in all Judea and Samaria, and to the ends of the earth."

After Jesus said this, He paused. Every believer living today has the opportunity to operate in the power of the Holy Spirit. But it has to do with whether you are willing to humble yourself.

Jesus said in Luke 14:11 quote: For everyone who exalts himself will be humbled, and he who humbles himself will be exalted.

Showing humility is like planting seeds; the more humility that is being sown in your life, the more the spiritual harvest is going to be.

Galatians 6:9 quote: Let us not become weary in doing good, for at the proper time we will reap a harvest if we do not give up.

As believers, we have to stop looking for ways to retaliate. If you want to retaliate, then you need to do it with an act of kindness. *Are you representing Christ or representing yourself?*

Philippians 2:3–4 quote: Do nothing out of selfish ambition or vain conceit, but in humility consider others better than yourselves. Each of you should not look only to your own interests, but also to the interest of others.

Whenever you are reading the Word of God, God's Holy Word is speaking directly to you. As you have heard before, God's Word is holding you accountable. Remember what the Lord said to Joshua when the Lord was preparing the Israelites to enter into the Promised Land?

Joshua 1:8 quote: Do not let this Book of the Law depart from your mouth; meditate on it day and night, so that you may be careful to do everything written in it. Then you will prosperous and successful.

Notice the keywords: "So that you may be careful to do everything written in it." The majority of the unsaved people of the world refer to themselves as being number one. They only think about themselves first. Everybody else is secondary or they can care less about them. As a pastor, I'm thinking about what is in the best interest of the members of the local church. And why do I do this? Because it is biblical. Any pastor who cares nothing about his congregation has no business in being a pastor.

1 Peter 5:2–3 quote: Be shepherds of God's flock that is under your care, serving as overseers-not because you must, but because you are willing, as God wants you to be; not greedy for money, but eager to serve; not lording it over those entrusted to you, but being examples to the flock.

Whether you like it or not, you are under my care. That's only if you are a member of this local church. The pastor who is the local shepherd is responsible for you to get the biblical training that you really need in your Christian walk.

Luke 6:40 quote: A student is not above his teacher, but everyone who is fully trained will be like his teacher.

If you are being taught under your pastor's anointing, most of the teachings that you receive from your pastor ought to confirm that you are getting the Word of God inside of you. And here's the reason why: Your pastor will be the one who will set the biblical examples for you to follow.

Philippians 4:8–9 quote: Finally, brothers, whatever is true, whatever is noble, whatever is right, whatever is pure, whatever is lovely, whatever is admirable-anything is excellent or praiseworthy-think about such things. Whatever you have learned from me or received or heard from me, or seen in me-put it into practice. And the God of peace will be with you.

If you have a Spirit-filled pastor, expect the God of Peace to rest on him. Because the God of Peace is going to rest on you also. You will also be concerned with what is in the very best interest of others. Salvation through the Lord Jesus Christ is in the very best interest of others who need to be saved. Whenever we see the unsaved people this way, it gives us as believers in Christ the opportunity to get our foot into the door when it comes down to witnessing and sharing our faith with them.

Colossians 4:6 says, "Let your conversation be always full of grace, seasoned with salt, so that you may know how to answer everyone." Church, you cannot expect to do this if you have self in the way. *Are you representing Christ or representing yourself?*

Philippians 2:3–5 quote: Do nothing out of selfish ambition or vain conceit, but in humility consider others better than yourselves. Each of you should look not only to your own interests, but also to the interest of others. Your attitude should be the same as that of Christ Jesus.

Just imagine what would have happened if Jesus had the very same attitude that the unsaved people of the world have. We would still be in our very own sins. It is a must that every believer in Christ have a complete spiritual attitude adjustment in their lives. If you come up with a ghetto attitude, you are not going to win anybody to Christ.

This is why Jesus tells us in Matthew 11:28–30, quote: Come to me, all you who are weary and burdened, and I will give you rest. Take my yoke upon you and learn from me, for I am gentle and humble in heart, and you will find rest for your souls. For my yoke is easy and my burden is light."

Church, Jesus has revealed Himself as humble. Where did Jesus come from? Jesus came from God. Jesus stripped Himself of His Heavenly glory so that He could take on human flesh.

John 1:14 quote: The Word became flesh and made his dwelling among us. We have seen his glory, the glory of the One and Only, who came from the Father, full of grace and truth.

Jesus did not come to this earth to be served, but to serve. The religious leaders of Jesus' day misunderstood this. They were looking for royalty and someone who could overthrow the government. Yes, Jesus was a King, but not of this world's system.

This is why we are told in 1 John 2:15–17 quote: Do not love the world or anything in the world. If anyone loves the world, the love of the Father is not in him. For everything in the world-the cravings of sinful man, the lust of the eyes and the boasting of what he has and does-comes not from the Father but from the world. The world and its desires pass away, but the man that does the will of God lives forever.

The world that we are to seek has to do with what we are told to do in Matthew 6:32–33 quote: For the pagans run after all these things, and your heavenly Father knows that you need them. But seek first his kingdom and his righteousness, and all these things will be given to you as well.

The Kingdom of God is very much different from what the people of this world seek. The Kingdom of God is God's right way of doing things for your life. In order for us as believers in Christ to enter into this Kingdom, our attitude should be the very same as that of Christ Jesus: Jesus did not have an attitude problem. Jesus knew exactly what He had come to do.

John 10:17–18 quote: The reason my Father loves me is that I lay down my life-only to take it up again. No one takes it from me, but I lay it down on my own accord. I have authority to lay it down and authority to take it up again. This command I received from Father.

Jesus was referring to giving His life as ransom for many. In order for Jesus to do this, He had to take the place of a servant. Jesus humbled Himself and became obedient to death. If we are going to represent the Lord Jesus Christ, then all believers need to be able to discipline themselves, so that they can remove self out of the way.

Galatians 2:20 quote: I have been crucified with Christ and I no longer live, but Christ lives in me. The life I live in the body, I live by faith in the Son of God, who loved me and gave himself for me.

The life that we now live in our bodies does not include self. Self has got to be removed off the throne of our hearts, so that the Lord Jesus Christ can rule. Colossians 3:15 says, "Let the peace of Christ rule in your hearts, since as members of one body you were call to peace." And be thankful.

Church, Jesus needs to be the umpire in every situation in your life. The King James version uses "the Mind of Christ"; the NIV uses "Your attitude should be the same as that of Christ Jesus." Either way we look at it, we should all be concentrating on becoming Christ-centered instead of self-centered. Jesus gave up heaven so that He could take our place on the cross on Calvary.

Hebrews 9:22 quote: In fact, the law requires that nearly everything be cleansed with blood, without the shedding of blood there no forgiveness.

This is why we ask you this question: *Are you representing Christ or representing yourself?*

Philippians 2:3–5: Do nothing out of selfish ambition or vain conceit, but in humility consider others better than yourselves. Each of you should look not only to your own interests, but also to the interest of others. Your attitude should be the same as Christ Jesus.

CONCLUSION

Selfish ambition can ruin a church, but genuine humility can build it. Being humble involves having a serious true perspective about ourselves. It does not mean that we should put ourselves down. Before God, we are sinners, saved only by God's grace, but we are saved and therefore have great worth in God's Kingdom. We are to lay aside selfishness and treat others with the utmost respect and common courtesy. Considering other interests as more important than our own links us with Christ, who was a true example of humility.

1 Peter 2:21 quote: To this you were called, because Christ suffered for you, leaving you an example, that you should follow in his steps.

Amen!

7

Are You Feeding on the Solid Food of the Word of God?

Hebrews 5:14. But solid food is for the mature, who by constant use have trained themselves to distinguish good from evil.

SERMON MESSAGE:

While the Lord Jesus Christ was being tempted by the devil, He was not being tempted for His benefit, but for ours. Jesus was showing us how to deal with the enemy when it comes down to being tempted. Jesus had nothing to prove to the devil. This is why the Scriptures were used for our benefit.

Matthew 4:4 quote: Jesus answered, "It is written: 'Man does not live by bread alone, but on every word that comes from the mouth of God.

Who is considered as the bread alone? We are told that Jesus is the Bread of Life.

John 6:35 quote: Then Jesus declared, "I am the bread of life. He who comes to me will never go hungry, and he who believes in me will never be thirsty.

Whenever you go to BJ's or Sam's Club, you need to show a membership card to get in the door. After you get in the door, you are free to purchase and to pay for whatever items you want. In order for you to be saved, you need to receive Jesus Christ as the Bread of Life because this is the only way that you can get into the Kingdom of God. And this is the only way that you can get the Kingdom of God to work for you on your behalf.

John 10:9 quote: I am the gate; whoever enters through me will be saved. He will come in and go out, and find pasture.

In order to be Born Again, you have to first of all be born of the water. What does this mean? Everyone who is born in human form has the opportunity to be Born Again.

John 1:12–13 quote: Yet to all who received him, to those who believed in his name, he gave the right to become children of God-children born not of natural descent, nor of human decision or husband's will, but born of God.

Now that you have received Jesus Christ as the Bread of Life, you need the Word of God to live by.

We are told in 1 Peter 2:2–3 quote: Like newborn babies, crave pure spiritual milk, so that by it you may grow up in your salvation, now that you have tasted that the Lord is good.

Once the newborn babies are delivered from their mothers' wombs, the very first thing they begin to crave is milk. They are given to their mothers, and they feed them the milk that they are craving from their breasts. When it comes down to the Word of God, we are to crave the sincere milk of the Word of God. This is where our spiritual growth in the Lord is coming from. In order to grow spiritually, you have got to have fruit.

John 15:1–3 quote: "I am the true vine, and my Father is the gardener. He cuts off every branch in me that bears no fruit, while every branch that does bear fruit he prunes so that it will be even more fruitful. You are already clean because of the word I have spoken to you.

Bearing fruit runs hand and hand with the Word of God. For this reason, you will find many Christians in the world today who attend their local churches regularly, but there is no fruit in their lives. You know that they are saved, but there is no evidence to see whether or not they are really growing.

The writer of Hebrews said it this way in Hebrews 5:11–13 quote: We have much to say about this, but it is hard to explain because you are slow to learn. In fact, though by this time you ought to be teachers, you need someone to teach you the elementary truths of God's word all over again. You need milk not solid food! Anyone who lives on milk, being still infant, is not acquainted with the teaching about righteousness.

Some of the people who I grew up with quit attending school in different grade levels. They just didn't see themselves moving ahead in life. And some of them were just looking for shortcuts.

Church, when it comes down to living the Christian life as a believer in Christ, there are no shortcuts. You must study God's Word. You must apply God's Word to your everyday life.

This is why we are told in 2 Timothy 2:15 quote: Do your best to present yourself to God as one approved, a workman who does not need to be ashamed and who correctly handles the word of truth.

If you want to truly live the Christian life as a believer in Christ, then you must study God's Word for all its worth. You cannot put a price on the Word of God, because it is priceless.

James 1:22–24 quote: Do not merely listen to word, and so deceived yourselves. Do what it says. Anyone who listens to the word but docs not do what it says is like a man who looks at his face in a mirror and, after looking at himself, goes away and immediately forgets what he looks like.

It is all well and good if you know how to quote the Scriptures. But it doesn't mean a hill of beans if you do not know exactly what the Scriptures are saying, so that you can apply the Word of God to your everyday life.

Luke 11:28 quote: "Blessed rather are those who hear the word of God and obey it.

Why did the Lord Jesus Christ use the word *blessed*? Because every time believers read and study and apply God's Holy Word to their lives, they will always have the opportunity to be blessed. While the believer is reading the Word of God, he is going to receive biblical godly wisdom while he understands God's Word.

James 1:5 quote: If any of you lacks wisdom, he should ask God, who gives generously to all without finding fault, and it will be given to him.

You can't go to man when it comes down to having the desire to understand godly wisdom. You have to go to God's Word so that the Holy Spirit can feed you the godly information that you need to grow up in your salvation.

Philippians 2:12–13 quote: Therefore my dear friends, as you have always obeyed-not only in my presence, but now much more in my absence-continue to work out your salvation with fear and trembling, for it is God that works in you to will and act according to his good purpose.

Church, how is God working in the will and act according to His purpose? God is doing it through the work of the Holy Spirit in our Christian walk.

So in order to do this, we have to do exactly what the Scripture says: Galatians 5:16–18 quote: So I say, live by the Spirit, and you will not gratify the desires of the sinful nature. For the sinful nature desires what is contrary to the Spirit, and the Spirit what is contrary to the sinful nature. They are in conflict with each other, so that you do not do what you want. But if you are led by the Spirit, you are not under law.

Church, it would be very difficult to live the Christian life apart from the Word of God on your own. This is why there are so many denominations among us today. Somewhere along the line, Christians have decided to go their own way, apart from the Word of God.

This why we are told in Proverbs 3:5–7 quote: Trust in the Lord with all of your heart and lean not unto your own understanding; in all your ways acknowledge him, and he will make your path straight. Do not be wise in your own eyes; fear the Lord and shun evil.

Whenever we become wise in our own eyes, we wind up walking in accordance to our sinful flesh. When this does happen, we find ourselves living away from the will of God for our lives.

In Romans 8:8, quote: Those controlled by the sinful nature cannot please God.

We know that God is not speaking to those who are unsaved, and the reason why is this: There is only one nature living inside of them. That nature is their sinful flesh. And this is because they are spiritually dead.

This is why we are told in 1 Corinthians 2:14 quote: The man without the Spirit does not accept the things that come from the Spirit of God, for they are foolishness to him, and he cannot understand them, because they are spiritually discerned.

In other words, you need to be born of the Spirit in order to understand the very things of God.

1 Corinthians 2:9–10 quote: However, as it is written: "No eye has seen, no ear has heard, no mind has conceived what God has prepared for those who love him"-but God has revealed it to us by his Spirit. The Spirit searches all things, even the deep things of God.

As for the believer, in Christ we can choose to be controlled by the Spirit, or we can choose to be controlled by the flesh. Each time we do not allow the Spirit to control us, then we are not pleasing God. To please God, we need to know God's will. So in order to do this, we have to get into the Word of God and be connected to the Holy Spirit's leading.

In John 15:5, Jesus tells us about himself, quote: I am the vine; you are the branches. If a man remains in me and I in him, he will bear much fruit; apart from me you can do nothing.

As long as the disciples remained with Jesus, they didn't lack anything. Jesus was everything that they needed and more. Today, we have Jesus all wrapped up in the Holy Spirit and the Word of God.

Hebrews 1:1-3 quote: In the past God spoke to our forefathers through the prophets at many times and in various ways, but in these last days he has spoken to us by his Son, whom he appointed heir of all things, and through whom he had made the universe. The Son is the radiance of God's glory and the exact representation of his being, sustaining all things by his powerful word. After he had provided purification for sins, he sat down at the right hand of the Majesty in heaven.

The Lord Jesus Christ has just as much of an impact with us as He had when He was with His disciples.

This is why we are told in Revelation 3:20 quote: Here I am! I stand at the door and knock. If anyone hears my voice and opens the door, I will come in and eat with him, and he with me.

The question for you is this: *Are you feeding on the solid food of the Word of God?*

Hebrews 5:14 quote: But solid food is for the mature, who by constant use have trained themselves to distinguish good from evil.

Once we become converted to the Christian faith, it is true that we have to feed on the milk of the Word of God first. But as we grow spiritually, while we are spiritually maturing in the Christian faith, we are going to desire the solid food of the Word of God. This is where our training will be coming from.

2 Timothy 3:16–17 quote: All Scripture is God-breathed and is useful for teaching, rebuking, correcting and training in righteousness, so that the man of God may be thoroughly equipped for every good work.

There is no other book that is on the market today that can train you like the Word of God can. How do believers mature? By constant feeding on the Word of God daily. It needs to become a habit. You are not going to learn everything in just one day. When we first started school, we went to grade school, then to elementary school, and then junior high and senior high school. We didn't start in just one day. But going to kindergarten all the way up to twelfth grade graduation, it takes years. When it comes down to feeding on the Word of God, it is an ongoing Christian life experience.

1 Corinthians 9:24–27 quote: Do you not know that in a race all the runners run, but only one gets the prize? Run in such a way to get the prize. Everyone who competes in the games goes into strict

training. They do it to get a crown that will not last; but we do it to get a crown that will last forever. Therefore I do not run like a man running aimlessly; I do not fight like a man beating the air. No, I beat my body and make it my slave so that after I have preached to others, I myself will not be disqualified for the prize.

What would be the sense in working out if you had no equipment to work out with? Today's runners need running equipment in order to run and exercise with. The same is true with a boxer, or any Olympic contender, who's in competition. Church, we need to have our equipment when it comes to living the Christian life. Our equipment is the Word of God.

Hebrews 4:12–13 quote: For the word of God is living and active. Sharper than any double-edged sword, it penetrates even to dividing soul and spirit, joints and marrow; it judges the thoughts and attitudes of the heart. Nothing in all creation is hidden from God's sight. Everything is uncover and laid bare before the eyes of him to whom we must give account.

God's Word is designed to touch you in such a way that whatever the Scripture or passage you are reading, it is designed for you, right at that very moment. It's just like a sword; it penetrates and cuts right through the heart. If you are doing something wrong, God's Word is going to warn you ahead of time.

For example, we are told in 1 Corinthians 10:13 quote: No temptation has seized you except what is common to man. And God is faithful; he will not let you be tempted beyond what you can bear. But when you are tempted, he will also provide a way out so that you can stand up under it.

By reading the Word of God, the believer can recognize temptation before giving into it. We live in a world where there are so many distractions. Lust, money, power, recognition, greed, selfish ambition, and vain conceit have become distractions for God's people.

This is why we are told in John 10:10 quote: The thief comes only to steal and kill and destroy; I have come that they may have life, and have it to the full.

Satan want to take a way our joy and destroy our testimonies. This can happen with trials, also the storms that we come in contact with throughout our Christian experiences. Just because we are going through these consequences in our lives doesn't mean that we throw in the spiritual towel. We go right back to the Word of God.

James 1:2–4 quote: Consider it pure joy, my brothers, whenever you face trials of many kinds, because you know that the testing of your faith develops perseverance. Perseverance must finish its work so that you may be mature and complete, not lacking anything.

Are you feeding on the solid food of the Word of God? Because if you are, you are going to do just fine as you get through the storms and the testing in your life. This is a sign of you maturing in the faith.

Hebrews 5:14 quote: But solid food is for the mature, who by constant use have trained themselves to distinguish good from evil.

The pastors are given a noble task when it comes to leading their congregation.

This is what they have all been instructed to do in Ephesians 4:12–13 quote: To prepare God's people for works of service, so that the body of Christ may be built up until we all reach unity in the faith and in the knowledge of the Son of God and become mature, attaining to the whole measure of fullness of Christ.

Church, God's Word tells us that we need to become mature. It is the pastor's duty that you mature. If there are people in the congregation that are mature, and you are struggling in the area of maturity, then you need to ask yourself this question: Am I'm feeding on the solid food of the Word of God? Or am I just going through the motions?

Hebrews 10:25 quote: Let us not give up meeting together, as some are in a habit of doing, but let us encourage one another-and all the more as you see the Day approaching.

Church, don't attend your local church just to be attending your local church. Expect to get something out of it whenever you attend. One of the main reasons why we are to encourage one another is to get them into the habit of reading and studying the Word of God for themselves. When Apostle Paul went to Berea, the people who came out to hear Paul preach paid very careful attention to what Paul was saying.

Acts 17:11 quote: Now the Bereans were of more noble character than the Thessalonians, for they receive the message with great eagerness and examined the Scriptures every day to see if what Paul said was true.

Church, your pastor is giving you some very serious information. And the information that is being given to you needs to be lined up with the Word of God. Anybody can talk a good game. But you need to pay very special attention to who you listen to. If what they are saying does not line up with the Word of God, then you need to back away and find another local church. This is what the pastors are told to do.

2 Timothy 4:2–4 quote: Preach the Word; be prepared in season and out of season; correct, rebuke and encourage-with great patience and careful instruction. For a time will come when men will not put up with sound doctrine. Instead, to suit their own desires, they will gather them around a great number of teachers to say what their itching ears want to hear. They will turn their ears away from the truth and turn aside to myths.

Without the Word of God, we all would be labeled not as pastors but as motivational speakers. We have enough of that going around in the local churches and on the television today, everybody being pumped up, leaving the church the very same way they came in: unchanged.

This is why we are told in Romans 12:1–2 quote: Therefore, I urge you brothers, in view of God's mercy, to offer your bodies as living sacrifices, holy and pleasing to God-this is your spiritual act of worship. Do not conform any longer to the pattern of this world, but be transformed by the renewing of your mind. Then you will be able to test and approve what God's will is-his good, pleasing and perfect will.

So how do we get our minds renewed? By getting into the reading of the Word of God. Mature believers can look at their life back when they were feeding on the milk of the Word. But since they have been feeding on the solid food of the Word of God, they know, without a shadow of doubt, there has been a change in the way that they have chosen how to live: godly.

Paul said to the saints in 1 Corinthians 3:1–2 quote: Brothers, I could not address you as spiritual but worldly-mere infants in Christ. I gave you milk, not solid food, for you were not yet ready for it. Indeed you are still not ready.

When it came down for the brothers at Corinth to move on to spiritual maturity, they had become so relaxed and so complacent that they didn't want to move on in the Christian faith. Christians are like this today. They have one foot in the world's system, and the other foot in the church. They are straddling the fence. They are not reading the Word of God. This is why the question is being asked, *Are you feeding on the solid food of the Word of God?* Church, there is no excuse.

Hebrews 5:14 quote: But solid food is for the mature, who by constant use have trained themselves to distinguish good from evil.

The very reason why we distinguish good from evil is because there are people out there who are bringing forth false teachings that don't line up with the Word of God. If they are not careful, Christians who are not matured in the faith will wind up having the wool pulled over their eyes.

Ephesians 4:14 quote: Then we will no longer be infants, tossed back and forth by the waves, and blown here and there by every wind of teaching and by the cunning and craftiness of men in their deceitful scheming.

While you are reading and studying the Word of God on your own, there needs to be a confirmation between you and your local pastor to make very sure that you understand exactly what you are reading.

1 Peter 4:11 quote: If anyone speaks, he should do it as one speaking the very words of God. If anyone serves, he should do it with the strength that God provides, so that in all things God may be praise through Jesus Christ.

Church, you cannot expect your pastor to speak the very Words of God to you if your pastor doesn't know anything about the biblical Scriptures. It doesn't make any biblical sense. Everybody wants to be a pastor, but not everybody wants to do whatever it takes to become one.

This is why we are told in Luke 6:40 quote: No student is above his teacher, but everyone who is fully trained will be like his teacher.

One of the biblical characteristics in being a pastor is that he must be able to teach. This means that a pastor must be feeding on the Word of God every day for the rest of his life. This is how the pastor can develop spiritual fruit in his life, so that he can pass his fruit along to others.

John 15:16 quote: You did not choose me, but I have chose you and appointed you to bear fruit-fruit that will last. Then the Father will give you whatever you ask in my name.

When I understood that my pastor was committed to reading the Word of God, it gave me the desire to want to read the Word of God on a continual basis. As I read the Word of God consistently, it give me an everlasting impact on my life, along with bearing fruit.

This is why Psalm 1:1–3 can also be quoted this way: quote: Blessed is the man who does not walk in the counsel of the wicked or stand in the way of sinners or sit in the seat of mockers. But his delight is in the law of the Lord, and on his law he meditates day and night. He is like a tree planted by streams of water, which yields its fruit in season and whose leaf does not wither. Whatever he does prospers.

A lot of Christians today do not realize how blessed that they can really become. If only they will take the time to go from the milk of the Word to the solid food of the Word. The solid food of the Word of God is the spiritual meat that we need to possess in our lives, daily. In fact, the Word of God is going to teach us how we can live and become godly.

1 Timothy 4:7 quote: Have nothing to do with godless myths and old wives' tales; rather, train yourself to be godly.

Living the Christian life doesn't just happen automatically. You have to want to live the Christian life; if you truly desire to do so, you have to train yourself to want it gladly enough.

The Lord God told Joshua this in Joshua 1:8 quote: Do not let this Book of the Law depart from your mouth; meditate on it day and night, so that you may be careful to do everything written in it.

Church, we need to be doing the same thing that Joshua was instructed to do by the Lord. We are to meditate on the Scriptures both day and night. Even though this was given to the Old Testament saints, it is still given to us today as believers.

In Romans 15:4 quote: For everything that was written in the past was written to teach us, so that through endurance and the encouragement of the Scriptures we might have hope.

Our hope is coming from the Scriptures that are from God's Word.

CONCLUSION

In order to grow from immature Christians to mature Christians, we must learn discernment. We must train our consciences, our senses, our minds, and our bodies to distinguish good from evil.

Philippians 4:8–9 quote: Finally, brothers, whatever is true, whatever is noble, whatever is right, whatever is pure, whatever is lovely, whatever is admirable-if anything is excellent or praiseworthy-think about such things.

Can you recognize temptation before it traps you? Can you tell the difference between a correct use of Scripture and a mistaken one? Jesus was able to do this with the Sadducees.

Matthew 22:29 quote. Jesus replied, "You are in error because you do not know the Scriptures or the power of God.

Our capacity to feast on deeper knowledge of God has to do with the solid food of the Word of God. Too often we want God's banquet before we are spiritually capable of digesting it. As you grow into the Lord, put into practice what you have learned; your capacity to understand the solid food of the Word of God will also grow. Question: *Are you feeding on the solid food of the Word of God?*

Hebrews 5:14 quote: But solid food is for the mature, who by constant use have trained themselves to distinguish good from evil.

Amen!

8

Worship and Glorify God and Enjoy Him Forever

Psalm 37:4–5 Delight yourself in Lord and he will give you the desires of your heart. Commit your way to the Lord; trust in him and he will do this.

SERMON MESSAGE:

Many of us today have favorite things that we like to do. And the very reason we like to do these things is because we are very good at doing them. It could be basketball, bowling, golf, singing, cooking, running, doing things on a computer, and so on, or just being alone reading a good book to feed your mind. Whether you are saved or unsaved, understand this: God gave us the ability to do these things and to become very good at what we do. What we need to do as individuals is to bring these talents out so that they can surface and we can excel in them. How do we do this?

Matthew 6:33 quote: But seek first his kingdom and his righteousness, and all these things will be given to you.

Seeking first the Kingdom of God and His righteousness in everything that we do will place us automatically into His

Kingdom. Worship should be on the very top of our list. Why worship? Because God has placed a desire in every believer's heart to worship Him. This is whether you choose to worship God or not. God has placed worship in your heart.

This is why Apostle Paul was able to tell us in Romans 12:1 quote: Therefore, I urge you brothers, in view of God's mercy, to offer your bodies as living sacrifices, holy and pleasing to God-this is your spiritual act of worship.

Church, we do not have to assemble ourselves anywhere any longer to worship our Heavenly Father. We do not have to go to the mountains or to the brooks and so on to worship the Lord. It all has to do with Who's dwelling inside of us, right at this very moment. We have God the Holy Spirit dwelling on the inside of us. And this is only if you are saved.

1 Corinthians 6:19–20 quote: Do you not know that your body is the temple of the Holy Spirit, who is in you, whom you have received from God? You are not your own; you were bought at a price. Therefore honor God with your body.

We are to honor God by the way that we live our lives before Him each day. We are always in the very presence of the Lord at all times. This is why we need to offer our bodies as living sacrifices holy and pleasing unto God. When Jesus told the woman at the well that a time was coming, and had now come, when the true worshipers will worship the Father in spirit and truth, He was revealing to her who God is.

John 4:24 quote: God is spirit, and his worshipers must worship in spirit and it truth."

We should acknowledge God's worth in Spirit and in truth. By God being Spirit means that God is not limited to just one place. What we need to understand is this: God is everywhere at the same time.

Hebrews 10:25 quote: Let us not give up meeting together, as some are in a habit of doing, but let us encourage one another-and all the more as you see the Day approaching.

Just because we enter into a place of worship during the week doesn't mean that we come to worship God as if God dwells in a building made with human hands. But we come to worship God together because God dwells in us.

This is why we are told in 1 John 4:4 quote: You dear children are from God and have overcome them, because the one who is in you is greater than the one who is in the world.

As believers in Christ, we have a greater alternative than what this world's system has to offer. One of the areas where we are able to operate in the Kingdom of God, when it comes to worship, is faith.

Hebrews 11:6 quote: And without faith it is impossible to please God, because anyone who comes to him must believe that he exist and that he rewards those who earnestly seek him.

If you do not believe that God exists, then you need to be saved. No questions asked. As a believer, when you have your back against the wall, and you have done all that you can, this is where your faith comes in.

Hebrews 11:1 quote: Now faith is being sure of what we hope for and certain of what we do not see.

I have eternal life right now. And it is because I have accepted Jesus Christ as my Savior and Lord. Even though I'm not in heaven right at this very moment, I know for certain, without a shadow of a doubt, I'm going. Church, this all has to do with my faith in the Lord.

Ephesians 2:8–9 quote: For it is by grace you have been saved, through faith-and this is not from yourselves, it is the gift of God-not by works, so that no one can boast.

Eternal life is a gift. All you need to do is act on receiving it by faith. Many religions and religious cults are trying to work their way to heaven. Heaven cannot be earned within itself. This is the very reason why God the Father sent His one and only Son to this world to die for us. Because every human being is born in sin.

Romans 5:8 quote: But God demonstrates his own love for us in this: While we were still sinners, Christ died for us.

An unsaved person cannot worship God until they can actually understand why they need to worship God. In Luke 17:12-19, the story of the ten lepers, nine were Jews and one was a Samaritan. Every one of them pleaded for Jesus to have pity on them. Jesus told them to go and show themselves to the priest. As they were on their way, they were all instantly cleansed. The Samaritan was the only one who came back and worshiped and thanked Jesus for the cleansing. Jesus asked, "Were not all ten cleansed? Where are the other nine? Was no one found to return and give praise to God except this foreigner?" Then He said to him, "Rise and go; your faith has made you well." Look at what Jesus said when He commended the Samaritan, who was a foreigner; this Samaritan who was a foreigner praised God for the cleansing. Church, shouldn't we as believers in Christ do the same thing for what Jesus did for us at Calvary?

John 8:34–36 quote: Jesus replied, "I tell you truth, everyone who sins is a slave to sin. Now a slave has no permanent place in the family, but a son belongs to it forever, So if the Son sets you free, you will be free indeed.

Just like Jesus freed the ten lepers from their leprosy, Jesus freed us from every sin. Our attitude of worship should be the same as the Samaritan, who was the foreigner, who returned to Jesus and began worshiping and praising Him. As believers, we have a reason and a purpose to worship and praise the Lord for all He has done for us. Church, our Heavenly Father is not going to twist our arms to get us to worship Him. The Lord has already done enough already.

2 Chronicles 7:14 quote: If my people, who are called by my name, will humble themselves and pray and seek my face and turn from their wicked ways, then will I hear from heaven and will forgive their sin and will heal their land.

When we seek God's face, we begin to worship Him. What are we doing? *Worshipping and glorifying God and enjoying Him forever.*

Psalm 37:4–5 quote: Delight yourself in the Lord and he will give you the desires of your heart. Commit your way to the Lord; trust in him and he will do this.

Whenever we are delighting ourselves in the Lord, our fleshly desires are going to change. We are not going to desire the same things that the people of world desire. Back in the heyday, many of us used to go out and party in the wee hours of the night. We'd come home on Sunday morning, only to sleep in all day long. Church, those days are long gone. In fact, we are told in 2 Corinthians 5:17 quote: Therefore, if anyone is in Christ, he is a new creation; the old has gone, the new has come.

The old way that we used to live is gone. The new way has come. Church, that new way is being in the willful act of worship.

1 Corinthians 13:11 quote: When I was a child, I talked like a child, I thought like a child, I reasoned like a child. When I became a man, I put childish ways behind me.

Instead of enjoying the things that we used to enjoy—drinking, smoking, doing drugs, using profanity, sleeping around and having unprotected sex, gambling, wild living, and so on—we no longer do them. We put childish ways behind us. As believers in Christ, we are now preparing ourselves for true genuine worship.

Ephesians 5:17–20 quote: Therefore, do not be foolish, but understand what the Lord's will is. Do not get drunk on wine, which leads to debauchery. Instead, be filled with the Spirit. Speak to one another with psalms, hymns and spiritual songs. Sing and make music in your heart to the Lord, always giving thanks to

God the Father for everything, in the name of our Lord Jesus Christ.

Whenever we are filled with the Spirit, we are preparing ourselves for an act of worship. True worship becomes a spiritual habit. Is there anyone in your life who you feel comfortable being around? If I could be self-employed or self-sufficient, I would want to spend all my time with my wife, at all times. We enjoy being in each other's presence. This is what our Heavenly Father wants from each of us: acknowledging His presence in our lives. From the time we get up to the time we go to bed.

1 Timothy 4:7 quote: Have nothing to do with godless myths and old wives' tales; rather, train yourself to be godly.

Getting in the habit of worshiping the Lord takes work. We have to be very serious in this area of worship. We are seeking God's face. We already got our Heavenly Father's attention at the very moment we gave our lives to Christ.

In fact, we are told in John 1:12–13 quote: Yet to all who received him, to those who believed in his name, he gave the right to become children of God-children born not of natural decent, nor of human decision or husband's will, but born of God.

Since we are children of God, God is our Heavenly Father. Our Heavenly Father is going to treat us as sons and daughters. God has no grandchildren. So whenever we mess up and go astray, expect your Heavenly Father to discipline you and bring you back home.

This is why Jesus tells us in John 15:1–2 quote: "I am the true vine, and my Father is the gardener. He cuts off every branch in me that bears no fruit, while every branch that does bear fruit he prunes so that it will be even more fruitful.

Our Heavenly Father disciplines us for our own good.

2 Timothy 4:5 quote: But you, keep your head in all situations, endure hardship, do the work of an evangelist, discharge all the duties of your ministry.

As believers, we are going to have to endure hardships whenever they occur. This is how we are able to be fit to share God's Holiness when we are disciplined.

Hebrews 12:7 quote: Endure hardship as discipline; God is treating you as sons. For what son is not disciplined by his father.

Now that we are adults, we can all look back on how our earthly parents raised us. They raised us the best that they could. If we did something wrong, they disciplined us by punishing us for our good. Why good? So that we would learn from the mistakes we made. Now that we have matured as adults, we do not do things we did when we were children and teenagers, thinking that we could get away with them.

Galatians 6:7–8 quote: Do not be deceived: God cannot be mocked. A man reaps what he sows. The one who sows to please his sinful nature, from that nature will reap destruction; the one who sows to please the Spirit, from the Spirit will reap eternal life.

The ones who are sowing to please the Spirit are the ones who will *worship and glorify God and enjoy Him forever.*

Psalm 37:4–5 quote. Delight yourself in the Lord and he will give you the desires of your heart. Commit your way to the Lord; trust in him and he will do this.

The most important time in the American family home is being in front of the television. The television gets more attention than God does.

Matthew 22:37 quote: Jesus replied: " 'Love the Lord your God with all your heart and with all your soul and with all your mind.

It is hard to love the Lord your God with all of your heart and soul and mind, when someone or something else has taken the place of the love of God in your life.

James 4:1–3 quote: What causes fights and quarrels among you? Don't they come from your desires that battle within you? You want something but don't get it. You kill and you covet, but you cannot have what you want. You quarrel and you fight. You do not have because you do not ask God. When you ask, you do not receive, because you ask with wrong motives, that you may spend what you get on your pleasures.

Whenever we ask with wrong motives, we must examine our motives and examine ourselves.

2 Corinthians 13:5 quote: Examine yourselves to see whether you are in the faith; test yourselves. Do you not realize that Christ Jesus is in you-unless, of course, you fail the test?

If you are saved, the Holy Spirit is there to lead and to guide you into all truth. If you are truly looking for the Lord to come through for you, when it comes to your desires, worship Him and glorify the Lord by giving Him glory in everything that you do.

1 Corinthians 10:31 quote: So whether you eat or drink or whatever you do, do it all for the glory of God.

If you can't give glory to God in everything that you do, then you should not do it. Myself included. Our life as believers in Christ ought to be seriously dedicated to the Lord. Dear Lord, today, this day, I dedicate my life to you. What does this mean? A celebrity who receives an award, such as an Oscar or Emmy or Grammy, may want to give this award to someone special to them; they dedicate the award to them or actually give it to them.

Romans 6:13 says, "Do not offer the parts of your body to sin, as instrument of wickedness, rather offer yourselves to God, as those who have been brought from death to life; and offer the parts of your body to Him as instruments of righteousness." When celebrities receive awards, these awards are made of genuine gold. Church, our Heavenly Father sees each of us as more expensive than gold. We are sacred in God's eyes. 1 Corinthians 3:16–17 says, "Don't you know that you yourselves are God's temple and that God's Spirit lives in you?" If anyone destroys God's temple, God will destroy him; for God's temple is sacred, and you are that temple. Church, our Heavenly Father has already set us up for true genuine worship. Worshiping God has now become our way of life. Worship is designed this way so that we can delight ourselves in the Lord, while we are in the midst of His presence. Our desires are going to change. We go from worldly desires to godly desires. Yes, there is a difference.

This is why we are told in Romans 12:2 quote: Do not conform any longer to the pattern of this world, but be transformed by the renewing of your mind. Then you will be able to test and approve what God's will is-his good, pleasing and perfect will.

The patterns of this world will keep us from *worshipping and glorifying God and enjoying Him forever.*

Psalm 37:4–5 quote: Delight yourself in the Lord and he will give you the desires of your heart. Commit your way to the Lord; trust in him and he will do this.

Church, we can't have it both ways.

Luke 16:13 quote: "No one can serve two masters. Either he will hate the one and love the other, or he will be devoted to the one and despise the other. You cannot serve both God and Money."

It is our Heavenly Father's will that we delight ourselves in Him. So how do we go about this? One of the reasons why we attend worship after we have been converted to faith in Christ is so that we can know God. If the Lord didn't want us to know Him, He wouldn't have allowed it to be written in His Word.

Listen to what Jesus says in Matthew 11:28–30 quote: Come to me, all you who are weary and burdened, and I will give you rest. Take my yoke upon you and learn from me, for I am gentle and humble in heart, and you will find rest for your souls. For my yoke is easy and my burden is light."

Jesus wants you to learn from Him. This is what it means to know Him. Jesus does not want to have a distant relationship with you. Many Christians today have distanced themselves from the Lord. Not only have some Christians distanced themselves, but they have also limited themselves from the Lord's presence.

Revelation 3:20 quote: Here I am! I stand at the door and knock. If anyone hears my voice and opens the door, I will come in and eat with him, and he with me.

Jesus wants to have a personal relationship with you. The people of the world need to see that in us as believers in Christ. You are the only Jesus that the people in your world will ever see. The very reason why Jesus reveals Himself to us through His Word is so that we can become like Him.

1 Corinthians 11:1 quote: Follow my example, as I follow the example of Christ.

Apostle Paul spent three and a half years in Arabia, being alone with Jesus. All those years, Paul was being taught by the Lord Jesus Christ Himself.

This was why Paul was able to say in Philippians 4:8–9 quote: Finally, brothers, whatever is true, whatever is noble, whatever is right, whatever is pure, whatever is lovely, whatever is admirable-if anything is excellent or praiseworthy-think about such things. Whatever you have learned or received or heard from me, or seen in me-put it into practice. And the God of peace will be with you.

The God of Peace was with Paul, and the God of Peace is being passed along to every believer who puts Christ's teachings into practice.

Hebrews 1:1–3 quote: In the past God spoke to our forefathers through the prophets at many times and in various ways, but in these last days he has spoken to us by his Son, whom he appointed heir of all things, and through whom he made the universe. The Son is the radiance of God's glory and the exact representation of his being, sustaining all things by his powerful word. After he had provided purification for sins, he sat down at the right hand of the Majesty in heaven.

Church, Jesus is still speaking to us today through His Word. The very reason why the Lord doesn't speak audibly to us today is because He doesn't need to. The Lord has given us His Word. The Word of God is all we really need to have God speak to us.

Hebrews 4:12–13 quote: For the word of God is living and active. Sharper than any double-edged sword, it penetrates even the dividing soul and spirit, joints and marrow; it judges the thoughts and the attitudes of the heart. Nothing in all creation is hidden from God's sight. Everything is uncovered and laid bare before the eyes of him to whom we must give account.

As long as you are reading and studying the Word of God, God is going to be the one speaking to you. How do we know this?

2 Peter 1:20–21 quote. Above all, you must understand that no prophecy of Scripture came about by the prophet's own interpretation. For prophecy never had its origin in the will of man, but men spoke from God as they were carried along by the Holy Spirit.

Are you ready for this? The more that you read and study and apply God's Word to your everyday life, the more you are delighting yourselves in the Lord.

Listen to what Peter says in 1 Peter 2:2–3: quote. Like newborn babies, crave pure spiritual milk, so that by it you may grow up in your salvation, now that you have tasted that the Lord is good.

Church, if the Lord is good, then you are delighting yourselves in Him. As we mature on the milk of the Word of God, we are prepare to move on to the very next level of our faith. The meat of the Word of God. There is no short cut to reading the Word of God.

We are told in 2 Timothy 2:15, quote: Do your best to present yourself to God as one approved, a workman who does not need to be ashamed and who correctly handles the word of truth.

This is God's approval only.

Our Heavenly Father wants us to share in the benefits when it comes to true genuine worship.

Proverbs 3:1–10 quote: My son, do not for get my teaching, but keep my commands in your heart, for they will prolong your life many years and bring you prosperity. Let love and faithfulness never leave you; bind them around your neck, write them on the tablet of your heart. Then you win favor and a good name in the sight of God and man. Trust in the Lord with all your heart and lean not on your own understanding; in all your ways acknowledge him, and he will make your paths straight. Do not be wise in your own eyes; fear the Lord and shun evil. This will bring health to your body and nourishment to your bones. Honor the Lord with your wealth, with the firstfruits of all your crops; then your barns will be filled to overflowing, and your vats will brim over with new wine.

As long as we delight ourselves in the very things of the Lord, the Lord is going to bring our desires to pass in our lives. We are not talking about worldly pleasures, but godly pleasures—things that glorify God. Colossians 3:16 says, "Let the Word of Christ dwell in you richly as you teach and admonish one another with all wisdom, and as you sing songs, hymns, and spiritual songs with gratitude in your hearts to God." *Worship and glorify God and enjoy Him forever.*

Psalm 37:4–5 quote. Delight yourself in the Lord and he will give you the desires of your heart, Commit your way to the Lord; trust in him and he will do this.

CONCLUSION

To delight in someone is to experience great pleasure and joy in his or her presence. This happens only when we know that person well. Thus, to delight in the Lord, we must know Him better.

Knowledge of God's great love will indeed give us delight. To commit ourselves to the Lord means entrusting everything—our lives, our families, our jobs, our possessions—to God's control and guidance. To commit ourselves to the Lord means to trust completely in Him, believing that the Lord can care for us better than we can care for ourselves. We should be willing to wait patiently for the Lord to work out what is best for us.

Romans 8:28 quote. And we know that in all things God works for the good of those who love him, who have been called according to his purpose.

Worship and glorify God and enjoy Him forever. Amen!

9

Being on the Top of Your Game Requires Discipline

1 Corinthians 9:24–27. Do you not know that in a race all the runners run, but only one gets the prize? Run in such a way as to get the prize. Everyone who competes in the games goes into strict training. They do it to get a crown that will not last; but we do it to get a crown that will last forever. Therefore I do not run like a man running aimlessly; I do not fight like a man beating the air. No, I beat my body and make it my slave so that after I have preached to others, I myself will not be disqualified for the prize.

SERMON MESSAGE:

Question: What comes to your mind whenever you think about the word *discipline*? When we were younger, we used to think about the word *discipline* as being something very bad because we thought that it was always lined up with us being punished for being caught in the very act of doing something we did wrong. When we got the beatings and the whippings and the spankings, we learned not to continue to get into the same trouble that we got into before. Before you allow yourselves to get caught up in that very same trouble spot again, you remember, Hey, I got a good whipping for that, I'm not doing that again. What just happened right then? You learned from it. If you are constantly getting yourself in the same trouble over and over again, then you have a very serious problem. You are eventually going to reap what you sow.

Galatians 6:7–8 quote: Do not be deceived: God cannot be mocked. A man reaps what he sows. The one who sows to please his sinful nature, from that nature will reap destruction; the one who sow to please the Spirit, from the Spirit will reap eternal life.

Church, sowing and reaping can work for you, or it can work against you. The choice is up to you. Because of the sin problem, life is full of mistakes. But just because you make a mistake doesn't mean that you are bad person. So when you make a mistake, what do you do? You learn from it. An unsaved person, as they go through life, will constantly make mistakes. Until they receive the help that they really need, they are always going to stumble and struggle. But in order for them to get around this, they need to be Born Again.

Jesus said to Nicodemus in John 3:3 quote: "I tell you the truth, no one can see the kingdom of God unless he is born again.

The Kingdom of God is God's right way of doing things for your life. There are no mistakes in the Kingdom of God, because God doesn't make any mistakes. As Christians, each time we do something wrong, we automatically step out of the Kingdom of God. What happened when Adam disobeyed God's only commandment? Adam stepped away from the very presence of God. Living a Christian lifestyle can keep you from living in sin and doing the wrong things. What is it that Christians need to help them live a Christian life? They need to have the understanding of the Word of God in their lives.

1 Peter 2:2–3 quote: Like newborn babies, crave pure spiritual milk, so that by it you may grow up in your salvation, now that you have tasted that the Lord is good.

Without the Word of God in our everyday lives, we may go astray and become influenced and polluted by this world's system. This is why no one can live the Christian life apart from the Word of God.

John 15:5 quote: "I am the vine; you are the branches. If a man remains in me and I in him, he will bear much fruit; apart from me you can do nothing.

How do we allow Jesus as the true vine to remain in us? By remaining in His Word.

John 15:7 quote: If you remain in me and my words remain in you, ask whatever you wish, and it will be given you.

This is why we are told in Hebrews 1:1-3 quote: In the past God spoke to our forefathers through the prophets at many times and in various ways, but in these last days he has spoken to us by his Son, whom he appointed heir of all things, and through whom he made the universe. The Son is the radiance of God's glory and the exact representation of his being, sustaining all things by his powerful word. After he provided purification for sins, he sat down at the right hand of the Majesty in heaven.

Church, Jesus is speaking to us as believers today through His Word. There are so many Scriptures that support this.

Matthew 4:4 quote: Jesus answered, "It is written: 'Man does not live by bread alone, but on every word that comes from the mouth of God.

When Jesus ministered on this earth during His earthly ministry, He was God's mouthpiece.

John 5:19 quote: Jesus gave them this answer: "I tell you the truth, the Son can do nothing by himself; he can do only what he sees his Father doing, because whatever the Father does the Son also does.

Every time Jesus opened His mouth, the Father spoke through Him. Jesus was God in the flesh.

John 1:1–3, 14 quote: In the beginning was the Word, and the Word was with God, and the Word was God. He was with God in the beginning. Through him all things were made; without him nothing was made that has been made. The Word became flesh and made his dwelling among us. We have seen his glory, the glory of the One and Only, who came from the Father, full of grace and truth.

As believers in Christ, we have all the help that we need to live the Christian life. We have the help of the Holy Spirit dwelling with us along with the Word of God. The Holy Spirit and the Word of God both work together in our lives. After the resurrection, Jesus' disciples could not do anything until He gave them the instructions that they needed to obey.

Acts 1:4–5 quote: On one occasion, while he was eating with them, he gave them this command: "Do not leave Jerusalem, but wait for the gift my Father promised, which you have heard me speak about. For John baptized with water, but in a few days you will be baptized with the Holy Spirit.

The three years that Jesus spent with His disciples, He was forced to limit Himself, because He was living in this earthly realm. But now that Jesus has been glorified, He can be everywhere at the same time.

Matthew 18:20 quote: For where two or three come together in my name, there am I with them.

Church, God is the active power of the Holy Spirit, who is working in our everyday lives, along with the Word of God. The Holy Spirit helps brings the Word of God to our memory. If you do not memorize Scriptures, you can't expect to know them.

This is why we are told in Joshua 1:8 quote: Do not let this Book of the Law depart from your mouth; meditate on it day and night, so that you may be careful to do everything written in it. Then you will be prosperous and successful.

File clerks collect very important information. The very reason why they carry out this task is so that when this information comes up again, they know exactly where to find it. They go to the files. Whether it is stored in a file cabinet or saved in a computer, they know exactly where to go. Memorizing the Scriptures is the same thing. But the Holy Spirit is attaining this biblical information for you. All you really need to do is meditate on the Word of God. How do you do this? You have to prepare yourself to study.

2 Timothy 2:15 quote: Do your best to present yourself to God as one approved, a workman who does not need to be ashamed and who correctly handles the word of truth.

Whenever we study the Word of God as believers, God's Holy Word is going to change our whole perspective on the way we look at our everyday life. We no longer see life from our point of view, but we now see life from God's point of view. The Lord God has compassion for lost souls. It is God's desire that everyone be saved.

2 Peter 3:9 quote: The Lord is not slow in keeping his promise, as some understand slowness. He is patient with you, not wanting anyone to perish, but everyone to come to repentance.

Salvation doesn't happen automatically. Not everyone is going to be saved. But the opportunity to be saved will always be there. This is where we come in as believers in Christ. We prepare ourselves to become faithful witnesses for Christ.

Acts 1:8 quote: But you will receive power when the Holy Spirit comes on you; and you will be my witnesses in Jerusalem, and in all Judea and Samaria, and to the ends of the earth."

We start out by the way we live as Christians. If we are not living a Christian life, nobody is going to have anything to do with us.

Ephesians 5:15–16 quote: Be very careful, then, how you live-not as unwise but wise, making the most of every opportunity, because the days are evil.

We cannot be mediocre Christians, but we have to be serious Christians. This is why *being on the top of your game requires discipline.*

1 Corinthians 9:24 quote. Do you not know that in a race all the runners run, but only one gets the prize? Run in such of the way to get the prize.

When the Cleveland Cavaliers were the hottest team in the NBA, they played like they had already taken it all. They were all at the top of their game. The Cavaliers were a professional basketball team. How did the Cavaliers become this good? They practiced strict discipline. Church, when it comes down to living the Christian life as a believer in Christ, it's going to take practice and strict discipline in the very lives that we live. To live a life as a Christian is to live a godly life.

1 Timothy 4:7 quote: Have nothing to do with godless myths and old wives' tales; rather, train yourself to be godly.

Many Christians today think that all they have to do is get saved, and that's it. They go on about their business and continue to live in sin. No. This is why it is a must that we discipline ourselves to live a godly life.

1 Peter 2:12 quote: Live such good lives among the pagans that, though they accuse you of doing wrong, they may see your good deeds and glorify God on the day he visits us.

We need to live the Christian life in such a way as to win the prize. You mean to tell me that God rewards us on earth for living a godly life? Yes. Because whenever you are living a godly life, the very life that you live is going to have an everlasting impact on others.

Proverbs 3:1-10 quote: My son do not forget my teaching, but keep my commands in your heart, for they will prolong your life many years and bring you prosperity. Let love and faithfulness never leave you; bind them around your neck, write them on the tablet of your heart. Then you will win favor and a good name in the sight of God and man. Trust in the Lord with all of your heart and lean not on your own understanding; in all your ways acknowledge him, and he will make your paths straight. Do not be wise in your own eyes; fear the Lord and shun evil. This will bring health to your body and nourishment to your bones. Honor the Lord with your wealth, with the first fruits of all your crops; then your barns will be filled to overflowing, and your vats will brim over with new wine.

Whenever we are living a godly life among the unsaved, the Lord is going to give us favor. Do you remember what happened in the life of Joseph? Joseph didn't realize it, but the Lord was working it all out for his good. Every situation that Joseph was placed in, God had always showed him favor. The very same can be said about each and every one of us, just as long as we are living godly lives.

Romans 8:28 quote: And we know in all things God works for the good of those who love him, who have been called according to his purpose.

So if you are living a godly life, then your Heavenly Father has a purpose for you.

Listen to what Jesus said in John 15:16 quote: You did not choose me, but I chose you and appointed you to go and bear fruit-fruit that will last. Then the Father will give you whatever you ask in my name.

Whether you know it or not, every believer was appointed to bear good fruit. If you choose to go through life without bearing any good fruit, then you can expect yourself to be cut off.

John 15:1–2 quote: "I am the true vine, and my Father is the gardener. He cut off every branch in me that bears no fruit, while every branch that does bear fruit he prunes so that it will be even more fruitful.

What does it mean to "prune" in the biblical sense? It means to discipline. Discipline is a word that we need to embrace, because it is our friend. It is not an act of punishment, it is act of correction. Church, while we are in training, we are going to make mistakes. But we are supposed to train ourselves not to.

2 Timothy 3:16–17 quote: All Scripture is God-breathe and is useful for teaching, rebuking, correcting and training in righteousness, so that the man of God may be thoroughly equipped for every good work.

We are to train ourselves in the area of righteousness, by getting into the Word of God. The Word of God is designed to equip the believer for every good work.

We are told in Ephesians 2:10 quote: For we are God's workmanship, created in Christ Jesus to do good works, which God prepared in advance for us to do.

This is why the Word of God is so very important to us today as believers in Christ. God's Word is more than just a book. It is Basic Instructions Before Leaving Earth.

In fact, we are told in Hebrews 4:12–13 quote: For the word of God is living and active. Sharper than any doubled-edged sword, it penetrates even the dividing soul and spirit, joints and marrow; it judges the thoughts and attitudes of the heart. Nothing in all creation is hidden from God's sight. Everything is uncovered and laid bare before the eyes of him to whom we must give account.

Every time we read the Word of God, we are being held accountable. This is what *being on the top of your game requires discipline* is all about.

1 Corinthians 9:25 quote. Everyone who competes in the games goes into strict training. They do it to get a crown that will not last; but we do it to get a crown that will last forever.

As believers, this is why we have to be on the top of our game when it comes to applying God's Holy Word to our lives every day.

James 1:22–24 quote: Do not merely listen to the word to deceive yourselves. Do what it says. Anyone who listen to the word but does not do what it says is like a man who looks at his face in a mirror and, after looking at himself, goes away and immediately forgets what he looks like.

Knowing the Word of God may be all well and good, but if you do not apply it to your life, all you are really doing is just talking loud and saying nothing. This is what the Pharisees and the teachers of the law were doing in Jesus' day. Jesus exposed them to His disciples.

Jesus said in Matthew 23:2-3 quote: "The teachers of the law and the Pharisees sit in Moses' seat. So you must obey them and do everything they tell you. But do not do what they do, for they do not practice what they preach.

All that they were really are doing was talking loud and doing nothing. Don't do as I do, do as I say. They taught the truth, but they did not live the truth by the very lives they were living. As we live the Christian life as believers, we have to set biblical examples for others to follow. But it starts with us. Don't teach it if you are not going to live it with your life.

1 Peter 2:21 quote. To this you were called, because Christ suffered for you, leaving you an example, that you should follow in his steps.

This is the very reason why the Lord gave us pastors. And here is the main reason: Ephesians 4:12–14 quote: To prepare God's people for works of service, so that the body of Christ may be built up until we all reach unity in the faith and in the knowledge of the Son of God and become mature, attaining to the whole measure, of the fullness of Christ. Then we will no longer be infants, tossed back and forth by the waves, and blown here and there by every wind of teaching and by the cunning and craftiness of men in their deceitful scheming.

In order for the local shepherds to prepare you, they have to be already prepared themselves. To be a pastor or a teacher, you have to be on the very top of your game.

The pastors are told in 1 Peter 5:2–3 quote: Be shepherds of God's flock that is under your care, serving as overseers-not because you must, because you are willing, as God wants you be; not greedy for money, but eager to serve; not lording it over those being entrusted to you, but being examples to the flock.

If you belong to a very good church, and your pastor is grounded in the biblical Scriptures of the Word of God, then you can expect to have the opportunity to become grounded in the Scriptures as well.

Luke 6:40 quote: A student is not above his teacher, but everyone who is fully trained will be like his teacher.

Church, you can only become as good as your teacher. If you have a teacher who knows the Word of God really well, then you are going to know the Word of God just as well. The Word of God is to teach you the dos and the don'ts.

James 4:17 quote: Anyone, then, who knows the good he ought to do and doesn't do it, sins.

Why are the things that we are to do so very important? Because the things that we do for Christ will be the only things we will get credit for when we get to heaven.

2 Corinthians 5:10 quote: For we must all appear before the judgment seat of Christ, that each one may receive what is due him for the things done while in the body, whether good or bad.

Most people know that the L.A. Lakers have won the NBA championship; they received the NBA World Championship trophy, along with the championship rings. The trophy and the rings are not going to last forever. But the things that we do for Christ will last forever.

This is why we are told in 2 Corinthians 4:18, "So we fix our eyes not on what is seen, but on what is unseen. For what is seen is temporary, but what is unseen is eternal." *Being on the top of your game requires discipline.*

1 Corinthians 9:26–27 quote: Therefore I do not run like a man running aimlessly; I do not fight like a man beating the air. No, I beat my body and make it my slave so that after I have preached to others, I myself will not be disqualified for the prize.

Tell your body no. You cannot allow your flesh to control you any longer, because you are now in control.

2 Corinthians 5:17 quote: Therefore, if anyone is in Christ, he is a new creation; the old has gone, the new has come.

The very moment that we were converted to faith in Christ, our Heavenly Father placed us as tenants in control of our bodies.

This is why we are told in 1 Corinthians 6:19–20 quote: Do you not know that your body is the temple of the Holy Spirit, that is in you, whom you have receive from God? You are not your own; you were bought at a price. Therefore honor God with your body.

Before we were saved, our five senses were taking advantage of us and controlling us. But now since we have been set free, we can choose whether or not to allow our fives senses to control us.

This is the very reason why Apostle Paul said in 1 Corinthians 9:26–27 quote: Therefore I do not run like a man running aimlessly; I do not fight like a man beating the air. No, I beat my body and make it my slave so that after I have preached to others, I myself will not be disqualified for the prize.

Whenever a man is running aimlessly, it shows one thing. This man is out of control. This is the reason why you hear about people robbing people, people cussing out people and telling them off, people killing people, and so on. It is because they are out of control. Many Christians today have disqualified themselves, because of the type of sinful lifestyle they live. They are still living worldly lives.

Paul wrote about the Christians at Corinth as being worldly, because they were still acting like spiritual infants. Apostle Paul addressed them this way: 1 Corinthians 3:1–2 quote: Brothers, I could not address you as spiritual but worldly-mere infants in Christ. I gave you milk, not solid food, for you were not ready for it. Indeed, you are still not ready.

These Christians were not on the top of their game. There was so much conflict and division among them. Paul wrote to them so that it could nipped in the bud. To be on the top of your game, you have to be in control at all times. Whenever you are in control, you give yourselves completely to the Spirit's leading, so He can lead you along.

Galatians 5:16–21 quote: So I say live by the Spirit and you will not gratify the desires of the sinful nature. For the sinful nature desires what is contrary to the Spirit, and the Spirit what is contrary to the sinful nature. They are in conflict with each other, so that you do not do what you want. But if you are led by the Spirit, you are not under law. The acts of the sinful nature are obvious: sexual immorality, impurity and debauchery; idolatry and witchcraft; hatred, discord, jealousy, fits of rage, selfish ambition, dissensions, factions and envy; drunkenness, orgies, and the like. I warn you, as I did before, that those who live like this will not inherit the kingdom of God.

Whenever you are operating in the Kingdom of God, you are allowing the Holy Spirit to lead and guide you into all truth.

Galatians 5:22–23 quote: But the fruit of the Spirit is love, joy, peace, patience, kindness, goodness, faithfulness, gentleness and self-control. Against such things there is no law.

But in order for you to allow the Holy Spirit to accomplish this task, your flesh has to become your slave. When sinful activities occur in your life that you do not agree with, you have to tell your flesh no, because you are going to be tempted.

This is why we are told in 1 Corinthians 10:13 quote: No temptation has seized you except what is common unto man. And God is faithful; he will not let you be tempted beyond what you can bear. But when you are tempted, he will also provide a way out so that you can stand up under it.

As long as we do what is right, there will always be a way for us to escape each time. In the world in which we live, there are so many distractions. Satan does not want us to succeed.

This is why Peter tells us in 1 Peter 5:8 quote: Be self-control and alert. Your enemy the devil prowls around like a roaring lion looking for someone to devour.

Church, if you are not grounded in the Scriptures, and you don't know the Word of God for your life, then the devil is going to have a field day with you. Because as he comes on to you, you must be ready to take him on. So how do you do this?

James 4:7 quote: Submit yourselves, then, to God. Resist the devil, and he will flee from you.

You resist the devil by submitting yourself to God. What does it mean to submit? It means to do the will of God for your lives.

Romans 12:1–2 quote: Therefore, I urge you, brothers, in the view of God's mercy, to offer your bodies as living sacrifices, holy and pleasing unto God-this is your spiritual act of worship. Do not conform any longer to the pattern of this world, but be transformed by the renewing of your mind. Then you will be able to test and approve what God's will is-his good, pleasing and perfect will.

As we renew our minds, as we get into the Word of God, we no longer will allow ourselves to be connected to this world's system.

1 John 2:15–17 quote: Do not love the world or anything in the world. If anyone loves the world, the love of the Father is not in him. For everything in the world-the cravings of sinful man, the lust of his eyes and the boasting of what he has and does-comes not from the Father but from the world. The world and its desires pass away, but the man who does the will of God lives forever.

Doing the will of God for your life will allow you to be on the very top of your game.

Listen to what it says in Colossians 3:23–24: quote: Whatever you do, work at it with all your heart, as working for the Lord, not for men, since you know you will receive your inheritance from the Lord as a reward. It is the Lord Christ you are serving.

CONCLUSION

Winning a race requires purpose and discipline. Apostle Paul uses the illustration of a race to explain that the Christian life takes hard work, self-denial, and grueling preparation. To live the Christian life is going to cost you. As Christians, we are running toward our heavenly rewards. Essential disciplines of prayer, Bible study, and worship equip us to run with vigor and stamina. Don't merely observe the grandstand; don't just turn out to jog a couple of laps each morning. Train diligently—your spiritual progress depends upon it.

1 Corinthians 15:58 quote: Therefore my dear brothers, stand firm. Let nothing move you. Always give yourselves fully to the work of the Lord, because you know that your labor in the Lord is not in vain.

Are you on the very top of your game? Amen!

10

Be Very Careful Who You Listen To

Ephesians 4:14. Then we will no longer be infants, tossed back and forth by the waves, and blown here and there by every wind of teaching and by the cunning and craftiness of men in their deceitful scheming.

SERMON MESSAGE:

Have you ever wondered why there are so many religions in the world today? Some societies think that it is all right for an individual to believe what they want to believe. They have a right to believe whatever they want to believe. But the question is, is it the right choice? There are certain countries where you can't practice just any ole' religion. In those countries, religion is a distraction to keep people from hearing the real truth about the Lord Jesus Christ. Some people are so caught up in everything, and they do not realize that they are bombarded with all types of distractions. These distractions are designed to pull the people of this world further and further away from God. Because of this, people have become atheists or agnostics. The atheist believes that God does not exist. The agnostic believes that there is no way to know whether God exists.

Hebrews 11:6 quote And without faith it is impossible to please God, because anyone who comes to him must believe he exists and he rewards those that earnestly seek him.

In order to believe that there is a God, and that God does exist, one has to have faith in God. Lord, if you are really there, show me. Reveal Yourself to me. And if you are really sincere, God will reveal Himself to you. The Lord has placed every one of us in the right place at the right time. Galatians 4:4 says, "But when the time had fully come, God sent His Son, born of a woman, born under law, to redeem those under the law, that we might receive the full rights as sons."

Just like it was the right time for Jesus to appear on the scene, today it is true with us; it was the right time for you to appear on the scene. It doesn't matter how you were conceived or how you got here. The only thing that matters now is that you are here. Something evil might have transpired that brought you here, you may have been conceived while your mother was raped, or you might have been conceived out of wedlock; it doesn't matter. But what does matter is you are here now. As long as you are willing to become Born Again, God has a plan for your life. And if you are not Born Again yet, then God is still waiting for you to become Born Again so that He can use you. And if you are already Born Again, then you are saved by the Blood of Lamb, the Lord Jesus Christ. Our Heavenly Father wants to use us in the area where we can have impact on the lives of others.

Acts 1:8 quote: But you will receive power when the Holy Spirit comes on you; and you will be my witnesses in Jerusalem, and in all Judea and Samaria, and to the ends of the earth."

Our Jerusalem is our comfort zone. This is an area in our lives where we feel very comfortable when it comes down to witnessing and sharing our faith. Where we share our faith is where we are going to let our light shine.

Jesus said it this way in Matthew 5:16: quote: In the same way, let your light shine before men, that they may see your good deeds and praise your Father in heaven.

Next, we have our Judea. This place of witnessing can be considered our own backyard: our neighborhood, our workplace, the places where we frequently visit from time to time, our in-laws, our associates, and so on. As believers in Christ, we need to ask the Lord to give us compassion for lost souls. When it comes down to being lost, hell is no place for a human being. It doesn't matter how sinful they are.

Peter tells us in 2 Peter 3:9, quote: The Lord is not slow in keeping his promise, as some understand slowness. He is patient with you, not wanting anyone to perish, but everyone to come to repentance.

If God is not willing that any should perish, then we should have the same desire, that none should perish either. We need to see people the same way that our Heavenly Father sees them, lost and in need of a Savior. This brings us to the next one: Samaria. Back in Jesus' day, the Jews didn't have anything to do with a Samaritan. They avoided these people as if they were the scum of the earth. They really despised them. If anyone didn't deserve to be saved in their eyes, it was Samaritans. When the Lord Jesus Christ told His disciples that they were witnesses in Jerusalem and

Judea, He made it very clear that He included Samaria as well. What is Samaria to a believer today? Our Samaria is people we do not want to have anything to do with. We think if these people were to die in their sins, we would say, so be it. Church, this is the wrong attitude to have. Especially when we call ourselves Christians.

Philippians 2:3–5 quote: Do nothing out of selfish ambition or vain conceit, but in humility consider others better than yourselves. Each of you should not look only to your own interests, but also the interests of others. Your attitude should be the same as that of Christ Jesus.

What is in the best interest of those who are considered lost? It is that they become saved. When Jesus was opposed by the religious leaders in His day, He still extended an invitation to them. John 8:23–24 says, "You are from below; I am from above. You are of this world; I am not of this world. I told you that you would die in your sins; if you do not believe that I am [the one I claim to be] you will indeed die in your sins."

Church, all that these religious leaders needed to do individually was to believe in who Jesus claimed to be and begin to receive Jesus as Lord. Here's the point: If Jesus could open Himself up, so the religious leaders could receive Him, then we should be able to open ourselves for others to receive Jesus as Lord as well. Just because we have the antidote to share Christ with others, doesn't give us the right to share our faith with just anybody we want. Your friends are not going to want to listen to you. They want you to continue on doing what you were doing before you became converted to your faith in Christ. Just like you are trying to influence them, they are still trying to influence you, so that you can continue to hang out with them. They have religion on their side, but you have the Lord Jesus Christ on your side. *Be very careful who you listen to.*

Ephesians 4:14 quote: Then we will no longer be infants, tossed back and forth by the waves blown here and there by every wind of teaching and by the cunning and the craftiness of men in their deceitful scheming.

Religion is having a field day in the world. But if you are grounded in the Word of God, you do not have to be tossed back and forth by the waves when it comes down to false doctrine. Christians today are leaving one local church and going to another. Many local churches today have become revolving doors. Just because a local church has become small doesn't mean that the Word of God is not being preached in it. Christians today will not sit still, and for this reason, they have become stumbling blocks for the unsaved. Find a Bible-believing Christ-centered church and stay there. If the Lord hasn't told you to move, then don't you move.

We are told in 1 Corinthians 15:58 quote: Therefore, my dear brothers, stand firm, Let nothing move you. Always give yourselves fully to the work of the Lord, because you know that your labor in the Lord is not in vain.

If you do not give yourself fully to the work of the Lord, expect to drift from church to church. Many Christians want to have it their way, and if they can't have it their way, they will leave and try to take as many Christians as they can with them. But if you are grounded in the Scriptures, you are not going to leave.

I experienced this in the ministry before I became a pastor. One church member told me that the pastor wasn't preaching and teaching the Word of God. This was not true, because I was taking notes each time the pastor was preaching. The same member who told me that the pastor wasn't teaching the Word was fondling her boyfriend while the pastor was preaching. Satan is rocking the boat in many local Bible-believing Christ-centered churches today.

1 Peter 5:8 quote: Be self-control and alert. Your enemy the devil prowls around like a roaring lion looking for someone to devour.

Who is Peter writing to? Peter is writing to Christians everywhere. He is not writing to the people of the world. The people of this world have no concept of what Satan is trying to do to Christians. The devil comes to church on Sundays, and his desire is to distract you from getting the Word of God in you. And many local churchgoers are playing right into his hands.

Hebrews 10:24–25 quote: And let us consider how we may spur one another on toward love and good deeds. Let us not give up meeting together, as some who are in a habit of doing, but let us encourage one another-and all the more as you see that Day approaching.

Why do we come to church in the first place? To worship and to fellowship with one another, and to feed on the Word of God together. What are we doing, Church? We are strengthening one another in the Body of Christ so that we can become mature in our faith in Christ, so that the believers in the church can be built up. You can't expect to be built up in the Christian faith, if you are constantly listening to anybody and everybody. You need to use discernment. Pay attention to who you listen to, and pay attention to what you hear. You have to consider the source, who you receive your information from. *Be very careful who you listen to.*

Ephesians 4:14 quote: Then we will no longer be infants, tossed back and forth by the waves, and blown here and there by every wind of teaching and by the cunning and craftiness of men in their deceitful scheming.

When Apostle Paul is speaking about infants, who's he referring to? Paul is speaking about the babes in Christ who haven't become grounded in the Word of God. You have Christians who have been saved for many years who are still acting like spiritual babies. They won't come to church regularly; they won't read and study their Bibles. The only time they pray is when they attend church or when something bad happens in their lives. They have never witnessed to someone about their faith in Christ, so when the enemy does come on the prowl, they become easily persuaded.

Matthew 23:2–3 quote. The teachers of the law and the Pharisees sit in Moses seat. So you must obey them and do everything they tell you. But do not do what they do, for they do not practice what they preach.

For religious reasons, these Jewish rulers and Pharisees were considered the official leaders of Jesus' day in Jerusalem. It was out of obedience that Jesus told His disciples to obey them. As believers, we have to obey the judicial law that is set before us. Even though some of our leaders may do something illegal and get away with it, it doesn't mean that we have the right to do the same. We set the examples by practicing what we preach. We do this not because we have a title as a pastor, or an important office in the local church, but we do this because we are Christians. A true Christian represents themselves as being followers of Christ.

1 Peter 2:21 quote: To this you were called, because Christ suffer for you, leaving you an example, that you should follow in his steps.

When was the last time you read or listened to the four Gospels? When the Lord Jesus ministered on this earth, He became a role model for all to see and to follow. In Matthew 4:18-19: As Jesus was walking beside the Sea of Galilee, he saw two brothers, Simon called Peter and his brother Andrew. They were casting a net into the lake, for they were fishermen. Come, follow me," Jesus said, and I will make you fishers of men." What did it mean for Peter to follow Jesus? Peter was to follow Jesus' lifestyle or way of life. Jesus was setting Peter and the rest of His disciples up to catch men, instead of catching fish.

Luke 9:23 quote: "If anyone would come after me, he must deny himself and take up his cross daily and follow me.

Make very sure that the teachings of the person you listen to are lined up with the Word of God.

1 Peter 4:11 quote: If anyone speaks, he should do it as one speaking the very words of God. If anyone serves, he should do it with the strength God provides, so that in all things God may be praised through Jesus Christ. To him be the glory and the power for ever and ever. Amen.

If you are going to speak the very words of God, then you have to study the Word of God. When Paul spent those three years in Arabia with the Lord, he was being taught the very things of God. After Paul's time spent with the Lord was over, he went up to Jerusalem and met with the disciples, and they were all on the same page. The pastors in the local churches have duties that have to be carried out. The Lord prepares them, and they in turn prepare the congregations in the local churches.

Ephesians 4:11–14 quote: It was he who gave some to be apostles, some to be prophets, some to be evangelists, and some to be pastors and teachers, to prepare God's people for works of service, so that the body of Christ may be built up until we all reach the unity of the faith and in the knowledge of the Son of God and become mature, attaining to the whole measure of fullness of Christ. Then we will no longer be infants, tossed back and forth by the waves, and blown here and there by every wind of teaching and by the cunning and craftiness of men in their deceitful scheming.

Everyone thinks that when it comes to carrying out the duties in the local church, everyone looks to the pastor. They think that the pastor does everything in the church. Church members are not being built up today. Many of them have lost their zeal when it comes down to carrying out their assignment for the work of the Lord. They never stay in a church long enough to find out what exactly it is that they need to be doing in the first place. Everything is centered around themselves, and not the Lord.

Ephesians 2:10 quote: For we are God's workmanship, created in Christ Jesus to do good works, which God prepared in advance for us to do.

Every believer who is a member of a local church needs to become an active member. Someone may tell you that you do not need to become an active member. If you are not actively involved in your local church, then expect to drift away. *Be very careful who you listen to.*

Ephesians 4:14 quote: Then we will no longer be infants, tossed back and forth by the waves, and blown here and there by every wind of teaching and by the cunning and craftiness of men in their deceitful scheming.

The serpent in Genesis Chapter 3:1; was considered more crafty than all the wild animals that the Lord God made. Satan used one of God's beautiful creatures to become wicked and filled it with all kinds of deceit. Church, Satan is using so-called Christians today for the same very purpose: for deception. The devil does not want the Church to be fed the Word of God, because if the believers ever get fed the Word of God, they would use the Word of God against the devil. The Word of God is our sword of Spirit. It is very powerful.

In fact, we are informed in Hebrews 4:12–13 quote: For the word of God is living and active. Sharper than any doubled-edge sword, it penetrates even the dividing soul and spirit, joints and marrow; it judges the thoughts and attitudes of the heart. Nothing in all creation is hidden from God's sight. Everything is uncovered and laid bare before the eyes of him to whom we must give account.

The Bible is not just a book; it is more important than that. God's Holy Word speaks to us individually, to our soul and spirit. God's Word cannot and will not speak to the flesh. God's Word speaks to an unsaved person's soul. This is when an unsaved person is without excuse. On the other hand, if you are truly a believer in the Lord Jesus Christ, you are going to have to make a very serious decision about who you listen to. Are you going to listen to your pastor, who has been placed as your local shepherd in the church, or are you going to listen to the craftiness of men in their deceitful scheming? The so-called Christians, who you are not supposed to be listening to, have their very own agendas. They are only in it for themselves to fleece the flock. They can care less about you or anyone else. They also can talk a good game. Use spiritual discernment. If it does not line up with the Word of God, then do not receive it.

Hebrews 13:17 quote: Obey your leaders and submit to their authority. They keep watch over you as men who must give account. Obey them so that their work will be a joy, not a burden, for that would be of no advantage to you.

Church, it is the pastor's duty in the local church to keep watch over his local flock, whenever he teaches and preaches God's Word.

Luke 6:40 quote. A student is not above his teacher, but everyone who is fully trained will be like his teacher.

I know for certain how well equipped I have become. I know exactly what it takes to become grounded in the Word of God. It takes serious commitment. It has nothing to do with how you or I feel.

Paul asked a question to the church at Galatia: Galatians 5:7 quote: You were running a good race. Who cut in on you and kept you from obeying the truth?

Be very careful who you listen to.

CONCLUSION

When Paul was getting ready to leave for Jerusalem, he warned the elders, who were the pastors, in Acts 20:28–31 quote: Keep watch over yourselves and the flock of which the Holy Spirit has made your overseers. Be shepherds of the church of God, which he bought with his own blood. I know that after I leave salvage wolves will come in among you and will not spare the flock. Even from your own number men will arise and distort the truth in order to draw away disciples after them. So be on your guard! Remember for three years I never stopped warning each of you night and day with tears.

Once the savage wolves come into the local church, the pastors have to be on guard at all times. Because the savage wolves are going to go after the local shepherd's flock. Their goal is to draw as many disciples as they can away from the truth. This is why it is a must that every church member who is a believer stays rooted and grounded in the Word of God.

James 4:7 quote: Submit yourselves, then, to God. Resist the devil, and he will flee from you.

How do we submit ourselves to God? By putting on the full armor of God. *Be very careful who you listen to.* Amen!

11

Live in the Center of God's Will in Christ Jesus

Luke 9:23. Then he said to them all: "If anyone would come after me, he must deny himself and take up his cross daily and follow me.

SERMON MESSAGE:

When the Lord Jesus Christ spoke with Nicodemus, He made it very clear what Nicodemus had to do. When Jesus made the following statement, He was not just referring to Nicodemus, but to all of us.

John 3:3 quote: In reply Jesus declared, "I tell you the truth, no one can see the kingdom of God unless he is born again.

Why do we have to be Born Again? Because this is the only way that God the Father has chosen to be connected with man. Jesus said this for a reason and a purpose. Jesus is God's mouthpiece. If anyone wants to connect with God, they have to be Born Again. If you are not Born Again, then you are just wasting your time.

John 1:12–13 quote: Yet to all who received him, to those who believed in his name, he gave the right to become children of

God-children born not of natural decent, nor of human decision or a husband's will, but born of God.

This is what it means to be Born Again, born of God. Religion doesn't teach this. The people in religion are too busy trying to question the Christian faith, when they should be stepping out on faith.

For this reason, it is written in Proverbs 16:25 quote: There is a way that seems right to a man, but in the end it leads to death.

In order for a religious person to be saved, they have to step out on faith.

Hebrews 11:6 quote: And without faith it is impossible to please God, because anyone that comes to him must believe that he exists and he rewards those that earnestly seek him.

If individuals have enough sense to believe that God can truly save them, then they need to step out on faith. God is going to reward those who seek after Him, the gift of eternal life through Jesus Christ. Eternal life cannot be earned. It wasn't given to us like that. Because if we had to earn it, then we wouldn't have it. Church, it is impossible for us to earn eternal life.

Ephesians 2:8–9 quote: For it is by grace you have been saved, through faith-and this is not from yourselves, it is a gift of God-not by works, so that no one can boast.

If you are here today, and you know without a shadow of a doubt that you are saved, then you should know that you have nothing to boast about before Almighty God. When we get to heaven, everyone we see will have gotten there by grace. When the Lord Jesus Christ came on the scene during the time of His ministry on this earth, how did He come? Jesus came by grace and truth.

Listen to what it says in John 1:14: quote: The Word became flesh and made his dwelling among us. We have seen his glory, the glory of the One and Only, who came from the Father, full of grace and truth.

What is grace? God giving us what we do not deserve. What is mercy? God not giving us what we do deserve. This is why grace is so important to every believer today. Grace is "God's Righteousness At Christ's Expense." So if you want to see the Kingdom of God, then you must be Born Again. When Jesus spoke about the Kingdom of God, it is now understood that He was talking to believers and not to the unsaved. Why not the unsaved?

1 Corinthians 2:14 quote: The man without the Spirit does not accept the things that comes from the Spirit of God, for they are foolishness to him, and he cannot understand them, because they are spiritually discerned.

As believers begin to read the Word of God once they've become Born Again, they are going grow spiritually.

1 Peter 2:2–3 quote: Like newborn babies, crave pure spiritual milk, so that by it you may grow up in your salvation, now that you have tasted that the Lord is good.

Getting into the milk of the Word of God at the very moment of their conversion allows believers to have the opportunity to enter into the Kingdom of God. Why the Kingdom of God? Because the Kingdom of God is God's right way of doing things for your life. The Kingdom of God offers a greater alternative than what this sinful world has to offer.

Matthew 6:32–33 quote: For the pagans run after all these things, and your heavenly Father knows that you need them. But seek first his kingdom and his righteousness, and all these things will be given to you as well.

The very moment that you give your heart to the Lord Jesus Christ, your Heavenly Father already knows exactly what your greatest needs are. The things that the pagans are chasing after, we need not be running after.

We are told in 1 Timothy 6:6–11 quote: But godliness with contentment is great gain. For we bought nothing in this world, and we can take nothing out of it. But if we have food and clothing, we will be content with that. People who want to get rich fall into temptation and a trap and into many foolish harmful desires that plunge men into ruin and destruction. For the love of money is the root of all kinds of evil. Some people, who have eager for money, have wandered from the faith and pierced themselves with many griefs. "But you man of God, flee from all of this, pursue righteousness, godliness, faith, love, endurance, and gentleness."

The very first thing that we are to pursue as believers in Christ is righteousness. Righteousness plays a very important role in the Christian life, providing that we continue to seek after it.

For instance, we are told in 2 Timothy 3:16–17 quote: All Scripture is God-breathed and is useful for teaching, rebuking, correcting and training in righteousness, so that the man of God may thoroughly equipped for every good work.

Every time that you are being taught the Word of God, or reading the Word of God on your own, you are receiving the training that you really need in the area of righteousness. Why is biblical Training so very important to every believer? It is so that we can be able to apply God's Word to our everyday lives.

This is why James 1:22–24 tell us, quote: Do not merely listen to the word, and so deceive yourselves. Do what it says. Anyone who listens to the word but does not do what it says is like a man who looks at his face in a mirror and, after looking at himself, goes away and immediately forgets what he looks like.

If you look in a mirror and notice that your hair needs combing, you comb it. Or if you have any type of dirt on your face, you use soap to wash it off. If you see your nose running, you blow it. If there are food particles on your mouth, you wipe them off. The same is true with the Word of God. If you see a change that needs to take place in your life, you look forward to making that change.

Romans 12:2 quote. Do not conform any longer to the pattern of this world, but be transformed by the renewing of your mind. Then you will be able to test and approve what God's will is-his good and pleasing and perfect will.

Whenever we read and apply the Word of God to our lives, we have the opportunity to be transformed by the renewing of our minds. This is a greater alternative to what this world's system has to offer.

This is why we are told in Ephesians 5:15–16 quote: Be very careful, then, how you live-not as unwise but wise, making the most of every opportunity, because the days are evil.

So how can we be very careful in how we live as believers? By changing the way that we live by getting into reading and applying the Word of God to our lives. If we say that we are Christians, then those who are unsaved need to see it. Talk is cheap. But your actions should speak louder than your words.

Matthew 5:16 quote: In the same way, let your light shine before men, that they may see your good deeds and praise your Father in heaven.

Whenever the unsaved see your light shining bright in you, you become an effective witness to them. The very life that you live for Jesus is designed for you to get your foot in the door so that you can share your faith with them.

This is why we are told in 1 Peter 3:15 quote: But in your heart set apart Christ as Lord. Always be prepared to give an answer to everyone who asks you to give the reason for the hope that you have. But do this with gentleness and respect.

We cannot expect to set apart Christ as Lord, if Jesus isn't Lord over the very life that we live as believers. What's going to happen is this: We will wind up causing others to stumble, while they are trying to live in the Christian faith. This is why every believer must be *living in the center of God's will in Christ Jesus.*

Luke 9:23 quote: Then he said to them all: "If anyone would come after me, he must deny himself and take up his cross daily and follow me.

Every one of us has a cross that we have to bear. James and John wanted to sit at Jesus' right and left when they came into His Kingdom. But Jesus asked them each a question. Were they willing to drink the exact cup that Jesus was going to drink? But when you look at it in reality, no one can drink the cup that was given to Jesus to drink.

The cup that Jesus had to drink had to do with John 3:16–17 quote: For God so loved the world that he gave his one and only Son, that whoever believes in him shall not perish but have eternal life. For God did not send his Son into the world to condemn the world, but to save the world through him.

Church, God the Father has made it very clear that He loves His one and only Son. The Father proved this right at the Baptism of Jesus before He went into the wilderness and also at the Mount of Transfiguration. Jesus Himself also made it very clear that He loves His Father. Jesus says this all throughout the four Gospels.

For example, Jesus said in John 10:17–18 quote: The reason my Father loves me is that I lay down my life-only to take it up again. No one takes it from me, but I lay it down on my own accord. I have authority to lay it down and the authority to take it up again. This command I received from my Father.

Why was Jesus able to say this? Because Jesus was fully connected to doing His Father's will. When it came down to Jesus ministering here on earth, He came to do one thing, and one thing only. Jesus came to carry out His Father's divine will for His life.

This is why Jesus was able to say in John 5:19 quote: Jesus gave them this answer: "I tell you the truth, the Son can do nothing by himself; he can only do what he sees his Father doing, because whatever the Father does the Son also does.

Jesus also said in John 8:28–29, "When you lifted up the Son of Man, then you will know that I Am the one I claim to be, and I do nothing on my own but speak just what the Father has taught me. The one who sent me; He is with me, He has not left me alone, for I always do what pleases Him." As believers, how do we go about pleasing God? By carrying out His commands in our lives. It all has to do with the way we live as believers in Christ.

This is why Jesus was able to say in Luke 11:28 quote: He replied, "Blessed rather are those who hear the word of God and obey it."

Obeying the Word of God should be very important to every believer. We need to discipline ourselves in order to obey it.

This is why Hebrews 5:14 says quote: But solid food is for the mature, who by constant use have trained themselves to distinguish good from evil.

As we are growing spiritually in the Christian faith, we are going to have the opportunity to receive all the spiritual nourishment that we need, providing that we do what we have been called to do.

1 Timothy 4:7 quote: Have nothing to do with godless myths and old wives tales; rather, train yourself to be godly.

When an individual becomes a Christian, he is not going to learn how to live a godly life all by himself. He has got to be taught how to live and to become a Christian. This is where God's Word comes in place.

2 Timothy 2:15 quote: Do your best to present yourself to God as one approved, a workman who does not need to be ashamed and who correctly handles the word of truth.

While you are studying the Word of God, the Scriptures are going to come to life inside of you.

For example, we are told in 2 Chronicles 7:14 quote: If my people, who are called by name, will humble themselves and pray and seek my face and turn from their wicked ways, then I will hear from heaven and will forgive their sin and will heal their land.

Believers who listen to this verse of Scripture will question themselves to make very sure that they are willing to do what God's Word says. This is what it means to be *living in the center of God's will in Christ Jesus.*

Luke 9:23 quote: Then he said to them all: "If anyone would come after me, he must deny himself and take up his cross daily and follow me.

You might say, "Pastor Rucker, 2 Chronicles 7:14 doesn't apply to us because it is Old Testament. And the Lord is speaking to the Jewish race." Church, the Lord is speaking to you too.

Romans 15:4 quote: For everything was written in our past was written to teach us, so that through endurance and the encouragement of the Scriptures we might have hope.

Also, the same blessings that God gave to Abraham, God has given to every believer.

Galatians 3:29 quote: If you belong to Christ, then you are Abraham's seed, and heirs according to the promise.

What is an heir? A person who inherits or is entitled to inherit another's property or title upon the other's death. Again, the same blessings that God gave to Abraham have also been given to every believer as well. We are also told in Galatians 3:14, "He redeemed us in order that the blessing given to Abraham might come to the Gentiles through Jesus Christ, so that by faith we might receive the promise of the Spirit." Jesus Christ has redeemed us from the curse of the law by becoming a curse for us.

This is why we are told in 2 Corinthians 5:21 quote: God made him who had no sin to be sin for us, so that in him we might become the righteousness of God.

The righteousness of God has been placed on every believer because of what Jesus Christ has done for us. This is why when the Lord sees you, He sees the righteousness of God that has been placed in you. We now begin to live the way that God wants us to live.

1 Peter 2:12 quote: Live such good lives among the pagans that, though they accuse you of doing wrong, they may see your good deeds and glorify God on the day he visits us.

The good deeds that we carry out in our lives are recognized as fruit. The good works or good deeds don't take place in our lives until after we have become Born Again.

Ephesians 2:10 quote: For we are God's workmanship, created in Christ Jesus to do good works, which God prepared in advance for us to do.

In the world in which we live, there are so many people who are talented and skilled and gifted in every walk of life. An artist can consider his paintings as a work of art or a masterpiece. Every believer in Christ is considered to be God's masterpiece or work of art. And this is because of what Jesus Christ has done for us.

2 Corinthians 5:17 quote: Therefore, if anyone is in Christ, he is a new creation; the old has gone the new has come!

We are to no longer live the way that we used to live. We used to live in the flesh, but we are to live in the center of God's will in Christ. So how do we begin to live in the center of God's will?

Luke 9:23 quote: Then he said to them all: "If anyone would come after me, he must deny himself and take up his cross daily and follow me.

You start out by giving up selfish desires. It is no longer about you anymore. Or what you want to do or the direction where you want to go with your life.

Philippians 2:3–5 quote: Do nothing out of selfish ambition or vain conceit, but in humility consider others better than yourselves. Each of you should look not only to your own interest, but also the interest of others. Your attitude should be the same as that of Christ Jesus.

If you are going to become a follower of Christ, then you need to become like Christ. "Christian" means follower of Christ.

Galatians 2:20 quote: I have been crucified with Christ and I no longer live, but Christ lives in me. The life I live in the body, I live by faith in the Son of God, who loved me and gave himself for me.

Every step that we live as believers is to be lived by faith. Whenever we are living by faith, things are not always going to appear as they seem.

This is why we are told in Proverbs 3:5–7 quote: Trust in the Lord with all your heart and lean not on your own understanding; in all your ways acknowledge him, and he will make your paths straight. Do not be wise in your own eyes; fear the Lord and shun evil.

If you say that you are a Christian, you cannot direct your pathway straight on your own. This is where we as believers have to follow the leading of the Holy Spirit, who has been placed inside of us.

Living in the center of God's will in Christ Jesus is going to allow us to follow the leading and the guidance of the Holy Spirit.

Luke 9:23 quote: Then he said to them all: "If anyone would come after me, he must deny himself and take up his cross daily and follow me.

Once we deny our fleshly desires, then we will be able to take up our crosses and become followers of the Lord Jesus Christ. How do we deny our fleshly desires? By walking in the Spirit.

Galatians 5:16–21 quote: So I say live by the Spirit, and you will not gratify the desires of the sinful nature. For the sinful nature desire what is contrary to the Spirit, and the Spirit what is contrary to the sinful nature. They are in conflict with each other, so that you do not do what you want. But if you are led by the Spirit, you are not under law. The acts of the sinful nature are obvious: sexual immorality, impurity and debauchery; idolatry and witchcraft; hatred, discord, jealousy, fits of rage, selfish ambition, dissensions, factions and envy; drunkenness, orgies, and the like. I warn you, as I did before, that those who live like this will not inherit the kingdom of God.

Church, you cannot walk in the Spirit and walk in the flesh at the same time. This is where we discipline ourselves when it comes to living the Christian life. We have the Holy Spirit along with the Word of God to help us to live the Christian life. The Holy Spirit that is dwelling inside of us is representing the Lord Jesus Christ. John 14:15–17 says, "As Jesus was speaking to His disciples, Jesus told them this: 'If you love me, you will obey my command. And I will ask the Father, and He will give you another Counselor to be with you forever—the Spirit of truth.'" While Jesus was on earth during His earthly ministry, while He lived in His physical body, He was limited. If Jesus wanted to, Jesus could have been present everywhere. During Jesus' ministry, Jesus was able to heal people from a distance, without ever going to them. This happened when Jesus healed the Canaanite woman's daughter who was demon possessed. Jesus also healed a royal official's son who laid sick and was close to death. Church, Jesus wasn't in their presence when He healed them. If Jesus wanted to be in every place at the same time, He could have been. This is why we have the Holy Spirit with us today. The Holy Spirit is everywhere at the same time. What is the Holy Spirit doing in our lives? He is guiding us into all truth. This is why we need to follow the Spirit's leading in our lives.

John 15:5 quote: "I am the vine; you are the branches. If a man remains in me and I in him, he will bear much fruit; apart from me you can do nothing.

As long as we remain in Christ, we can expect to bear much fruit. We have the combination of the Word of God along with the help of the Holy Spirit dwelling in our lives.

John 15:16 quote: You did not choose me, but I chose you and appointed you to go and bear fruit-fruit that will last. Then the Father will give you whatever you ask in my name.

The very reason why so many Christians have unanswered prayers in their lives is because they have refused to bear fruit. Not bearing fruit can place you out of the center of God's will.

John 15:1–2 quote: "I am the true vine, and my Father is the gardener. He cuts off every branch in me that bears no fruit, while every branch that does bear fruit he prunes so that it will be even more fruitful.

What is the reason for pruning? It is so that Christians can endure discipline. While living the Christian life as believers, we can expect to go through many storms and trials in our lives. To live the Christian life, it's going to cost you.

This is why James 1:2–4 tells us, quote: Consider it pure joy, my brothers, whenever you face trials of many kinds, because you know that the testing of your faith develops perseverance. Perseverance must finish its work so that you may be mature and complete, not lacking anything.

As we become mature and complete in the Christian faith, then can we expect to be in the center of God's will in Christ. We are not going to face these storms and trials and testing alone. The Lord Jesus Christ is going through these storms along with us. But every believer in Christ has to be in the center of God's will in Christ.

Ephesians 5:17 quote: Therefore do not be foolish, but understand what the Lord's will is.

Our will, will not work.

CONCLUSION

People are willing to pay a high price for something they value. Is it any surprise that Jesus demands this much commitment from

His followers? There are at least three conditions that must be met by people who want to follow Jesus: They must be willing to deny self, to take up their crosses, and to follow Jesus daily. Anything less is superficial lip service.

Jesus said it this way in Luke 9:62: quote: Jesus replied, "No one who puts his hand to the plow and looks back is fit for service in the kingdom of God."

Are you *living in the center of God's will in Christ Jesus*? Amen!

12

Believe that God Exists by the Faith that You Have

Hebrews 11:6. And without faith it is impossible to please God, because anyone who comes to him must believe that he exists and that he rewards those who earnestly seek him.

SERMON MESSAGE:

As Moses was at the entrance of the burning bush, the place that was considered Holy Ground, he asked the Lord God a question. In Exodus 3:13–14, Moses said to God, "Suppose I go to the Israelites and say to them, 'The God of your fathers has sent me to you,' and they ask me, 'What is your name?' Then what shall I tell them?" God said to Moses, "I AM WHO I AM. This is what you are to say to the Israelites: 'I AM has sent me to you.'"

The same I Am that spoke to Moses at the burning bush now resides inside of the hearts of every believer who has accepted Jesus Christ as Lord and Savior. Why is this so very important? It is because God wants us to know Him. God has given us the opportunity to really know Him. And this is by knowing His one and only Son. The Lord Jesus Christ.

John 1:1–3, 14 quote: In the beginning was the Word, and the Word was with God, and the Word was God. He was with God in the beginning. Through him all things were made; without him nothing was made that has been made. The Word became flesh and made his dwelling among us. We have seen his glory, the glory of the One and Only, who came from the Father, full of grace and truth.

Jesus has given his invitation to know him to the whole world. If an unsaved person really wants to know Jesus, they have the opportunity to do so. During Jesus' ministry on earth, he was reaching out to everyone. Even the teachers of law.

John 8:23–24 quote: But he continued, "You are from below; I am from above. You are of this world; I am not of this world. I told you that you would die in your sins; if you do not believe that I am the one I claim to be, you will indeed die in your sins."

Jesus appeared on the scene and showed them, and told them exactly who he was, yet they refused to believe in him. And these leaders were without excuse, because they saw all the miracles and signs that Jesus had done. Instead of putting their complete faith in Jesus, they criticized Jesus.

And yet we are told in John 20:30-31 quote: Jesus did many other miraculous signs in the presence of his disciples, which are not recorded in this book. But these are written that you may believe that Jesus is the Christ, the Son of God, and that by believing you may have life in his name.

Just believing exactly what the four Gospels recorded is all that is truly needed to give the unsaved the evidence that they really need to be saved. Not only did the Lord Jesus die for our sins, but there needed to be enough proof to show that Jesus actually accomplished this task. This is why we have the Gospel writers. While they were writing the four Gospels, they actually fulfilled prophesy. How do we know this?

2 Peter 1:20–21 quote: Above all, you must understand that no prophecy of Scripture came about by the prophet's own interpretation. For prophecy never had its origin in the will of man, but men spoke from God as they were carried along by the Holy Spirit.

These biblical writers were being inspired by God as they were being led to write down the Words.

In fact, we are told in Hebrews 1:1–3 quote: In the past God spoke to our forefathers through the prophets at many times and in various ways, but in these last days he has spoken to us by his Son, whom he has appointed heir of all things, and through whom he made the universe. The Son is the radiance of God's glory and the exact representation of his being, sustaining all things by his powerful word. After he provided purification for sins, he sat down at the right hand of the Majesty in heaven.

Did you hear that? But in these last days, God now speaks to us by His Son. Jesus is speaking to us today. Jesus is speaking to us through His Word. Jesus is also speaking to us through those who are believers, who know His Word. Now if you do not know His Word, then you cannot expect Jesus to speak through you. You need to be lined up to the Word of God.

This is why we are told in 1 Peter 4:11 quote: If anyone speaks, he should do it as one speaking the very words of God. If anyone serves, he should do it with the strength God provides, so that in all things God may be praised through Jesus Christ. To him be the glory and the power for ever and ever, Amen.

You hear some people say that God has spoken to them. If this is true then it is a must that what they are saying lines up with the Word of God. And if it doesn't, then consider the source as to where the information is coming from. This is why we must understand exactly what we are reading when it comes down to biblical Scriptures of the Word of God. Before Jesus' Ascension, He had given His remaining disciples the final instructions that they needed to carry out.

Matthew 28:18–20 quote: Then Jesus came to them and said, "All authority in heaven and on earth has been given to me. Therefore go and make disciples of all nations, baptizing them in the name of the Father and of the Son and of the Holy Spirit, and teaching them to obey everything I have commanded you. And surely I am with you always, to the very end of the age."

The very reason why these instructions were so important for Jesus' disciples to obey is because each of them were considered as eyewitnesses to what Jesus had accomplished while He was ministering on earth. This was the reason why Thomas needed to see the resurrected Christ. Thomas wanted a confirmation because the Lord Jesus had already told them about His death, burial, and resurrection.

Once Thomas had seen Jesus, He told Thomas this in John 20:29: quote: Then Jesus told him, "Because you have seen me, you have believed; blessed are those who have not seen and yet have believed."

Who was Jesus referring to? Jesus is talking to every person who has completely put their trust and faith in Him.

John 1:12–13 quote: Yet to all who received him, to those who believed in his name, he gave the right to become children of God-children born not of natural decent, nor of human decision or a husband's will, but born of God.

Church, we do not need any proof to see exactly what Jesus looked like. Our salvation isn't based upon what Jesus looked like. But it is based upon faith in Christ.

Ephesians 2:8–9 quote: For it is by grace you have been saved, through faith-and this is not from yourselves, it is the gift of God-not by works, so that no one can boast.

We do not need any proof to what our Heavenly Father looks like. [Show a picture of Jesus.] You see this picture here? This is idolatry. Some folks say that Jesus is white, some folks say that Jesus is black, others say that Jesus is Hispanic or Italian and so on.

In Acts 1:8 quote: But you will receive power when the Holy Spirit comes on you; and you will be my witnesses in Jerusalem, and in all Judea and Samaria, and to the ends of the earth.

These early Church people were considered as eyewitnesses of the Lord Jesus Christ. We have the evidence to show that these disciples were with Jesus.

Acts 4:12–13 quote: Salvation is found in no one else, for there is no other name under heaven given to men by which we must be saved. " When they saw the courage of Peter and John and realized that they were unschooled, ordinary men, they were astonished and they took note that these men had been with Jesus.

This is how the people during the early Church era were able to believe. It was from the testimony of Jesus' disciples as they were witnessing to the people. What do we have today? Church, we have the Word of God in written format; this is all the evidence that we really need to show that Jesus actually existed. Why is the Word of God so important to us today?

We are told in Hebrews 4:12–13 quote: For the word of God is living and active. Sharper than any double-edged sword, it penetrates even the dividing soul and spirit, joints and marrow; it judges the thoughts and attitudes of the heart. Nothing in all creation is hidden from God's sight. Everything is uncovered and laid bare before the eyes of him to whom we must give account.

The Word of God is going to convince you, without shadow of a doubt, that God truly exists. You do not have to defend the Word of God. The Word of God is capable of defending itself. As believers, all we need to do is read it and apply it to our lives.

In Luke 11:28 quote:" Blessed rather are those who hear the word of God and obey it."

Every time we read and study and apply God's Word, we are being held accountable. The blessings are going to be given to everyone who obeys the teachings.

James 4:17 quote: Anyone, then, who knows the good he ought to do and doesn't do it, sins.

The Word of God will always be centered around God's goodness. This is exactly who God is. This is the very reason why we read God's Word, so that we can have the opportunity to reach spiritual maturity.

Hebrews 5:14 quote: But solid food is for the mature, who by constant use have trained themselves to distinguish good from evil.

As you continue to read God's Holy Word, you will continue *believing that God exists by the faith that you have.*

Hebrews 11:6 quote: And without faith it is impossible to please God. Because anyone who comes to him must believe that he exists and that he rewards those who earnestly seek him.

Throughout the Word of God, we find that there are so many ways that we are to please God. One way that we please God is by the way that we present our bodies to God.

Romans 12:1 quote. Therefore, I urge you, brothers, in the view of God's mercy, to offer your bodies as living sacrifices, holy and pleasing to God-this is your spiritual act of worship.

From the time that you get up, until the time that you go to your bed, you are to be a living sacrifice, holy and pleasing to God. This is why we have to be very careful as to what we do with our bodies. Your body doesn't belong to you anymore.

If you are a Christian, you are told in 1 Corinthians 6:19–20 quote: Do you not know that your body is a temple of the Holy Spirit, who is in you, whom you have received from God? You are not your own; you were bought at a price. Therefore honor God with your body.

Our parents used to get on us when we did something wrong in the Lord's house: talking loud, not behaving ourselves, chewing gum in the Lord's house. Under the dispensation of grace, this local church is not the Lord's house. Neither is the mega church the Lord's house. But if you are saved and have accepted Jesus Christ as your Lord and Savior, then your body is representing, right at this very moment, the Lord's house. 1 Corinthians 3:16–17 says, "Don't you know that you yourselves are God's temple and that God's Spirit lives in you? If anyone destroys God's temple, God will destroy him; for God's temple is sacred, and you are that temple." You cannot do as you please, or as you see fit. Your body now belongs to the Lord and not to you. The Lord has placed you as the tenant of your body. Whenever we are renting an apartment or house, the landlord holds us responsible for anything that we damage in the place that we are renting. This is why we have to deal with the consequences at hand. The same is true when it comes down to our bodies. If we or anybody does anything wrong to our body, they are going to be held accountable, or have to suffer the consequences. For this is reason why we need to be pleasing to the Lord with our bodies. Another area we can be pleasing to God is when we renew our minds in God's Holy Word.

Romans 12:2 quote: Do not conform any longer to the pattern of this world, but be transformed by the renewing of your mind. Then you will be able to test and approve what God's will is-his good, pleasing and prefect will.

Whenever we are becoming transformed by the renewing of our minds, we get rid of the old, improper, sinful data that we really do not need. How do we do this?

Philippians 4:8 quote: Finally, brothers, whatever is true, whatever is noble, whatever is right, whatever is pure, whatever is lovely, whatever is admirable-if anything is excellent or praiseworthy-think about such things.

We are to line our thoughts up with the biblical Scriptures of the Word of God, because we are operating in the faith realm.

Hebrews 11:1 quote: Now faith is being sure of what we hope for and certain of what we do not see.

The moment that you became saved was by faith. This was the very first step that every believer who is now saved had to make. Now that we are saved, what happens next? You continue *believing that God exists by the faith that you have.*

Hebrews 11:6 quote: And without faith it is impossible to please God, because anyone who comes to him must believe he exist and that he rewards those who earnestly seek him.

Christians today are getting saved only to return back into their old sinful state of mind again. We need to be reminded of what took place in our lives at the moment of our conversion.

We are told in 2 Corinthians 5:17 quote: Therefore, if anyone is in Christ, he is a new creation; the old has gone, the new has come!

We are to no longer continue to live our lives in sin. The Christian life that we are to live is to be lived by faith.

2 Corinthians 5:7 quote: We live by faith, not by sight.

When it comes to living in the faith realm, whose report are you going to believe? We live in a very negative world's system. As believers, we need to not be part of it because whenever we become a part of it, we wind up doing the very same things that the unsaved people of this world are doing.

1 John 2:15–17 quote: Do not love the world or anything in the world. If anyone loves the world, the love of the Father is not in him. For everything in the world-the cravings of sinful man, the lust of his eyes and the boasting of what he has and does-comes not from the Father but from the world. The world and its desires pass away, but the man who does the will of God lives forever.

For this reason, if we truly want to do the will of God, then we have to take our eyes off this world's system and place them on Lord Jesus Christ. This is when we begin to live the Christian life by faith.

Galatians 2:20 quote: I have been crucified with Christ and I no longer live, but Christ lives in me. The life I live in the body, I live by faith in the son of God, who loved me and gave himself for me.

Living the Christian life by faith is very much different than living in accordance to this world's system. Things are not going to always appear as they seem in the faith realm. And the reason is because we have stepped away from this world's system and into the Kingdom of God. This world's system can bring about worrying. But as believers in Christ, we are told not to worry.

Matthew 6:32–33 quote: For the pagans run after all these things, and your heavenly Father knows that you need them. But seek first his kingdom and his righteousness, and all these things will be given to you as well.

This country today is dealing with home foreclosures, unemployment, job layoffs, salary pay cuts, and so on. And everyone who is affected by this is worried. But for believers, this should not be the case. Things may not work out the way that we plan them. But we must understand that the Lord is working it all out for us.

Romans 8:28 quote: And we know that in all things God works for the good of those who love him, who have been called according to his purpose.

In the life of Joseph, nothing was going right for him in the physical sense. But Joseph continued to place his complete trust in the Lord. And this was regardless of what he went through. The Lord saved the best for last. Joseph was promoted to prime minister of Egypt. God's purpose for Joseph was to save the whole world through a seven-year drought. Listen to what Joseph said to his brothers, after Jacob their father died: In Genesis 50:20 quote: You intended to harm me, but God intended for the good to accomplish what is now being done, the saving of many lives.

As we continue to live by faith, we do not know what the Lord has in store for us. But we can certainly know for sure, the Lord is working it all out for our good. This is the reason why we must keep our lives free from sin.

Hebrews 12:1–2 quote: Therefore, since we are surrounded by such a great cloud of witnesses, let us throw off everything that hinders and the sin that so easily entangles, and let us run with perseverance the race marked out for us. Let us fix our eyes on Jesus, the author and perfecter of our faith, who for the joy set before him endured the cross, scorning its shame, and sat down at the right hand of the throne of God.

We have a cloud of witnesses. Who are these people? These are people every believer needs to be around. You need to learn from everyone you know who's living a godly life.

Philippians 4:9 quote: Whatever you have learned or received or heard from me, or seen in me-put it into practice. And the God of peace will be with you.

Because whenever you do this, you're *believing that God exists by the faith that you have.*

Hebrew 11:6 quote: And without faith it is impossible to please God, because anyone who comes to him must believe that he exists and that he rewards those who earnestly seek him.

Genuine true believers know without a shadow of a doubt that God exists. Their prayer life is going to be consistent with faith. Their Christian life is going to be consistent with faith. These believers are God seekers. We seek God when we worship Him and praise Him (not so that we can get what we want).

Psalm 37:4–5 quote: Delight yourself in the Lord and he will give you the desires of your heart. Commit your way to the Lord; trust in him and he will do this.

Whenever we delight ourselves in the Lord, our Heavenly Father already knows exactly what we really need. But whenever we are seeking after God, we are giving the Lord our undivided attention.

Proverbs 3:3–10 quote: Let love and faithfulness never leave you; bind them around your neck, write them on the tablet of your heart. Then you will win favor and a good name in the sight of God and man. Trust in the Lord with all your heart and lean not on your own understanding; in all your ways acknowledge him, and he will make your paths straight. Do not be wise in your own eyes; fear the Lord and shun evil. This will bring health to your body and nourishment to your bones. Honor the Lord with your wealth, with the first fruit of all your crops; then your barns will be filled to overflowing, and your vats will brim over with new wine.

Church, there are benefits whenever we are seeking the Lord by faith. To be blessed of God, we need to seek God earnestly. We need to go out of our way to seek after Him. What are you willing to give up to seek after the Lord? Let's start out by giving up ourselves.

In the Gospel, Luke 9:23, Jesus tells us, quote: "If anyone would come after me, he must deny himself and take up his cross daily and follow me.

Whenever we are operating in the faith realm, it is a must that we deny our flesh every day. We learn to give up sinful habits and fleshly desires every day.

This was the reason Apostle Paul made this statement in 1 Corinthians 9:24–27 quote: Do you not know that in a race all the runners run, but only one gets the prize? Run in such a way to get the prize. Everyone who competes in the games goes into strict training. They do it to get a crown that will not last; but we do it to get a crown that will last forever. Therefore I do not run like a man running aimlessly; I do not fight like a man beating the air. No, I beat my body and make it my slave so that after I have preached to others, I myself will not be disqualified for the prize.

Living a sinful lifestyle can disqualify us from receiving the prize.

This is where we come in as believers; we are told in 1 Timothy 4:7 quote: Have nothing to do with godless myths and old wives' tales; rather, train yourselves to be godly.

To live a godly and pure and a holy life doesn't come natural. We have to train ourselves to become godly. This is the reason why we come to worship.

Hebrews 10:25 quote: Let us not give up meeting together, as some are in the habit of doing, but let us encourage one another-and all the more as you see the Day approaching.

The very reason why so many teens today are illiterate is because they drop out of junior high and senior high school. When they become adults, no one wants to hire them because they have nothing to show for themselves. But when it comes down to a believer in Christ, the Lord wants you to have something to show for yourselves.

1 Peter 2:2–3 quote: Like newborn babies, crave pure spiritual milk, so that by it you may grow up in your salvation, now that you have tasted that the Lord is good.

This is why we have the opportunity to go from spiritual infancy to spiritual maturity. If you do not get into the reading and the studying of the Word of God, you will not be able to move up to the very next level of your faith.

2 Timothy 2:15 quote: Do your best to present yourself to God as one approved, a workman who does not need to be ashamed and who correctly handles the word of truth.

Church, it is your Heavenly Father who does the promoting from within the Body of Christ. Your faith will be increased as long as you stay in the Word of God.

2 Timothy 3:16–17 quote: All Scripture is God-breathed and useful for teaching, rebuking, correcting and training in righteousness, so that the man of God may be thoroughly equipped for every good work.

Every time that we are reading God's Word, we are without excuse. This is where we become trained. Bible study, Sunday school, and regular church attendance all play a very important role in the Christian faith. Every time we are participating as believers, in the very things of God, it becomes a step of faith as we live as believers. Living the Christian life by faith is an alternative to what this world has to offer us.

1 John 5:4–5 says, "For everyone born of God overcomes the world." This is the victory that has overcome the world, even our faith. Who is it that overcomes the world? Only he who believes that Jesus is the Son of God.

CONCLUSION

When it comes to believing that God exists, God will not settle for mere acknowledgment of His existence.

Matthew 10:32-33 quote: Whoever acknowledge me before men, I also will acknowledge him before my Father in heaven. But whoever disowns me before men, I will disown him before my Father in heaven.

God wants a personal dynamic relationship with each and every one of us that will transform our lives. Those who seek God will find that they will be rewarded with God's intimate presence.

The Lord Jesus said in Revelation 3:20 quote: Here I am! I stand at the door and knock. If anyone hears my voice and opens the door, I will come in and eat with him, and he with me.

Sometimes we wonder about the fate of those who haven't heard of Christ or don't even have a Bible to read. God has assured us that all who honestly seek Him—who act on the faith in the knowledge of God that they possess—will be rewarded. This is what is called *believing that God exists by the faith that you have.*

Hebrews 11:6 quote: And without faith it is impossible to please God, because anyone who comes to him must believe that he exists and that he rewards those who earnestly seek him.

Amen!

13

God Breaks His Connection to Bring Us Together

Matthew 27:46, About the ninth hour Jesus cried out in a loud voice, "Eloi, Eloi, lama sabachthani?"-which means, "My God, my God, why have you forsaken me?"

Sermon for Passion Week

SERMON MESSAGE:

In the world in which we live, there are many crimes that are committed that we think go unpunished. This may be the case in criminology, but this is not the case for God. In God's eyes, no crime goes unpunished.

This is why we are told in Galatians 6:7–8 quote: Do not be deceived: God cannot be mocked. A man reaps what he sows. The one who sows to please his sinful nature, from that nature will reap destruction; the one who sows to please the Spirit, from the Spirit will reap eternal life.

No matter how we look at it, these verses of Scriptures can work for you, or they can work against you. You can run, but you can't hide. Someone has to pay. Such was the case in the Garden of Eden. There was a crime committed. No, it wasn't murder. No, it wasn't robbery. And neither was it rape, or any filthy or disgusting crime that you can think of. But the crime that was committed in the Garden of Eden was the crime of disobedience. What was so special about this crime that was committed? It opened up the door to every sin that mankind would ever commit. If disobedience was never committed in the Garden of Eden in the first place, sin would not exist today. This is why someone has to pay.

In Genesis 3:15, God said to the serpent, quote: And I will put enmity between you and the woman, and between your offspring and hers; he will crush your head, and you will strike his heel."

The seed that comes from the woman will crush the serpent's head with the final blow. As we are living currently, we can actually say, as believers, that devil is now defeated. The only difference is this: sin has got to reach its course. But what happened for this to occur? The very moment that Adam and Eve sinned, the Lord God brought forth His divine plan into action. Before sin came into existence, Adam and Eve never needed a mediator to stand between them and God. Because of Adam's sin, Adam could no longer enter into the very presence of God without a mediator, or a go-between. And this is because of who God is. God is Holy, and for this reason, God cannot and will not look at sin.

This is why we are told in Hebrews 9:22 quote: In fact, the law requires that nearly everything be cleansed with blood, and without the shedding of blood there is no forgiveness.

This was the very reason why the Lord God shed the blood of animals in order to make coats of skin for Adam and Eve's nakedness. The blood of the animals became a type of mediator to intercede for Adam and Eve. These animals were considered as a type of Christ. The animals were innocent. They were only designed to cover the sin. This is why the word *atonement* is used. Atonement means to cover, and not to take away. The sacrifice of animals would turn out to become a way of life. But at the very moment that Jesus would appear on the scene, He would open up the door to bring about an end to all the Old Testament animal sacrifices. Only God, and God alone, can intercede on man's behalf.

This is why we are told in Matthew 1:23 quote: "The virgin will be with child and will give birth to a son, and they will call him Immanuel" –which means, "God with us."

God became a man in the very person of the Lord Jesus Christ Himself.

John 1:1–3 quote: In the beginning was the Word, and the Word was with God, and the Word was God. He was with God in the beginning. Through him all things were made; without him nothing was made that has been made.

Also we are told in John 1:14 quote: The Word became flesh and made his dwelling among us. We have seen his glory, the glory of the One and Only, who came from the Father, full of grace and truth.

Why are these verses of Scriptures so very important to the individual? These Scriptures are designed to show us that only

God, and God alone, can forgive sin. This was the very reason why the Old Testament prophecies concerning the Messiah all had to be fulfilled in the Lord Jesus Christ.

2 Peter 1:20–21 quote: Above all, you must understand that no prophecy of Scripture came by the prophet's own interpretation. For prophecy never had its origin in the will of man, but man spoke from God as they were carried along by the Holy Spirit.

This explains why we have Jacob, Moses, David, Isaiah, Ezekiel, Jeremiah, and Daniel, along with the rest of the minor prophets. They all had something in common. They all prophesied the coming of Christ. The Lord Jesus Christ was God's divine plan for redeeming the whole human race. When John the Baptist was with some of his disciples, he pointed to Jesus and said, "Look, the Lamb of God, who takes away the sins of the world!" Notice what John the Baptist did not say, "Who covers the sins of the world!" No. Who takes away the sins of the whole world! The very purpose for Jesus to take away the sins of the whole world is so that everyone under the Dispensation Age of Grace can have the opportunity to receive eternal life through the forgiveness of sin.

Jesus said it this way in John 8:34–36 quote: "I tell you the truth, everyone who sins is a slave to sin, Now a slave have no permanent place in the family, but a son belongs to it forever. So if the Son sets you free, you will be free indeed.

When Jesus made this statement, He had not yet been glorified. Jesus knew exactly what He came to do. When Jesus walked this earth during His earthly ministry, He came only to do one thing, and one thing only. Jesus came to do His Father's divine will. Hebrews 10:5–7 says, "Therefore, when Christ came into the world, He said, 'Sacrifices and offerings you did not desire, but a body you prepare for me; with burnt offerings and sin offerings you were not pleased. Then I said, Here I am—it is written about me in the Scroll—I have come to do your will, O God.'" God was not pleased with the animal sacrifices, along with the sin offerings, and the burnt offerings. And here's the reason why: They were bringing lame and sick animals with all kinds of defects to the altar for sacrifices. God was not pleased. The Lord said to the Israelites through the Prophet Malachi, in Malachi 1:8 "Try to offer them to your governor! Would he be pleased with you? Would he accept you?" says the Lord Almighty." But when the Lord Jesus Christ came into the world, there was no question as to what He had come to do.

Matthew 5:17 quote: Do not think that I have come to abolish the law or the Prophets; I have not come to abolish them but to fulfill them.

The law first had to be fulfilled. Then Matthew 20:28 would become a reality, quote: Just as the Son of Man did not come to be served, but to serve, and to give his life as a ransom for many.

The law was God's moral standard for the entire human race to obey. Church, only God and God alone could fulfill the law. This was why God the Father and God the Son were completely connected.

John 5:19 quote: Jesus gave them this answer: I tell you the truth, the Son can do nothing by himself; he can do only what he sees his Father doing, because whatever the Father does the Son also does.

But a day would come when this connection would be temporarily broken. This is called *God breaks his connection to bring us together.*

Matthew 27:46 quote: About the ninth hour Jesus cried out in a loud voice, "Eloi, Eloi, lama sabachthani?"-which means, "My God, my God, why have you forsaken me?"

The Lord Jesus was not ignorant when it came to the cross.

This was why Jesus said it this way in John 10:17–18: quote. The reason my Father loves me is that I lay down my life-only to take it up again. No one takes it from me, but I lay it down of my own accord. I have the authority to lay it down and the authority to take it up again. This command I received from my Father.

When it came down to the cross that Jesus was to bear, Jesus knew exactly what He was to go through. The thought of Jesus enduring separation from God the Father would become a reality within itself. In Matthew 20:20-22, John and James's mother came to Jesus to ask a favor. She said, "Grant that one of these two sons of mine may sit at your right and the other at your left in your Kingdom." Jesus' answer was this: "You don't know what you are asking. Can you drink the cup I am going to drink." These two disciples were going to drink from the cup, but they were not going to "drink the cup." The cup that Jesus had to drink was the cup of suffering.

1 Peter 2:21 quote: To this you were called, because Christ suffered for you, leaving you an example, that you should follow in his steps.

This is the reason why Jesus wanted His disciples to keep watch and pray when He went into the garden of Gethsemane. It was right there when Jesus prayed as a man. In Matthew 26:39-44, three times Jesus prayed to have the cup taken away from Him. "My Father, if it is possible, may this cup be taken from me. Yet not as I will, but as you will." Being separated from His Father would play a very important role in Jesus' sufferings.

2 Corinthians 5:21 quote: God made him who had no sin to be sin for us, so that in him we might become the righteousness of God.

Our Heavenly Father broke His connection with His one and only Son so that we could become the righteousness of God through His Son. Don't ever stand in the presence of God in your own self-righteousness.

This is why we are told in Philippians 2:3–5, quote: Do nothing out of selfish ambition or vain conceit, but in humility consider others better than yourselves. Each of you should look not only to your own interests, but also to the interests of others. Your attitude should be the same as that of Jesus Christ.

Even though you may be saved, you can still have an attitude problem, be selfish, or be filled with vain conceit. When Jesus went to the cross, He humbled Himself and became obedient to death. Now that Jesus has humbled Himself, He is lifted up higher in authority. At the name of Jesus, every knee is going to bow and every tongue is going to confess that Jesus Christ is Lord. What does *Lord* means? Jehovah God.

We are told in 1 Peter 5:6, quote. Humble yourselves, therefore, under God's mighty hand, that he may lift you up in due time.

Church, this is what it means to have the same attitude of the Lord Jesus Christ. Jesus was already declared righteous from the very beginning of His earthly ministry. In order for God the Father to break His connection with God the Son, God the Father had to have a connection. What was God doing? *Breaking his connection to bring us together.*

Matthew 27:46 quote: About the ninth hour Jesus cried out in a loud voice, "Eloi, Eloi, lama sabachthani?"-which means, "My God, my God, why have you forsaken me?

At the baptism of Jesus, John the Baptist gave the eyewitness account of what happened. In Matthew 3:16-17, at the very moment John the Baptist baptized Jesus, heaven was opened, and he saw the Spirit of God descending like a dove and lighting on Him. And a voice from heaven said, "This is my Son, whom I love; with Him I am well pleased." The very reason why the Father was able to say this about His one and only Son was because of the connection they both had with one another. How powerful and effective was this connection between Jesus and His Father? In John 7:16–17, Jesus said, "My teaching is not my own. It comes from Him who sent me. If anyone chooses to do God's will, he will find out whether my teaching comes from God or whether I speak on my own." Also, Jesus tells us in John 14:10, "Don't you believe that I am in the Father, and that the Father is in me? The Words I say to you are not just my own. Rather it is the Father, living in me, who is doing His work."

John 14:8–9 quote: Philip said, "Lord, show us the Father and that will be enough for us." Jesus answered: "Don't you know me, Philip, even after I have been among you such a long time? Anyone who has seen me has seen the Father. How can you say show us the Father?

Jesus and His Father were in complete unity and oneness with one another. Jesus' teaching was not of human origin, and there was no inseparable connection between Jesus' Words and His work that He had received from His Father.

When Jesus spoke of every believer being His sheep, He said it this way: John 10:27–30 quote: My sheep listen to my voice; I know them and they follow me. I give them eternal life, and they shall never perish; no one can snatch them out of my hand. My Father, who has given them to me, is greater than all; no one can snatch them out of my Father's hand. I and my Father are one."

When it comes down to our salvation in the Lord Jesus Christ, we have been given double security. Some might argue that you can lose salvation. But I beg to differ with them. We had nothing to do with our salvation.

This is why we are told in Ephesians 2:8–9 quote: For it is by grace that you have been saved, through faith-and this is not from yourselves, it is the gift of God-not by works, so that no one can boast.

When it comes down to receiving salvation that's been offered to us by grace through faith in Christ Jesus, we had nothing to do with it in the first place. We are sealed at the very beginning of our conversion to faith in Christ.

Ephesians 1:13 quote: And you also were included in Christ when you heard the word of truth, the gospel of your salvation. Having believed, you were marked in him with a seal, the promised Holy Spirit.

Every believer is sealed until the day of redemption. And this is because of what Jesus did for us at the cross on Calvary.

Romans 6:23 quote: For the wages of sin is death, but the gift of God is eternal life in Christ Jesus our Lord.

God's gift to us is eternal life in Jesus Christ, His one and only Son. What went on at the cross when Jesus cried out in a very loud voice? Everyone who was present heard Him. The connection was broken between the Father and the Son. The perfect unity was broken. At that very moment, fellowship was broken. Right at that very moment, darkness covered the face of the entire earth.

Matthew 27:46 quote: "Eloi, Eloi, lama sabachthani?" which means, "My God, My God, why have you forsaken me?

God the Father had to turn His Face away from God the Son. The four Gospels—Matthew, Mark, Luke, and John—all gave eyewitness accounts as to what Jesus went through that led up to His crucifixion. This connection was now broken. We call this *God breaks his connection to bring us together.*

Matthew 27:46 quote: "Eloi, Eloi, lama sabaachthani?" which means, "My God, My God, why have you forsaken me?"

Through God's written Holy Word, it is written as to what Jesus went through. But do you understand what God had to do with His only begotten Son?

John 3:16–17 quote: "For God so loved the world that he gave his one and only Son, that who ever believes in him shall not perish but have eternal life. For God did not send his Son into the world to condemn the world, but to save the world through him.

Church, the judgment of mankind had fallen upon Jesus. Jesus had to endure the wrath of God on that cruel, wicked cross. No human being could imagine what Jesus had to endure on that cross. It doesn't come close. Isaiah 53:6 says, "We all, like sheep, have gone astray, each of us has turned to his own way; and the Lord has laid on Him the iniquity of us all." Jesus took each and every one of our places, individually, at the cross. And the very reason why Jesus did this was because of love.

Romans 5:8 quote: But God demonstrates his own love for us in this: While we were still sinners, Christ died for us.

It was as if someone had it in for you and decided to take your very life, by running you over with a car, and Jesus saw it coming and pushed you out of harm's way (and was run over in your place).

The evidence to show exactly what Jesus had to endure is found in John 19:28 quote: Later, knowing that all was now completed, and so that the Scripture would be fulfilled, Jesus said, "I am thirsty."

The punishment for the whole human race was now over. We hear about criminals sentenced to capital punishment, being shot by a firing squad, being strapped to an electric chair and electrocuted, or being forced to endure lethal injection. They cannot be compared to what Jesus had to endure on the cross. Because of what Jesus endured on the cross, we now have a cross to bear.

Luke 9:23 quote: Then he said to them all: "If anyone would come after me, he must deny himself and take up his cross daily and follow me.

When Jesus walked this earth, He didn't have to die. Jesus could have kept on living and kept on living. But Jesus came here for a reason and a purpose.

John 12:32 quote: But I, when I am lifted up from the earth, will draw all men to myself." What does it mean to be drawn to Jesus? It means salvation.

Acts 4:12 quote. Salvation is found in no one else, for there is no other name under heaven given to men by which we must be saved."

Jesus has made it easy for everyone within the sound of my voice to receive eternal life. In America, everything that you and I purchase today, we have to pay for, regardless of what it is. Nothing in this country is free. But the real Good News is this: Salvation through Jesus Christ is free.

Matthew 11:28–30 quote: Come to me, all who are weary and burdened, and I will give you rest. Take my yoke upon you and learn from me, for I am gentle and humble in heart, and you will find rest for your souls. For my yoke is easy and my burden is light."

Today's religion carries a heavy burden. And the reason why religion has a very heavy burden is because it is based on false teachings and false doctrines.

John 10:1 quote: "I tell you the truth, the man who does not enter the sheep pen by the gate, but climbs in by some other way, is a thief and a robber.

The religion of this world is telling you that you can climb in another way in order to be saved.

John 14:6 quote: Jesus answered, "I am the way and the truth and the life. No one comes to the Father except through me.

Jesus Christ now has connections with His Father. The connection between God the Father and God the Son is back together again. It was all designed to bring us together.

John 14:1–3 quote: "Do not let your heart be troubled. Trust in God; trust also in me. In my Father's house are many rooms; if it were not so, I would have told you. I am going there to prepare a place for you. And if I go and prepare a place for you, I will come back and take you to be with me that you also may be where I am.

Jesus is now with the Father. When the time comes and we breathe our last, we too will be with the Father. How do we know this?

2 Corinthians 5:8 quote: We are confident, I say, and would prefer to be away from the body and at home with the Lord.

CONCLUSION

The Lord Jesus Christ felt deep anguish when He took on the sins of the world, which caused Him to be separated from His Father. *God breaks his connection to bring us together.*

Matthew 27:46 quote: "Eloi, Eloi, lama sabachthani?-which means, "My God, My God, why have you forsaken me?

This is what Jesus dreaded as He prayed in the garden of Gethsemane to take the cup from Him. The physical agony was horrible, but even worse was the period of spiritual separation from God. Jesus had to experience this double death so that we would never have to experience eternal separation from God. For those who have already died in their sins, it is too late.

Proverbs 16:25 quote: There is a way that seems right to a man, but in the end it leads to death.

But it is not too late for you, my friend.

Romans 10:9-10 quote: That if you confess with your mouth, "Jesus is Lord," and believe in your heart that God raised him from the dead, you will be saved. For it is with your heart that you believe and are justified, and it is with your mouth that you confess and are saved.

Whoever calls upon the name of the Lord will automatically be connected to the Lord Jesus Christ. Amen!

14

God's Act of Forgiveness for the Whole Human Race

Luke 23:34 Jesus said, Father, forgive them, for they do not know what they are doing."

SERMON FOR PASSION WEEK:

SERMON MESSAGE:

What comes to your mind whenever you think about the meaning of forgiveness? Forgiveness took place in the Garden of Eden after sin came into existence, through disobedience. Man broke his relationship with God. For this reason Adam could not go into the presence of God, unless there was a mediator present. When we are reading and studying the Word of God, we must use discernment when it comes down to understanding the Word of God. The Lord God forgave Adam and Eve by making coats of skin for both of them. There was a blood sacrifice that took place in that garden to bring about forgiveness. The Lord took an animal and shed its blood in order to make coats of skin for both of them.

Hebrews 9:22 quote: In fact, the law requires that nearly everything be cleanse with blood, and without the shedding of blood there is no forgiveness.

This sacrifice was not a one-time event. But the sacrificing of animals would become a way of life. Why use animals? Animals were considered as blameless and innocent. The sacrificing of animals would become a type of Christ. But when the Lord Jesus Christ had appeared on the scene, it would bring about the fulfillment of the law, and open up the door of grace.

When speaking about Jesus, the Word of God tells us in John 1:1–2, and John 1:14 quote: In the beginning was the Word, and the Word was with God, and the Word was God. He was with God in the beginning. The Word became flesh and made his dwelling among us. We have seen his glory, the glory of the One and Only, who came from the Father, full of grace and truth.

When Jesus came to this earth, He brought grace and truth with Him, and this is because of who He is. Full of grace and truth. Jesus did not come to condemn and judge the people of the world, He came to save them.

John 3:16–17 quote: "For God so loved the world that he gave his one and only Son, that whoever believes in him shall not perish but have eternal life. For God did not send his Son into the world to condemn the world, but to save the world through him.

We are living today under the Dispensation Age of Grace. Before this Dispensation Age of Grace, the Old Testaments saints were living under the Dispensation Age of the Law, in which no one could fulfill but the Lord Jesus Himself. The Ten Commandments are God's moral standard for all mankind. Because of man's sinful nature, it was very difficult to live God's moral standard of keeping the law.

James 2:10 quote: For whoever keeps the whole law and yet stumbles at just one point is guilty of breaking all of it.

There is not a man or woman living today who has kept God's moral standard.

Romans 3:23 quote: For all have sinned and fall short of the glory of God.

This was why the ultimate sacrifice was needed. The Lord Jesus Christ Himself, who would be the only one to fulfill God's Ten Commandments for the whole entire human race. Listen to what John the Baptist said when he approached Jesus while John walked on with his disciples: "Behold the Lamb of God who takes away of the sins of the whole world." Whenever the Old Testament saints offered their sacrifice unto the Lord, the animal sacrifices were only temporary. All that the animal sacrifices did, was to cover the Old Testament saints' sins. They were only atoned for. To atone means to cover, and not to take away.

Matthew 5:17 quote: "Do not think that I have come to abolish the Law or the Prophets; I have not come to abolish them but to fulfill them.

Jesus came to fulfill the law and to give His life as a ransom for many. Why ransom? Because since the fall of Adam and Eve, the whole human race was held captive in sin. Jesus came to set the captives free.

John 8:34–36 quote: Jesus replied, "I tell you the truth, everyone who sins is a slave to sin. Now a slave has no permanent place in the family, but a son belongs to it forever. So if the Son sets you free, you will be free indeed.

What this mean is this: Once we have been converted to faith in Christ, we no longer are bound to our sinful nature, or sinful flesh any longer, because we have all been set free.

2 Corinthians 5:17 quote: Therefore, if anyone is in Christ, he is a new creation; the old has gone, the new has come.

If you are saved, and have repented and have accepted Jesus Christ as your Lord and Savior, then your Heavenly Father has brought your dead spirit to life. That spirit that is in you cannot, and will not sin, no matter what you do. Whenever we give in to sin, we are sinning according to our flesh. But how do we, as believers, keep from living in sin?

Galatians 5:16–21 quote: So I say, live by the Spirit, and you will not gratify the desires of the sinful nature. For the sinful nature desires what is contrary to the Spirit, and the Spirit what is contrary to the sinful nature. They are in conflict with each other, so that you do not do what you want. But if you are led by the Spirit, you are not under law. The acts of the sinful nature are obvious: sexual immorality, impurity and debauchery; idolatry and witchcraft; hatred, discord, jealousy, fits of rage, selfish ambition, dissensions, factions and envy; drunkenness, orgies, and the like. I warn you, as I did before, that those who live like this will not inherit the kingdom of God.

Apostle Paul is directing this message to those who are believers, and not to those who are unsaved. A person who is unsaved cannot inherit the Kingdom of God. Jesus made this very clear when He was speaking to the Pharisee that went by the name of Nicodemus.

John 3:3 quote: In reply Jesus declared, "I tell you the truth, no one can see the kingdom of God unless he is born again.

The Kingdom of God can only operate for those who are believers. We are to no longer chase after the things that people of the world are chasing after.

For this reason, Jesus told us in Matthew 6:32–33 quote: For the pagans run after all these things, and your heavenly Father knows that you need them. But seek first his kingdom and his righteousness, and all these things will be given to you as well.

We call this God's right way of doing things for our lives. We cannot expect for the Kingdom of God to work on our behalf if we are still constantly living sin, by walking in the flesh instead of the Spirit. Under the Dispensation Age of Grace, we no longer use animal sacrifices. When Jesus gave up His spirit when He died on the cross, the curtains in the Temple were torn in two, from top to bottom. Jesus' death brought an end to all animal sacrifices. The shedding of blood no longer became a cover-up. Jesus' shed blood at the Calvary cross took care of everyone's sins. How can we be sure of this?

John 19:30 quote: When Jesus received the drink, Jesus said, "It is finished." With that, he bowed his head and gave up his spirit.

Some well-known television evangelists teach and believe that Jesus did not finish our sins at the cross. They believe that He had to go to hell to finish off the punishment for our sins. Do you know what "It is Finished" means? It means paid in full. Jesus was in agony while God the Father poured out His wrath on His only Son. Why do you think Jesus cried out in a loud voice?

We are told in Matthew 27:26 quote: Then he released Barabbas to them. But he had Jesus flogged, and handed him over to be crucified.

At that very moment, Jesus became the Lamb of God that has taken away the sins of the world. He was the ultimate sacrifice. At this point, Jesus had become separated from His Father. And the reason was to be punished for the sins of the entire world. This is called *God's act of forgiveness for the whole human race.*

Luke 23:34 quote: Jesus said, "Father, forgive them, for they do not know what they are doing."

Jesus was not only referring to those who falsely accused Him, and beat Him beyond recognition, and nailed His hands and His feet to the cross, and thrust a crown of thorns on His head, while one of the thieves alongside of Him hurled insults at Him. Jesus had included everyone in this statement: Father, "forgive them, for they do not know what they are doing." The word *forgiveness* plays a very important role in our lives today. This is the very reason why we are assembled here today as believers in Christ.

We have been forgiven. The only way that our Heavenly Father has chosen to forgive us is through His Son Jesus Christ. Jesus Christ is our salvation.

Act 4:12 quote: Salvation is found in no one else, for there is no other name under heaven given to men by which we must be saved."

Jesus came to give us salvation, which is found in Jesus Christ alone.

John 14:6 quote: Jesus answered, "I am the way the truth and the life. No one comes to the Father except through me.

Today's religions among the pagans are telling you that there are other ways that you can get to heaven. These ways are false.

In fact, we are warned in Galatians 1:8 quote: But if we or an angel from heaven should preach a gospel other than the one we preached to you, let him be eternally condemned!

These religious organizations are teaching false doctrines that have no merits to themselves whatsoever.

In John 10:1 quote: "I tell you the truth, the man who does not enter the sheep pen by the gate, but climbs in by some other way, is a thief and a robber.

Man-made religion is telling you that you can climb in by another way. The very reason why the world is full of so many false religions is because they refuse to accept what has been made easy for the whole human race.

Matthew 11:28–30 quote: "Come to me, all you who are weary and burdened and I will give you rest. Take my yoke upon you and learn from me, for I am gentle and humble in heart, and you will find rest for your souls. For my yoke is easy and my burden is light."

Did you hear that? Jesus said that His yoke is easy, and His burden is light. Jesus had switched places with each and every one of us. We cannot atone for our own sins. To do so, we would have to spend eternity in hell and the in the Lake of Fires. This was the reason why Jesus came. Jesus came to keep each and every one of us from going to hell and the Lake of Fires. In order for an individual to keep from going to hell, they have to repent. What does it mean to repent?

2 Peter 3:9 quote: The Lord is not slow in keeping his promise, as some understand slowness. He is patient with you, not wanting anyone to perish, but everyone to come to repentance.

The purpose of repenting is so that God can forgive you and create in you a new heart. Beloved God wants to forgive you, so that you can receive the gift of eternal life. Eternal life is a free gift. You cannot earn it by working for it. Eternal life is not for sale. You can't buy it, and the reason is, you can't afford it. But yet, you can still receive this gift free of charge.

Those who are saved, we are told in Ephesians 2:8–9 quote: For it is by grace you have been saved, through faith-and this not from yourselves, it is the gift of God-not by works, so that no one can boast.

As believers in Christ we have nothing to boast about before Almighty God. It is through God's grace that we've been saved. And this all has to do with the Lord Jesus Christ shedding His precious blood on the cross for each and every one of us. This was called *God's act of forgiveness for the whole human race.*

Jesus said in Luke 23:34 quote: Jesus said, "Father, forgive them, for they do not know what they are doing."

The grace of God's forgiveness comes by one condition, and one condition only. It is that we all come through the Lord Jesus Christ and be saved. This is the only way that God the Father has chosen to forgive us. As denominations, we can disagree when it comes down to different biblical doctrines. Once we get to heaven, God is going to straighten all that out. But when it comes down to salvation through Jesus Christ, we all have to be on the same page. Why salvation through the Lord Jesus Christ? Because only God, and God alone, can forgive our sins. God became a man in the very person of Jesus Christ.

Romans 6:23 quote: For the wages of sin is death, but the gift of God is eternal life in Christ Jesus our Lord.

When a person I know comes to me and asks to borrow a specific amount of money, which I know that I can afford to lend to him, knowing that it's going to be hard for him to pay it back to me, I let him know that I'm giving it to him as a gift. They can either accept it or reject it. The choice is up to them. When it comes down to salvation through the Lord Christ Jesus, God knows that there is nothing that we can do to earn it. So we accept the free gift of eternal life that is being offered to us. By you receiving eternal life that's in Christ Jesus has become God's confirmation that you have been forgiven. It's called faith.

Hebrews 11:1 and Hebrews 11:6 quote: Now faith is being sure of what we hope for and certain of what we do not see. And without faith it is impossible to please God, because anyone who comes to him must believe that he exists and that he rewards those who earnestly seek him.

With faith, the believer can knock down all the fiery darts of doubts. This also includes doubting their salvation. There have been times when some believers have doubted their salvation. If you are saved, then you have been forgiven. If you happen to slip and stumble, or get sidetracked, or fall short of God's best, pick yourselves up and get right back into the race. Did you know that you are in a spiritual race? As Christians, we are not competing against each other. And the reason is, we are cheering and we are encouraging one another on.

This is why we are told in 1 Corinthians 9:24–27 quote: Do you not know that in a race all the runners run, but only one gets the prize? Run in such a way as to get the prize? Everyone who competes in the games goes into strict training. They do it to get a crown that will not last; but we do it to get a crown that will last forever. Therefore I do not run like a man running aimlessly; I do not fight like a man beating the air. No, I beat my body and make it my slave so that after I have preached to others, I myself will not be disqualified for the prize.

Many Christians today have disqualified themselves from the prize. Because they have failed to understand that they have already been forgiven. So they go right back and begin living their old sinful lifestyle all over again. Whenever this happens, they begin to grieve the Holy Spirit.

We are told as believers in Ephesians 4:30 quote: And do not grieve the Holy Spirit of God, with whom you were sealed for the day of redemption.

If you are grieving the Holy Spirit in your life, it can only mean one thing. You have put the Holy Spirit's fire out in your life. You began to ignore the correcting and discipline in your life. You stop bearing fruit, which has to do with fruit of the Spirit.

The fruit of the Spirit is mention in Galatians 5:22–23: quote: But the fruit of the Spirit is love, joy, peace, patience, kindness, goodness, faithfulness, gentleness and self-control. Against such things there is no law.

When Jesus began His earthly ministry, He was baptized by John the Baptist to fulfill all righteousness. As Jesus was being baptized, a voice from heaven spoke. It was the voice of His Father in heaven. Matthew 3:17 says, "And a voice from heaven said, 'This is my Son, whom I love; with Him I am well pleased.'" At everything that Jesus did and set out to do, God the Father was very pleased. Jesus did His Father's will.

John 5:19 quote: Jesus gave them this answer: "I tell you the truth, the Son can do nothing by himself; he can do only whatever he sees his Father doing, because whatever the Father does the Son also does.

Jesus and His Father were in complete unity with each other. But when Jesus came to the cross, God the Father and God the Son were completely separated from each other.

Before Jesus would receive the full strength of God's wrath poured upon Him, Jesus would say, Luke 23:34 quote: Jesus said, "Father, forgive them, for they do not know what they are doing."

This was considered as *God's act of forgiveness for the whole human race.* Jesus did not come to this earth to die for Himself. Church, understand this. Jesus didn't have to die. Jesus could have kept on living and kept on living. But Jesus came to earth for a purpose. To seek and to save that which was lost. You and I. Jesus knew exactly what His purpose was.

John 10:17–18 quote: The reason my Father loves me is that I lay down my life-only to take it up again. No one takes it from me, but I lay it down of my own accord. I have the authority to lay it down and authority to take it up again. This command I received from my Father.

Why did the Father love Jesus? Because Jesus came to do and to fulfill His Father's will. Church, Jesus laid down His life for us as believers to follow as well.

1 Peter 2:21 quote: To this you were called, because Christ suffered for you, leaving you an example, that you should follow in his steps.

Once the individual has been forgiven, the next step is doing the will of God for their life. Find a local Bible-believing Christ-centered church. Spend time in prayer and in the Word of God.

Then you will be able to do exactly what is mentioned in Romans 12:1–2 quote: Therefore, I urge you brothers, in view of God's mercy, to offer your bodies as living sacrifices, holy and pleasing unto God-this is your spiritual act of worship. Do not conform any longer to the pattern of this world, but be transformed by the renewing of your mind. Then you will be able to test and approve what God's will is-his good, pleasing and perfect will.

As the Lord Jesus sacrificed His life, we as believers need to sacrifice our lives, so that we can become living sacrifices, holy and pleasing unto God. Now that we have been forgiven, we are to be holy.

Matthew 5:16 quote: In the same way, let your light shine before men, that they may see your good deeds and praise your Father in heaven.

If you are constantly living in sin, living a sinful lifestyle, you are not going to let your light shine. All this will do will allow others to question whether or not you are truly saved. Whenever we let our light shine, we are identifying with Christ.

Jesus said in Luke 9:23 quote: Then he said to them all: "If anyone would come after me, he must deny himself and take up his cross daily and follow me.

The cross that we are to carry has to do with our sinful lifestyle, which we have to say no to. When Jesus endured the cross, He wasn't enduring the cross for Himself, because He was considered as being innocent. Since we as believers have been forgiven, we no longer allow our flesh to control us any longer. In order for a believer to live a godly life in Christ Jesus, they are going to have to get into the reading and studying of the Word of God.

John 15:1–3 quote: "I am the true vine, and my Father is the gardener. He cuts off every branch in me that bears no fruit, while every branch that does bear fruit he prunes so that it will be even more fruitful. You are already clean because of the word I have spoken to you.

It is the Word of God that cleans up our lives. If Jesus says that we are forgiven, then we need to live like we are. How do we accomplish this task? By reading and studying God's Word for your life.

2 Timothy 2:15 quote: Do your best to present yourself to God as one approved, a workman who does not need to be ashamed and who correctly handles the word of truth.

CONCLUSION

Jesus said in Luke 23:34 quote: Jesus said, "Father, forgive them, for they do not know what they are doing."

Jesus let us know that all of us who are now saved, have been forgiven. We have all repented and have received Christ Jesus as our Lord and Savior. If you are here tonight and you haven't received Christ Jesus as your Lord and Savior, then you now have the opportunity to truly be forgiven. The first step is to repent of your sins; admit that you are a sinner and you cannot save yourself. Then begin to confess with your mouth that Jesus Christ is Lord. Believe in your heart that God raised Jesus from the dead. For with the heart you believe and are justified, and with your mouth you confess and you are saved. For whosoever calls upon the name of the Lord will be saved.

John 20:30-31 quote: Jesus did many other miraculous signs in the presence of his disciples, which are not recorded in this book. But these are written that you may believe that Jesus is the Christ, the Son of God, and that by believing you may have life in his name. Luke 23:34 quote: Jesus said, "Father, forgive them, for they do not know what they are doing."

This is called *God's act of forgiveness for the whole human race.* Amen!

15

Jesus Has a Word for Spiritual Mothers and Others

John 19:25–27: Near the cross of Jesus stood his mother, his mother's sister, Mary the wife of Clopas, and Mary Magdalene. When Jesus saw his mother there, and the disciple whom he loved standing nearby, he said to his mother, "Dear woman, here is your son," and to the disciple, "Here is your mother." From that time on, this disciple took her into his home.

MOTHER'S DAY SERMON

SERMON MESSAGE:

What is the definition of a mother? A woman who has a child, whether by birth, or adoption, or fostering, who is able to care for this child's welfare.

When it comes down to raising a child, or children, we are told in Proverbs 22:6 quote: Train a child in a way he should go, and when he is old he will not turn from it.

This verse of Scripture can be applied to everyone, providing that they are saved. And if the mother is not saved, she is going to try to raise her child up the very best that she knows how. I didn't come up out of a Christian home. Along with my brothers and sisters, my parents raised us the very best way that they knew how. Whatever it was that they were teaching us, it became our upbringing. We did not know any better. I went to church every now and then. My parents could care less about us going to church. They were not bad people, they just raised us the best that they could. But on the other hand, if the mother is saved, she's going to raise up children up in the very best ways of the Lord. So if you really want to raise up your children in the ways of the Lord, then you need to be saved.

Romans 10:9–10 quote: That if you confess with your mouth, "Jesus is Lord," and believe in your heart that God raise him from the dead, you will be saved. For it is with your heart that you believe and are justified, and it is with your mouth that you confess and are saved.

The very reason why the Lord wants people to be saved right now is so they can be used for right now. There have been many deathbed conversions to salvation, but the saddest thing of all is this: those who go on to be with the Lord will miss out on receiving their heavenly rewards.

2 Corinthians 5:10 quote: For we must all appear before the judgment seat of Christ, that each one may receive what is due him for the things done while in the body, whether good or bad.

The more time that we spend on this earth, the more opportunity we have to bear spiritual fruit.

This is why Apostle Paul said it this way in Philippians 1:21–24 quote: For to me, to live is Christ and to die is gain. If I am to go on living in the body, this will mean fruitful labor for me. Yet what shall I choose? I do not know! I am torn between the two: I desire to depart and be with Christ, which is better by far; but it is more necessary for you that I remain in the body.

Paul wasn't raised up in a Christian background. He was raised up in Judaism. Paul's name was Saul; he was a Pharisee and was taught by and brought up under Gamaliel's teachings. Since Paul's conversion to the Christian faith in Christ, he continued bearing fruit. Christian mothers today are to continue to bear fruit. Some of you mothers have already raised children who are already grown and have children of their own. This doesn't mean that your work is over. Your Heavenly Father isn't done with you yet.

Philippians 1:6 quote: Being confident of this, that he who began a good work in you will carry it on to completion until the day of Christ Jesus.

While you are here on earth, you can still touch the lives of others with the Gospel of Jesus Christ. If you have children who are not saved yet, the Lord is still working on you to touch their lives. So do not give up.

Acts 16:31 quote: "Believe in the Lord Jesus, and you will be saved-you and your household."

If you truly believe that God has saved you, then you also can believe that God will save your entire household as well. When Rahab the prostitute hid the spies, they promised to protect

221

her and everyone she brought into her house. This harlot was no longer considered as a harlot. But Rahab became an Old Testament believer in the Lord. She did everything that she could to get all of her people into her house. When the Lord God sent Joshua to destroy the city of Jericho, he was able to spare Rahab's entire household. That meant everyone in her house had their lives spared. This was called faith.

Hebrews 11:6 quote: And without faith it is impossible to please God, because anyone who comes to him must believe that he exists and that he rewards those who earnestly seek him.

All throughout Jesus' ministry, He had traveled all over Judea healing the sick and raising the dead and preaching the Good News. But when Jesus came to His own hometown, the people there took offense at Him.

Matthew 13:57 quote. And they took offense at him. But Jesus said to them, "Only in his hometown and in his own house is a prophet without honor."

This was because of the lack of faith by the people living in Jesus' hometown. Did you know that at that time, Jesus' own brothers did not believe in Him? So if Jesus' family members had felt this way about Him, just imagine how your family members feel about you. Even though this message is directed to mothers in honor of Mother's Day, this message still can also be directed to each individual here today. While mothers raise their children and teach them to do what is right, children are placed under so much peer pressure.

Mothers today still have to encourage their children and nurture them up in the ways of the Lord: 1 Corinthians 15:58 quote: Therefore, my dear brothers, stand firm. Let nothing move you. Always gives yourselves fully to the work of the Lord, because you know that your labor in the Lord is not in vain.

So do not give up, and do not quit. Everyone has something good waiting for them at the very end of the tunnel. It all has to do with doing that which is right. When it comes down to living a Christian life, there are no short cuts.

Jesus said it this way in Luke 9:23 quote: "If anyone would come after me, he must deny himself and take up his cross daily and follow me.

Whenever mothers are teaching their children, they are not teaching in a one-shot deal. They have to stay constantly on them every day. Because there are going to be days that they are going to do some things wrong. This is where discipline comes in.

And this is where the teaching of the Word of God comes in; 2 Timothy 3:16–17 quote: All Scripture is God-breathed and is useful for teaching, rebuking, correcting and training in righteousness, so that the man of God may be thoroughly equipped for every good work.

Mothers, you may not be aware of this, but you are raising a child of God, so that they can be labeled as a man of God or a woman of God. This happened at the very moment that you dedicated them unto the Lord. My son Kevin is a grown man, but whenever he comes home and is under my roof, I do not have to ask him if he's going to church. It all has to do with the way that we raised him. Kevin honors his parents by going to church.

Ephesians 6:1–3 quote: Children, obey your parents in the Lord, for this is right. "Honor your father and mother"-which is the first commandment with a promise-"that it may go well with you and that you may enjoy long life on the earth.

The saddest thing that is going on among today's younger generation is that they are disrespecting their parents; they like to have their own way and do what they want. And because of this, so many young lives are ended in tragedy. Colossians 3:20 says, "Children, obey your parents in everything, for this pleases the Lord." *Jesus has a word for spiritual mothers.*

John 19:26–27 quote: When Jesus saw his mother there, and the disciple whom he loved standing nearby, he said to his mother, "Dear woman, here is your son," and to the disciple," "Here is your mother." From that time on, this disciple took her into his home.

While He was on the cross, Jesus said to Mary, "Dear woman, here is your son," and He said to the disciple, "Here is your mother." From that time on, John took her into his home. Jesus had brothers and sisters, but there was no spiritual relationship there among them. John, the beloved disciple, was a devoted follower of the Lord Jesus Christ. Jesus taught His disciples how to become fishers of men, fishing for lost souls and bringing them into the family of God. Church, this is what we have been called to do when it comes to leading lost souls to Christ.

Galatians 6:10 quote: Therefore, as we have the opportunity, let us do good to all people, especially to those who belong to the family of believers.

It is very good to look out for anyone who crosses your pathway. But it is also very good to watch out for those who are believers in Christ all the more. This is what Jesus did with His mother, Mary, when He singled her out to John, His disciple. We have spiritual mothers in our local churches who need our support and our help. Jesus had placed the care of His mother into the hands of one of His disciples. You have heard the old saying, Blood is thicker than water. Not in God's eyes.

John 1:12–13 quote: Yet to all who received him, to those who believed in his name, he gave the right to become children of God- children born not of natural decent, nor of human decision or husband's will, but born of God.

If everyone can, just take a moment and look around you. These are your spiritual family members, right here. You might as well get used to them, because these are the ones you are going to see in heaven all throughout eternity. So if you have any earthly family members you want to see in heaven, then you need to lead them to Christ.

1 Peter 3:15 quote: But in your hearts set apart Christ as Lord. Always be prepared to give an answer to everyone who asks you to give the reason for the hope that you have. But do this in gentleness and respect.

The way that we live our lives for Christ is the way that we ought to lead others to the Lord. You can know God's Word from cover to cover, but if you are not practicing exactly what you are preaching, you can't expect to lead anyone to the Lord.

James 1:22–24 quote: Do not merely listen to the word, and so deceive yourselves. Do what it says. Anyone who listens to the word but does not do what it says is like a man who looks at his face in a mirror and, after looking at himself, goes away and immediately forgets what he looks like.

All you are doing is fooling no one but yourself. Just acting like hypocrites. Whenever you attend your local churches on regular basis, the local churches are mostly filled with women. These women are considered as spiritual mothers.

This why we are told in Hebrews 10:25 quote: Let us not give up meeting together, as some are in a habit of doing, but let us encourage one another-and all the more as you see the Day approaching.

These spiritual mothers are your real encouragers, because that day is quickly approaching, and we need to be encouraging as many lost souls as we can. Jesus wants the lost to be saved.

Acts 1:8 quote: But you will receive power when the Holy Spirit comes on you; and you will be my witnesses in Jerusalem, and in all Judea and Samaria, and to the ends of the earth."

Just as the Lord Jesus Christ commissioned His apostles, He has also commissioned every believer as well. But *Jesus has a word for spiritual mothers.*

In Matthew 12:48–50, Jesus is speaking: "He replied to him, 'Who is my mother, and who is my brothers?' Pointing to His disciples, He said, 'Here is my mother and brothers. For whoever does the will of my Father in heaven is my brother and sister and mother.'" The main key to what the Lord Jesus was saying is to do the will of His Father. Church, Jesus wasn't putting His mother and brothers down when they wanted to see him, but while Jesus was speaking to the crowd, Jesus was just making a statement to what every believer needs to be doing: doing the will of God. When Jesus speaks to the mothers, Jesus is speaking to others as well.

This is why we are told in Romans 12:1–2 quote: Therefore, I urge you, brothers, in view of God's mercy, to offer your bodies as living sacrifices, holy and pleasing to God-this is your spiritual act of worship. Do not conform any longer to the pattern of this world, but be transformed by the renewing of your mind. Then you will be able to test and approve what God's will is-his good, pleasing and perfect will.

There are certain things that you have to do in order for you to do the will of God. But it starts with you. Jesus defended Himself against the Pharisees and the teachers of the law when they falsely accused Him of being Beelzebub. And while Jesus was defending Himself, a woman in the crowd called out, "Blessed is the mother who gave you birth and nursed you."

But Jesus told her in Luke 11:28 quote: He replied, "Blessed rather are those who hear the word of God and obey it."

Church, this is what God's will really is. God's will is that every believer obey the Word of God. The majority of us all have Bibles.

And the very thing that we need to do with our Bibles is to read and study them.

2 Timothy 2:15 quote: Do your best to present yourself to God as one approved, a workman who does not need to be ashamed and who correctly handles the word of truth.

But it doesn't stop there. We need to apply God's Word to our everyday lives.

This is why Paul tells us in 2 Corinthians 5:21 quote: God made him who had no sin to be sin for us, so that in him we might become the righteousness of God.

Church, our Heavenly Father has already declared us as what God's Word says we are: the righteousness of God. Our next step is for every believer to live like God's Word says we are. Where do you go to do this? You go to your local church, where there is someone who is there to teach and to train you in the very things of God when it comes down to doing the will of God. This is why you have pastors and teachers. They are given to the church for this purpose.

Ephesians 4:12–13 quote: To prepare God's people for works of service, so that the body of Christ may be built up until we all reach unity in the faith and in the knowledge of the Son of God and become mature, attaining to the whole measure of fullness of Christ.

If you have spent years in a local church, there needs to be some evidence to show that you have matured in the Christian faith.

1 Peter 2:2–3 quote: Like newborn babies, crave pure spiritual milk, so that by it you may grow up in your salvation. Now that you have tasted that the Lord is good.

Church, this is where it all begins: right here while you are being taught the Word of God. Spiritual mothers are those who have matured in the Christian faith. Apostle Paul referred to Timothy's grandmother and his mother for their great Christian faith. It was because of their spiritual maturity. Paul tells Timothy this in 2 Timothy 1:5, "I have been reminded of your sincere faith, which first lived in your grandmother Lois and in your mother Eunice and, I am persuaded, now lives in you also." The Christian upbringing that Timothy received came from his mother and grandmother. But *Jesus has a word for spiritual mothers.* John 19:26-27 quote: When Jesus saw his mother there, and the disciple whom he loved standing nearby, he said to his mother, "Dear woman, here is your son, "and to the disciple, "Here is your mother." From that time on, this disciple took her into his home.

In Mark 10: 28–31, Peter speaking to Jesus said, "We have left everything to follow You!"

"I tell you the truth," Jesus replied, "no one who has left home or brothers or sisters or mother or father or children or fields for Me and the Gospel will fail to receive a hundred times as much in this present age [homes, brothers, sisters, mothers, children, and fields—and with them, persecutions] and in the age to come, eternal life." To become a follower of Christ, it's going to cost you. What are you willing to give up to follow Jesus? Your life may be very valuable to you. Mothers, brothers, sisters, and fathers, are you willing to give up your life to follow Christ?

To the unsaved we are told in Matthew 16:26, quote: What good will it be for a man if he gains the whole world, yet forfeits his soul? Or what can a man give in exchange for his soul?

People today are holding on and trusting in the things that can't satisfy them, things they cannot take with them when they leave. Christians today are also doing the very same thing. What should profit a Christian, if they should gain the whole world and miss out on their heavenly rewards?

1 John 2:15–17 quote: Do not love the world or anything in the world. If anyone loves the world, the love of the Father is not in him. For everything in the world-the cravings of sinful man, the lust of his eyes and the boasting of what he has and does-comes not from the Father but from the world. The world and its desires pass away, but the man who does the will of God lives forever.

Our focus and our aim ought to be centered around doing the will of God. The very reason why we are following Christ is because our Heavenly Father has something far better than what the world's system has to offer us.

This is why we are told to do what the Lord says in Matthew 6:32–33 quote: For the pagans run after all these things, and your heavenly Father knows that you need them. But seek first his kingdom and his righteousness, and all these things will be given to you as well.

In order to leave everything to follow the Lord Jesus Christ, the Lord Jesus Christ must have first place in your life. The very reason why Peter denied Jesus three times was because Peter was still holding on to his life. Peter wasn't ready to give it up. Are you ready to give up the stuff in your life to follow Jesus? Are you ready to give up your life for Jesus?

Jesus told Peter in Luke 22:31–32 quote: "Simon, Simon, Satan has ask to sift you as wheat. But I have prayed for you, Simon, that your faith may not fail. And when you have turned back, strengthen your brothers."

Jesus wasn't done with Peter. And Jesus isn't done with you. Understand exactly who you are.

Ephesians 2:10 quote: For we are God's workmanship, created in Christ Jesus to do good works, which God prepared in advance for us to do.

The very moment that you accepted the Lord Jesus Christ as your Savior and Lord, God had programmed you to do good works.

2 Corinthians 5:17 quote: Therefore, if anyone is in Christ, he is a new creation; the old has gone, the new has come!

The things that you do for Christ will be the only things that will matter when we get to glory. We no longer live for ourselves any longer. But now we are to live for Christ.

Ephesians 5:15–17 quote: Be very careful, then, how you live-not as unwise but as wise, making the most of every opportunity, because the days are evil. Therefore do not be foolish, but understand what the Lord's will is.

God's Word teaches you how to do God's will. Jesus showed us how to do this in John 5:19 quote: Jesus gave them this answer: "I tell you the truth, the Son can do nothing by himself; he can do only do what he sees his Father doing, because whatever the Father does the Son also does.

No matter what it was that Jesus did, Jesus always placed His direct focus on doing His Father's will. How do we recognize the spiritual mothers? We recognize them as they are doing God's will for their lives.

Proverbs 3:5–7 quote: Trust in the Lord with all your heart and lean not on your own understanding; in all your ways acknowledge him, and he will make your paths straight. Do not be wise in your own eyes; fear the Lord and shun evil.

The spiritual mothers' paths are being guided along by the Lord.

CONCLUSION

Who is my mother? Who is my brother? Jesus was not denying His responsibility to His earthly family. Remember when Jesus criticized the religious leaders for not following the Old Testament command to honor their parents. How soon we forget. Jesus provided for His mother's security as He hung on the cross. Also, after Jesus had ascended on high, on the day of Pentecost, Jesus' mother and brothers were present in the upper room. When Jesus said, "Who is my mother? Who is my brother?" He was pointing out that spiritual relationships are as binding as physical ones.

Jesus was paving the way for a new community of believers, the Universal Church, which Jesus is still building today.

Matthew 16:18 quote. And on this rock I will build my church, and the gates of Hades will not overcome it.

This is God's spiritual family. Amen!

16

Accept Salvation through the Resurrected Christ

John 11:25–26. Jesus said to her, "I am the resurrection and the life. He who believes in me will live, even though he dies; and whoever lives and believes in me will never die. Do you believe this?

EASTER SUNDAY SERMON

SERMON MESSAGE:

Whenever you plant a seed of any kind, it is a must that you bury it. Why should you bury it? Because this is the only way that it can grow and produce a harvest after its very own kind. Whether this seed be physical, spiritual, or financial, they all need to be buried. Whenever you plant a seed, you are burying it. If you do not plant it, you cannot expect to receive a harvest from it. Jesus gave a statement in John 12:24, "I tell you the truth, unless a kernel of wheat falls to the ground and dies, it remains only a single seed. But if it dies, it produces many seeds." Jesus likened Himself as a kernel of wheat, to show the fact that He Himself had to die, and be buried, in order to produce many spiritual seeds after His kind.

John 1:12–13 quote: Yet to all received him, to those who believed in his name, he gave the right to become children of God-children born not of natural decent, nor of human decision or husband's will, but born of God.

Jesus had to die to pay the penalty for our sins, but also to show His power over death. Death had no hold over Jesus because Jesus was without sin.

John 10:17-18 quote: The reason my Father loves me is that I lay down my life-only to take it up again. No one takes it from me, but I lay it down on my own accord. I have the authority to lay it down and the authority to take it up again. This command I received from my Father. "

Why is this so important to every individual? When Jesus came to this world, He didn't commit any sin. This made Jesus exempt from death. Jesus could have kept on living and kept living in His physical body all throughout eternity if He wanted to. But Jesus came here for a reason and a purpose.

To fulfill God's moral standards for all mankind, Matthew 5:17 quote: "Do not think that I have come to abolish the Law or the Prophets; I have not come to abolish them but to fulfill them.

Jesus came also to give His life as a ransom for many.

Matthew 20:28 quote: Just as the Son of man did not come to be served, but to serve, and to give his life as a ransom for many."

Why would Jesus use the word *ransom*? It is because the entire human race is held captive in the jaws of sin. This captivity took place at the very beginning during the time of Adam and Eve. When Adam and Eve disobeyed God, they sinned, and by their sin, they placed every human being in jeopardy. Every person who has lived has inherited Adam's sinful nature. Placing our faith in the Lord Jesus Christ allows us to turn all of this around.

John 8:34–36 quote: Jesus replied, "I tell you the truth, everyone who sins is a slave to sin. Now a slave has no permanent place in the family, but a son belongs to it forever. So if the Son sets you free, you will be free indeed.

Why do we have to put our faith in the Lord Jesus Christ? Because other than Adam and Eve, Jesus Christ is the only one who was born free.

Listen carefully to the statement that Jesus gives in John 8:23 quote: But he continued, "You are from below; I am from above. You are of this world; I am not of this world.

Jesus made it very clear to the Pharisees, as to where He came from. The Lord created Adam from the dust of the ground, which makes it clear that every human being came from the dust of the ground. We are considered as descendants of Adam. But for our Lord and Savior Jesus Christ, this was not the case. Jesus came from above.

We are told in Luke 1:29–32, as the Angel Gabriel was speaking to Mary, who was a virgin at the time, Mary was greatly troubled at his words and wondered what kind of greeting this might be.

But the angel said to her, "Do not be afraid, Mary, you have found favor with God. You will be with child and give birth to a Son, and you are to give Him the name Jesus. He will be great and will be called the Son of the Most High." These verses of Scripture prove that Jesus is from above. Because Jesus is referred to as the Son of the Most High.

Also we are told in Matthew 1:23 quote: "The virgin will be with child and will give birth to a son, and they will call him Immanuel"-which means, "God with us."

Jesus is not the Son of the most below, but the Most High God. Jesus was considered as God in the flesh.

This is why we are told in John 1:1–3, quote: In the beginning was the Word, and the Word was with God, and the Word was God. He was with God in the beginning. Through him all things were made; without him nothing was made that has been made. Also we are told in John 1:14 quote: The Word became flesh and made his dwelling among us. We have seen his glory, the glory of the One and Only who came from the Father, full of grace and truth.

John, the beloved Apostle of Jesus Christ, testified that he saw the Glory of the Lord Jesus Christ. During those three very important years that Jesus spent on earth during His earthly ministry, Jesus showed John, Peter, and James His glory. This all took place on the Mountain of Transfiguration. Jesus knew exactly what he was talking about. Listen to John's testimony of Jesus Christ in 1 John 1:1: "That which was from the beginning, which we have heard, which we have seen with our eyes, which we have looked at and our hands have touched—this we proclaim concerning the Word of Life." The very reason Jesus came from above is to offer the gift of eternal life to everyone who wants to receive it. But in order for us to receive eternal life, we must believe that Jesus Christ is exactly who He says He is.

Hebrews 11:6 quote: And without faith it is impossible to please God, because anyone who comes to him must believe that he exists and that he rewards those who earnestly seek him.

For those who are first timers, the reward that is being offered is the free gift of eternal life through Jesus Christ. This is a reward that an unsaved person cannot earn. And here's the reason why: Ephesians 2:8–9 quote: For it is by grace you have been saved, through faith-and this not from yourselves, it is the gift of God-not by works, so that no one can boast.

There are a very large number of religious groups today. They are lying to people by teaching them that they can work their own way to heaven by their own self-righteous merits. This is a lie that comes straight from the devil.

Proverbs 16:25 quote: There is a way that seems right to a man, but in the end it leads to death.

For those of you who are already saved, you can continue to keep on doing what Hebrews 11:6 says. Because the more that we as believers in Christ continue to seek after God, God our Heavenly Father will continue to reward us with earthly blessings. These blessings are designed so that they can wet our appetites until the Lord calls us home to glory.

This why we are told in 2 Corinthians 5:7 quote: We live by faith, not by sight.

Things are not always as they appear to be. Also, we are told in 2 Corinthians 4:18, "So we fix our eyes not on what is seen, but on what is unseen. For what is seen is temporary, but what is unseen is eternal." But in order for this to be accomplished in our lives, we need to first agree by *accepting salvation through the resurrected Christ.*

John 11:25–26 quote: Jesus said to her, "I am the resurrection and the life. He who believes in me will live, even though he dies; and whoever lives and believe in me will never die. Do you believe this?"

When it comes down to Jesus' resurrection, the four Gospel writers are all on the same page. Jesus' resurrection is very important to every believer, because the resurrection of the Lord Jesus Christ secures our salvation. And it also secures our hope.

John 10:27–30 says quote: My sheep listen to my voice; I know them, and they follow me. I give them eternal life, and they shall never perish; no one can snatch them out of my hand. My Father, who has given them to me, is greater than all; no one can snatch them out of my Father's hand. I and the Father are one."

So how do you become one of Jesus' sheep? By repenting of your sins and by accepting Jesus Christ as Savior and Lord.

Romans 10:9–10 quote: That if you confess with your mouth, "Jesus is Lord," and believe in your heart that God raised him from the dead, you will be saved. For it is with your heart that you believe and are justified, and it with your mouth that you confess and are saved.

Before you confess with your mouth that Jesus is Lord, you need to first of all know something about Jesus. And all it takes is someone explaining to you in a nutshell what Jesus has already accomplished for you individually at the cross on Calvary.

2 Corinthians 5:21 quote: God made him who had no sin to be sin for us, so that in him we might become the righteousness of God.

God took someone who was very precious and dear to Him. Someone who was considered perfect, and blameless, and without sin. Someone who was innocent. Someone who went by the name of Jesus, and placed Him on the cross, so He could become our sin offering. John the Baptist called Jesus the Lamb of God, who takes away the sins of the whole world. Every sin that all mankind would ever commit would be placed upon Jesus. All four Gospels go into details as to what Jesus had to endure in the physical sense, but while Jesus hung on that cross, God the Father was still pouring out His wrath on His one and only begotten Son.

John 3:16–17 quote: For God so loved the world that he gave his one and only Son that whoever believes in him shall not perish but have eternal life. For God did not send his Son into the world to condemn the world, but to save the world through him.

How many of you understand that Jesus is still saving the people of the world today? An unsaved person already stands condemned, while they are condemning themselves for hell's judgment. Whenever they are given the opportunity to accept Jesus, but instead reject Him, they bring judgment on themselves.

Matthew 12:37 quote: For by your words you will be acquitted, and by your words you will be condemned."

When an individual dies in their sins, God is not the one at fault, but they are. The unsaved person has made a decision not to believe in the resurrected Christ. This is the very reason they allow God's wrath to remain on them.

John 3:36 quote: Whoever believes in the Son has eternal life, but whoever reject the Son will not see life, for God's wrath remains on him.

Many times we watch many different types of commercials on the television. They are constantly promoting their products to the consumers who watch these commercials. But the disappointing part of it is this: they do not stand by their products.

Matthew 23:1–3 quote: Then Jesus said to the crowds and to his disciples: "The teachers of the law and the Pharisees sit in Moses' seat. So you must obey them and do everything they tell you. But do not do what they do, for they do not practice what they preach.

The CEO of Ford Motor Corporation showed up at a hearing in Washington, DC, when his corporation needed a bail-out. This Ford executive showed up in a Lexus, when he should have been driving his own company's product, the Lincoln Navigator. This executive did not practice what he preached. In other words, he did not stand by his product. Jesus gave a statement about the hypocrites: "I tell you the truth, they have already received their rewards in full."

Galatians 6:7–8 quote: Do not be deceived: God cannot be mocked. A man reaps what he sows. The one who sows to please his sinful nature, from that nature will reap destruction; the one who sows to please the Spirit, from the Spirit will reap eternal life.

The Lord Jesus Christ has a product. And the Lord Jesus Christ stands by His product 100 percent. The product that the Lord Jesus Christ is promoting has been tried on Himself. The Lord Jesus Christ is not only the CEO of His product, He is also a client. The product that the Lord Jesus Christ is marketing to this entire world is eternal life. *Accepting salvation through the resurrected Christ* is all about giving an individual eternal life. And the only way that an individual can receive eternal life is by going through the head CEO Himself, the Lord Jesus Christ.

John 11:25–26 quote: Jesus said to her, "I am the resurrection and the life. He who believes in me will live, even though he dies; and whoever lives and believes in me will never die. Do you believe this?"

What Jesus is saying here is this: whoever believes in Him will not have to experience the second death. If you die in your sins, and you make it to the White Throne Judgment, it's already too late.

Matthew 7:13–14 quote: "Enter through the narrow gate. For wide is the gate and broad is the road that leads to destruction, and many enter through it. But small is the gate and narrow the road that leads to life, and only a few find it.

Today's religion is pointing people in all directions, telling them that there are other ways to get to heaven.

But Jesus said it this way in John 10:1 quote: "I tell the truth, the man who does not enter the sheep pen by the gate, but climbs in by some other way, is a thief and a robber.

There is only one way that person can get to heaven, and that is through the Lord Jesus Christ. This is why the resurrection of the Lord Jesus Christ is so very valuable to us today. Even though you cannot afford to purchase eternal life because of its value, it is free of charge.

This is why Jesus tells us in Matthew 16:26 quote: What good would it be for a man if he gain the whole world, yet forfeit his soul? Or what can a man give in exchange for his soul?

If an unsaved person was to gain the whole world, he still could not take it with him. Those who are unsaved may own a fleet of nice cars. The unsaved might even live in a mansion or even have a very large bank account. The unsaved might even have affordable health care through their entire life. But once it's over, it's over. But once the Lord calls their name, they won't have anything. Not even themselves.

This is why for the believers we are told in 1 Corinthians 6:19–20 quote: Do you not know that your body is a temple of the Holy Spirit, who is in you, whom you have received from God? You are not your own; you were bought at a price. Therefore honor God with your body.

How can we truly say that we own something, when as believers, we do not even own ourselves? Church, Jesus purchased every one of us at a very high price. When a very important person is being held for ransom, the captors place a high price tag on their head for ransom. This has nothing to do with the cost. God the Father was willing to do whatever it takes to purchase lost souls that were held in the captive jaws of sin. God could have sent a dog, or a cat, or a sick human being, or a tree, or an ocean of water to accomplish this task if He wanted to. But God the Father sent forth His very best.

Romans 5:8 quote: But God demonstrates his own love for us in this; while we were still sinners, Christ died for us.

The Lord Jesus Christ is God's very best. You cannot get any better than this. There is no one else when it comes down to God's very best. This is what it is called *accepting salvation through the resurrected Christ.*

John 11:25–26 quote: Jesus said to her, "I am the resurrection and the life. He who believes in me will live, even though he dies; and whoever lives and believes in me will never die. Do you believe this?"

The very reason why we as Christians celebrate Resurrection Sunday every year after the Passover is to show that there is eternal life in Jesus Christ, who rose from the dead and will give life to all believers who place their complete trust in Him. If the Rapture doesn't take place in our lifetime, we can expect to experience a physical death.

2 Corinthians 5:8 quote: We are confident, I say, and would prefer to be away from the body and at home with the Lord.

The very moment that we breathe our last breath on earth, our body is going to remain here on the earth. Our soul and our spirit are going to be with the Lord.

This is why Apostle Paul was able to tell us in Philippians 1:21–24 quote: For to me, to live is Christ and to die is gain. If I am to go on living in the body, this will mean fruitful labor for me. Yet what shall I choose? I do not know! I am torn between the two, I desire to depart and be with Christ, which is better by far; but it is more necessary for you that I remain in the body.

For the believer in Christ, who dies in the Lord, death can only become a welcome mat. Whether you are alive or have gone on to be with the Lord, there will be a resurrection for the believers in Christ. At the resurrection for the believers, we will meet the Lord in the air at the Rapture of the Church. 1 Corinthians 15:50 says, "I declare to you, brothers, that flesh and blood cannot inherit the Kingdom of God, nor does perishable inherit the imperishable." Something has to happen in order for the Rapture to take place. We have to be changed. From perishable, to imperishable. From mortal, to immortality. Church, we are going to receive glorified heavenly bodies. What is the purpose of the heavenly bodies? It is so that we will be able function within the heavenly realms all throughout eternity. While we remain in the body, we remain limited to what we can do and where we can go. When we receive our glorified bodies, we are told in Revelation 21:4, "There will be no more death or mourning or crying or pain, for the old order of things has passed away." There will be no more sin or evil in our presence.

This is the very reason why we are told as believers in Christ in Ephesians 5:15–17 quote: Be very careful, then, how you live-not as unwise but wise, making the most of every opportunity, because the days are evil. Therefore do not be foolish, but understand what the Lord's will is.

As believers, we have to monitor how we live, so that we do not become a stumbling block to those we want to lead to Christ.

Galatians 2:20 quote: I have been crucified with Christ and I no longer live, but Christ lives in me. The life I live in the body, I live by faith in the Son of God, who loved me and gave himself for me.

If we have been crucified with Christ, then we are going to be united together in Christ. *Accepting salvation through the resurrected Christ* brings about redemption.

Ephesians 1:13-14 quote: And you also were included in Christ when you heard the word of truth, the gospel of your salvation. Having believed, you were marked in him with a seal, the promised Holy Spirit, who is deposit guaranteeing our inheritance until the redemption of those who are God's possession—to the praise of His glory." This can be applied to you, only if you are saved and have accepted Jesus Christ as Lord.

CONCLUSION

Jesus has power over life and death as well as power to forgive sins. This is because He is the Creator of life.

John 14:6 quote: Jesus answered, "I am the way and the truth and the life. No one comes to the Father accept through me.

He who is life can surely restore life. Whoever believes in Christ has a spiritual life that death cannot conquer or diminish in any way. When we realize Jesus' almighty power and how wonderful His offer to us really is, how can we help but commit our lives to the Lord Jesus Christ? To those of us who believe, what a wonderful assurance and certainty we have: John 14:19 says, "Before long, the world will not see me anymore, but you will see me. Because I live, you also will live." This is what *accepting salvation through the resurrected Christ* is all about. In John 11:25–26, Jesus said, "I am the Resurrection and the Life. He who believes in Me will live, even though he dies; and whoever lives and believes in Me will never die." Do you believe this? Amen!

17

Why Spiritual Footwashing Is Very Important Today

John 13:1–11; It was just before the Passover Feast. Jesus knew that the time had come for him to leave this world and go to the Father. Having loved his own who were in the world, he now showed them the full extent of his love. The evening meal was being served, and the devil had already prompted Judas Iscariot, the son of Simon, to betray Jesus. Jesus knew that the Father had put all things under his power, and that he had come from God and was returning to God; so he got up from the meal, took off his outer clothing, and wrapped a towel around his waist. After that, he poured water into a basin and began to wash his disciples' feet, drying them with towel that was wrapped around him. He came to Simon Peter, who said to him, "Lord, are you going to wash my feet?" Jesus replied, "You do not realize now what I am doing, but later you will understand." No," said Peter, "you shall never wash my feet?" Jesus answered, "Unless I wash you, you have no part with me." Then, Lord," Simon Peter replied, "not just my feet but my hands and my head as well!" Jesus answered, "A person who has had a bath needs only to wash his feet; his whole body is clean. And you are clean, though not every one of you." For he knew who was going to betray him, and that was why he said not every one was clean.

SERMON MESSAGE:

What comes to your minds whenever you think about taking a bath? You are dirty and smelly, and you really want to get cleaned up. In a spiritual sense, this is exactly what every individual need to do with their lives. Every human being living today, needs to have a spiritual bath. It doesn't matter who you are. What race you are. How important you are, or how wealthy you are, or what color you are. You still need a spiritual bath. One of the very reason you were born; was so that you can have spiritual bath.

2 Peter 3:9 quote: The Lord is not slow in keeping his promise, as some understand slowness. He is patient with you, not wanting anyone to perish, but everyone to come to repentance.

Whenever an individual repents of their sins, and have acknowledge that they are a sinner, it opens the door to them receiving a spiritual bath. Jesus said to Nicodemus in John 3:3 quote: In reply Jesus declared, "I tell you the truth, no one can see the kingdom of God unless he is born again.

The Kingdom of God is personal. But in order for an individual to enter into it, they must be Born Again.

John 1:12–13 quote: Yet to all who received him, to those who believed in his name, he gave them the right to become children of God-children born not of natural decent, nor of human decision or a husband's will, but born of God.

Being children of God can only mean one thing, that God our Creator has now become our Heavenly Father. God has become our Heavenly Father through the very person of the Lord Jesus Christ. People today are still looking for many ways to approach God. And the very thing that is keeping people from coming to God is looking right at them in their faces. It's called sin. God's divine Holiness will not allow Him to look at sin. All our righteousness in God's eyes is as filthy rags.

Romans 3:23 quote: For all have sinned and fall short of the glory of God.

If an unsaved person thinks that they have the right to approach Almighty God, they are mistaken. They have it all wrong.

For this reason we are told in Proverbs 16:25 quote: There is a way that seems right to a man, but in the end it leads to death.

Once an unsaved person dies in their sins, it's already too late. As human beings, we are capable in making mistakes all the time, because no one is considered as being perfect. But once we make a mistake that is not life threatening, we might have the opportunity to correct it. But when it comes down to where an individual spends their eternity, if they make the wrong choice, they are stuck with it for all eternity.

Matthew 16:26 quote: What good will it be for a man if he gains the whole world, yet forfeits his soul? Or what can a man give in exchange for his soul.

Every human being who have reached the age of accountability needs a spiritual bath. It doesn't matter if you are a Baptist. Being Baptist can't save you. It doesn't matter if you were baptized. Being baptized can't save you. It doesn't matter if you speak in tongues. Speaking in tongues can't save you. It doesn't matter what Denomination, or religion you are in. There is a difference between Denomination and Religion. Denomination identifies an individual to a particular faith that they are in, but it doesn't mean that they are saved. Religion points you to God. But each time religion reaches to God, it misses God as the target each time.

Listen to what Jesus says in John 14:6: quote: Jesus answered, "I am the way and the truth and the life. No one comes to the Father except through me.

God is represented as the Father in heaven. If you want to get to the Father in heaven, it has got to be through Jesus, His Son. And here's the reason why.

John 3:16–17 quote: "For God so loved the world that he gave his one and only Son, that whoever believes in him shall not perish but have eternal life. For God did not send his Son into the world to condemn the world, but to save the world through him.

What does this mean? God the Father gave up His very best. Whenever you acknowledge Jesus Christ, you are acknowledging God's very best. And God's very Best connect you to His Father in heaven. The very reason why God gave His very Best, was because of His love.

Romans 5:8 quote: But God demonstrates his own love for us in this: While we were still sinners, Christ died for us.

Jesus died for us, so that each and every one of us, individually can be saved. What needs to happen for each individual person to receive eternal life and be saved? Repentance, and Acknowledgment when it come to receiving Jesus Christ as Savior and Lord. An individual having a change of heart concerning sin, that brings forth repentance.

Luke 13:3 quote: But unless you repent, you too will all perish.

Acknowledging Jesus Christ as Lord, Jesus said in Matthew 10:32-33 quote: Whoever acknowledge me before men, I will also acknowledge him before my Father in heaven. But whoever disowns me before men, I will disown him before my Father in heaven.

So how do we acknowledge Jesus before His Father in heaven?

Romans 10:9–10 quote: That if you confess with your mouth, "Jesus is Lord, "and believe in your heart that God raised him from the dead, you will be saved. For it is with your heart that you believe and are justified, and it is with your mouth that you confess and are saved.

We acknowledge Jesus Christ by receiving Jesus as Lord and Savior of our lives at the very moment we repent of our sins. What does it mean to receive Jesus as Lord? Whenever you receive Jesus Christ as Lord, you are receiving Jesus as Jehovah God. This is what Lord means. This is the spiritual bath that Jesus was actually referring to when Jesus speaking to Peter. In John 13:10, Jesus answered, "A person who has had a bath needs only to wash his feet; his whole body is clean. And you are clean, though not every one of you. Jesus had considered Peter and the other disciples clean. But when Jesus said, "Not every one of you," He was referring to Judas Iscariot. Jesus had washed Judas feet. Because if Jesus hadn't wash Judas's feet, then the rest of the disciples would have singled Judas out. Church, no one knew who it was that was going to betray Jesus, until after it had already happened.

This is why we are as believers in 2 Corinthians 13:5 quote: Examine yourselves to see whether you are in the faith; test yourselves. Do you realize that Christ Jesus is in you-unless, of course, you fail the test?

There are times in our lives where we have to put our salvation to self-examination. Just because we attend church on Sunday, and weekly Bibles studies, doesn't mean that we are saved.

Philippians 2:12–13 quote: Continue to work out your salvation with fear and trembling, for it is God who works in you to will and to act according to his good purpose.

If we are not working out our own salvation with fear and trembling, then we need to really question our salvation very seriously. Now that we have settle the issue of having a spiritual bath, which has to do with salvation and being Born Again, we can now move on to understanding *why spiritual footwashing is very important today.* While Jesus was washing His disciples feet, He came to Peter. But Peter could not see Jesus washing his feet. It was considered as the same statement that John the Baptist had made when Jesus ask to be Baptized. Matthew 3:14 says, "But John try to deter Him, saying, 'I need to baptized by you, and you come to me.'" But when it came down to Peter, Peter was very uncomfortable about the Lord Jesus Christ washing his feet. But also at the same time Peter was ignorant to exactly what Jesus was doing. But Jesus told Peter this: Unless I wash you, you have no part with me. Jesus did not have to break this down to Peter, Peter had understood exactly what Jesus was talking about. When Jesus was washing His disciples feet, Jesus was illustrating at this time, that He, and He alone, could forgive the confess sins of those who are saved.

This is why we are told in 1 John 1:9 quote: If we confess our sins, he is faithful and just and will forgive us our sins and purify us from all unrighteousness.

I can remember repeating the sinner's prayer, over and over again. It was because I didn't have the complete assurance that I thought I had. I kept hearing how I could lose my salvation, to I eventually gave up thinking that I was really saved. Because of my ignorance, I went back into the world, and remain in a back sliding state. I stay out there until I was delivered from this ignorance.

Jesus tells us in John 10:27–30 quote: My sheep listen to my voice; I know them, and they follow me. I give them eternal life, and they shall never perish; no one can snatch them out of my hand. My Father, who has given them to me, is greater than all; no one can snatch them out of my Father's hand. I and the Father are one."

This is what it means to have double security as a believer in Christ. It would surprise you of how many Christians today, do not recognize 1 John 1:9. Many do not know that this Scripture actually exist. This is the reason why we have so many spiritual babies living today, who are unaware of 1 John 1:9.

When Apostle Paul was speaking to the Church at Corinth, Paul addressed them in this way in 1 Corinthians 3:1–2 quote: Brothers, I could not address you as spiritual but as worldly-mere infants in Christ. I gave you milk, not solid food, for you were not yet ready for it. Indeed, you are still not ready.

These Christians brothers were considered as saved, but at the very same time they were considered as worldly, spiritual babies. Whenever a Christian that is worldly, it's very hard to tell if they are truly believers. Because of this, they have one foot in the world and the other in the church. And all that they are doing is playing church. After a while these worldly Christians began to unmask themselves where everyone can see right through them.

1 John 2:15–17 quote: Do not love the world or anything in the world. If anyone loves the world, the love of the Father is not in him. For everything in the world-the cravings of sinful man, the lust of his eyes and the boasting of what he has and does-comes not from the Father but from the world. The world and its desires pass away, but the man who does the will of God lives forever.

As long as you continue to love the world and the very things in the world, worldly Christians are going to continue to drift away into sin. There are a lot of temptations in the world to get us to sin. This is where the Word of God comes in.

1 Corinthians 10:13 quote: No temptation has seized you except what is common unto man. And God is faithful; he will not let you be tempted beyond what you can bear. But when you are tempted, he will provide a way out so that you can stand up under it.

We live in a world where sin is always visible, and if we are not careful, we will find ourselves given into it. In the High Priestly prayer, Jesus prays for the believers.

John 17:15 quote: My prayer is not that you take them out of the world but you protect them from the evil one.

The Lord has left us on this earth for purpose, and that purpose is to witness and share our faith with others. But while we are here, we are placed in the midst evil.

This is why we are told in Ephesians 5:15–17 quote: Be very careful, then, how you live-not as unwise but as wise, making the most of every opportunity, because the days are evil. Therefore do not be foolish, but understand what the Lord's will is.

Church, we are in the world, but we are not to be of it. This is *why spiritual footwashing is very important today.* The point is this, we need to confess our sins. Again, Jesus said to Peter, "Unless I wash you, you have no part with me." The same is true with every believer. Spiritual footwashing is just as important as having a spiritual bath. Having a spiritual bath needs to be first. Continuous footwashing comes afterwards. When you confess your sins, do not go to a priest. They cannot forgive your sins, but only God can. In God's Word, we are told exactly who to go to. 1 John 1:10–2:2–2 says, "If we claim we have not sinned, we make Him out to be a liar and His Words has no place in our lives. My dear children, I write this to you so that you will not sin. But if anybody does sin, we have one who speaks to the Father in our defense—Jesus Christ, the righteous one. He is the atoning sacrifice for our sins, and not only for ours but also for the sins of the whole world. Without a shadow of a doubt, you go to the Lord Jesus Christ to confess your sins. By grace through faith is where we accept the cleansing of sin in our lives." Church, this doesn't mean that we go on living in sin.

Galatians 6:7 quote. Be not deceived: God cannot be mocked. A man reaps what he sows.

Whenever we walk in the flesh, we open up the door to walk into sin. This doesn't mean that every time we are walking in the flesh we are going to sin, but the desire to sin will always be there.

Galatians 5:16–21 quote. So I say, live by the Spirit, and you will not gratify the desires of the sinful nature. For the sinful nature desires what is contrary to the Spirit, and the Spirit what is contrary to the sinful nature. They are in conflict with each other, so that you do not do what you want. But if you are led by the Spirit, you are not under law. The acts of the sinful nature are obvious: sexual immorality, impurity and debauchery; idolatry and witchcraft; hatred, discord, jealousy, fits of rage, selfish ambition, dissensions, faction and envy; drunkenness, orgies, and the like. I warn you, as I did before, that those who live like this will not inherit the kingdom of God.

Also, whenever we are walking in the flesh, we miss out on receiving the inheritance to the Kingdom of God. Whenever we sin, it brings a halt to our blessings. But the moment that we confess our sins, we are placed right back under God's umbrella of protection. Every believer needs to be seeking first the Kingdom of God in everything that we do.

Matthew 6:32–33 quote: For the pagans run after all these things, and your heavenly Father knows that you need them. But seek first his kingdom and his righteousness, and all these things will be given to you as well.

This is how the Kingdom of God works for the believers. You cannot expect to seek first the Kingdom of God if you are constantly living in sin. For some Christians who claim their conversion in faith in the Lord Jesus Christ, are not bearing any fruit in their lives whatsoever. They are not reading or studying the Word of God, they do not attend the worship services regularly.

This is why we are told in 2 Chronicles 7:14 quote: If my people, who are called by my name, will humble themselves and pray and seek my face and turn from their wicked ways, then will I hear from heaven and will forgive their sin and will heal their land.

When it comes down to salvation, our Heavenly Father doesn't leave us stranded. But our Heavenly Father wants us to always remain in fellowship with Him. 1 John 1:6, If we claim to have fellowship with Him yet walk in darkness, we lie and do not live by the truth. Spiritual darkness has to do with the sin in our lives. This is the very reason *why spiritual footwashing is very important today.* We need to always continually confess our sins; unto the Lord. Un-confess sin can hinder our ministry.

Ephesians 2:10 quote: For we are God's workmanship, created in Christ Jesus to do good works, which God prepared in advance for us to do.

As believers we cannot expect to do good work while we are constantly living in sin.

James 4:17 quote: Anyone, then, who knows the good he ought to do and doesn't do it, sins.

As believers in Christ we are really without excuse. And the very reason that we are without excuse is because we have the Word of God that makes us held accountable for our very own actions.

Hebrews 4:12–13 quote: For the word of God is living and active. Sharper than any double-edge sword, it penetrates even the dividing soul and spirit, joints and marrow; it judges the thoughts and the attitudes of the heart. Nothing in all creation is hidden from God's sight. Everything is uncovered and laid bare before the eyes of him to whom we must give account.

If you have a Bible, and you choose not to read it, and not to understand it, then, that's on you. Why do you come to church, if you are not going to pay attention. All you really doing is just wasting your time. Your time is very valuable, you could be doing something else. The only reason why I am here, is because I believe my time is valuable. Someone is going to benefit from the preaching of the Word of God. 1 Timothy 4:7 says, "Have nothing to do with godless myths and old wives tales; rather train yourself to be godly." Church, your Heavenly Father is not going to twist your arm and make you live a godly life. That's got to be up to you. We have to discipline ourselves if we truly want to live a godly life.

Our Heavenly Father has done His part in 2 Corinthians 5:17: quote: Therefore, if anyone is in Christ, he is a new creation; the old has gone, the new has come!

Now it is up to each and every one of us to do our part. When it comes to sin, we can't say that the devil made me do it. We now have a brand new spiritual nature living inside of us. We also have the Holy Spirit living inside of us too. Church, what more can we ask for? If our Heavenly Father wanted us to be robots, He would have created us to be robots. But God has given us a choice to choose on our own. And as we choose, our Heavenly Father is there to help us to make the right choice. For example, we are told in Deuteronomy 30:19–20, "This day I call heaven and earth as witnesses against you that I have set before you life and death, blessings and curses. Now choose life, so that you and your children may live and that you may love the Lord your God, listen to His voice, and hold fast to Him." Even though Moses is the one who is speaking, God is still the one speaking through Moses. And the Lord is the One that's helping us to make the right choice, by choosing life. Church, the same is true when it comes to learning *why spiritual footwashing is very important today.* It is so that we can move on to the very next level of our faith. This is what we call spiritual growth along with spiritual maturity. We cannot expect to move to spiritual maturity if we are still living in continuous sin.

We're told in Hebrews 12:1–2 quote: Therefore, since we are surrounded by such a great cloud of witnesses, let us throw off everything that hinders and the sin that so easily entangles, and let us run with perseverance the race marked out for us. Let us fix our eyes on Jesus, the author and the perfecter of our faith, who for joy set before him endured the cross, scorning its shame, and sat down at the right hand of the throne of God.

Every believer living a Christian life is running a spiritual race. Sin is a distraction and can entangle us and keep us from running the race that God has allowed us to run.

CONCLUSION

When Jesus came to wash Peter's feet, Peter failed to realize that he needed a spiritual cleansing. Peter had already had a spiritual bath through the cleaning of the Word of God.

John 15:3 quote: You are already clean because of the word I have spoken to you.

As believers, we need to undergo a spiritual cleansing in our lives every day. Especially when it comes down to sin in our lives.

If you are still living the same sinful lifestyle that you were living before you were saved, then Revelation 2:5 is for you, quote: Remember the height from which you have fallen! Repent and do the things you did at first. If you do not repent, I will come to you and remove your lampstand from its place.

Expect our Heavenly Father to bring about judgment on your life.

1 Corinthians 11:30–32 says, "That is why many among you are weak and sick, and a number of you have fallen asleep." But if we judge ourselves, we would not come under judgment. When we are judged by the Lord, we are being disciplined so that we will not be condemned with the world. This is *why spiritual footwashing is very important today.* Amen!

18

Carry Out God's Good Work that's Inside of You

Ephesians 2:10. For we are God's workmanship, created in Christ Jesus to do good works, which God prepared in advance for us to do.

SERMON MESSAGE:

During Jesus' ministry while He was on earth, Jesus did a lot of healings and miracles and signs while being in the very presence of the current generation of people living at that time. While Jesus was doing this, the religious leaders of His day became offended at what Jesus was doing. And they began to criticize Jesus for the many healings that He was performing. But these religious leaders had failed to understand the reason and the purpose to the reason why Jesus was doing these things.

This is why we are told in John 20:30 quote: Jesus did many other miraculous signs in the presence of his disciples, which are not recorded in this book. But these are written that you may believe that Jesus is the Christ, the Son of God, and that by believing you may have life in his name.

The good works that Jesus was doing among the people pointed people to himself. The very things that Jesus was doing cannot be accomplished today. Jesus healed the blind and the paralytic, raised the dead, healed those with deformity, and so on. And the reason why Jesus was able to do this, was because of the statement that He had made concerning His Father.

John 5:19 quote: Jesus gave this answer: "I tell you the truth, the Son can do nothing by himself; he can do only what he sees his Father doing, because whatever the Father does the Son also does.

Church, Jesus kept His eyes focus on His Father in heaven so that He could accomplish the very task in which Jesus was given to do. All throughout Jesus ministry on earth, Jesus spoke very highly of His Father. And Jesus' Heavenly Father spoke very highly of Him. This is my Beloved Son in whom I Am well pleased. Why was the Father pleased about His Only Son? Because Jesus Is the Son of God.

John 1:1–3 quote: In the beginning was the Word, and the Word was with God, and the Word was God. He was with God in the beginning. Through him all things were made; without him nothing was made that has been made.

Jesus was with God in the beginning, and Jesus was God, and still is God; and always will be God. But keep this in mind Church, the very reason why Jesus came to this earth was to do and to carry out His Father's will.

John 3:16–17 quote: "For God so loved the world that he gave his one and only Son, that whoever believes in him shall never perish but have eternal life. For God did not send his Son into the world to condemn the world, but to save the world through him.

Jesus came to give eternal life to each and every one. It doesn't matter if you are caught up a certain religion. Religion can't save you, but Jesus Christ really can save you.

In fact, we are told in 2 Peter 3:9 quote: The Lord is not slow in keeping his promise, as some understand slowness. He is patient with you, not wanting anyone to perish, but everyone to come to repentance.

All of this has to do with anyone who has been created in the Image of God and in His Likeness. It is God's desire for everyone to be saved, and for all to come to repentance. God is not leaving anyone out. Another reason why God the Father was well pleased about His Son the Lord Jesus Christ, was because of God's love for His one and only Son.

John 10:17–18 quote. The reason my Father loves me is that I lay down my life-only to take it up again. No one takes it from me, but I lay it down on my own accord. I have the authority to lay it down and the authority to take it up again. This command I received from my Father."

God could have used anything that He wanted to, to redeem the whole human race. God could have chosen a dog, or a tree, or a mountain, or some dirt, or some water, or so on to redeem all mankind. But the Lord God had chosen someone who is very valuable and very special to Himself to redeem the whole human race. God the Father had chosen His one and only Son. This was all done out of love.

Romans 5:8 quote: But God demonstrates his own love for us in this: While we were still sinners, Christ died for us.

The Lord Jesus Christ perform a greatest task of such good work that He gave up His life for us all. All the miraculous signs that Jesus had done throughout His entire ministry was considered as good works. Church, these miraculous signs were design to point the people of the world to Jesus Himself.

To show the people that Jesus was God in the flesh, John 1:14 quote: The Word became flesh and made his dwelling among us. We have seen his glory, the glory of the One and Only, who came from the Father, full of grace and truth.

In order for you to save yourself, you had to be Jesus. But Jesus did not have to be saved, because He was never lost in the first place. The whole human race was considered as lost through Adam's seed. Every human being that was born and ever lived, all have inherited Adam's sinful nature that Adam and Eve had received after they had sinned.

Romans 3:23 quote: For all have sinned and fall short of the glory of God.

God the Father has given the whole world the opportunity to receive the antidote for the forgiveness of sins. And His name is the Lord Jesus Christ, His one and only begotten Son.

John 8:34–36 quote: Jesus replied, "I tell you the truth, everyone who sins is a slave to sin. Now a slave has no permanent place in the family, but a son belongs to it forever. So if the Son sets you free, you will be free indeed.

As an individual, you cannot perform any good works until you have been set free from sin, or delivered from sin. In order for this to take place in your life, you first have to be Born Again.

John 3:3 quote: In reply Jesus declared, "I tell you the truth, no one can see the kingdom of God unless he is born again.

Seeing the Kingdom of God in the midst of you, is going to allow you to carry out the good work in your Christian life, that you have been call to do. This is why being Born Again is so very important.

John 1:12–13 quote: Yet to all who received him, to those who believed in his name, he gave the right to become children of God-children born not of natural decent, nor of human decision or a husband will, but born of God.

Everyone who is born into this world is first of all, is born in the flesh. This took place at the very moment that our birth mother gave birth to us. The next step in line, is to be born of the Spirit.

Ephesians 1:13 quote: And you also were included in Christ when you heard the word of truth, the gospel of your salvation. Having believed, you were marked in him with seal, the promised Holy Spirit.

Not everyone is born of the Spirit. But the opportunity to be born of the Spirit is there. People from every religion are being told that they can work their way, or earn their way to heaven. Do you know what the Word of God says about this lie?

Proverbs 16:25 quote: There is a way that seems right to a man, but in the end it leads to death.

Before you breathe your very last breath, make very sure that you have made the right decision. Because once it is over for you here on earth, its over. As long as we are all living and breathing, we can make all kinds of mistakes. We have time to make up for them, and correct them. But when it comes down to stepping into eternity, that's the choice that you have to make. Apostle Paul understood this, and he passes it along to us.

Philippians 1:21–24 quote: For to me, to live is Christ and to die is gain. If I am to go on living in the body, this will mean fruitful labor for me. Yet what shall I choose? I do not know! I am torn between the two, I desire to depart and be with Christ, which is better by far; but it is more necessary for you that I remain in the body.

When Paul was talking about fruitful labor, what's he talking about? Good works. Paul was already a believer in Christ. The more that Paul would live, the more Paul would have the opportunity to gain more in his fruitful labor. Church, the same thing can be said about you, that's only if you saved. Each one of you have the opportunity to *carry out God's good work that's inside of you.*

Ephesians 2:10 quote: For we are God's workmanship, created in Christ Jesus to do good works, which God prepared in advance for us to do.

Many Christians today have become so unproductive in their Christian life. And the reason is after they become saved, they go right back out and continue to live the very same sinful lifestyle.

Hebrews 10:25 quote: Let us not give up meeting together, as some are in the habit of doing, but let us encourage one another-in all the more as you see the Day approaching.

Just because you attend your local church on regular basis doesn't mean that you are doing good works. There is more to it than that. It starts with you. Your good works has got to be seen outside of the walls of your local church.

Matthew 5:16 quote: In the same way, let your light shine before men, that they may see your good deeds and praise your Father in heaven.

Church, everyone you come into contact with in your local church is going to see your light. Because there is nothing that you are going to do to disrespect yourselves, or disgrace yourselves, or embarrass yourselves. The unsaved needs to see the real you outside the walls of your local church.

2 Corinthians 5:20–21 quote: We are therefore Christ's ambassadors, as though God were making his appeal through us. We implore you on Christ's behalf: be reconciled to God. God made him who had no sin to be sin for us, so that in him we might become the righteousness of God.

Two things you need to know. You are representing the Lord Jesus Christ, and you are the righteousness of God. Seeing that this is the case, then how do you need to be living? You need to *carry out God's good work that's inside of you.*

Ephesians 2:10 quote: For we are God's workmanship, created in Christ Jesus to do good works, which God prepared in advance for us to do.

Whenever you think of someone who has great workmanship in what they do, what comes to your mind? Someone who has been gifted with a professional craft. Church, God has gifted each and every one of us as believers into becoming a workmanship created in Christ Jesus to do good work. We all have many different gifts that has been given to us in the Body of Christ.

This is why we are told in 2 Timothy 4:5 quote: But you, keep your head in all situations, endure hardship, do the work of an evangelist, discharge all the duties of your ministry.

Whenever we are faced with so many hardships of all kinds, doesn't mean that we throw in the towel, or quit and give up. For all you know, you could be right at the tip of your breakthrough.

Galatians 6:9 quote: Let us not become weary in doing good, for at a proper time we will reap a harvest if we do not give up.

I can remember when I first started out as a pastor, fourteen years ago. I had to depend upon sermon outlines in order to work on my sermons. I do not have a need for sermon outlines anymore. I haven't used sermon outlines in years. I now depend upon strictly on the Word of God to do my sermons. As a pastor, I believe that God is perfecting me.

269

2 Timothy 4:2–3 quote: Preach the Word; be prepared in season and out of season; correct, rebuke and encourage-with great patience and careful instruction. For the time will come when men will not put up with sound doctrine. Instead, to suit their own desires, they will gather around them a great number of teachers to say what their itching ears want to hear.

The same is true with you, as you continue to grow up in your spiritual gifts, God is going to see to it, that you bring your good work to its completion until the day of Christ Jesus. Beloved, God is not finish with you yet.

John 15:1–3 quote: "I am the true vine, and my Father is the gardener. He cuts off every branch in me that bears no fruit, while every branch that does bear fruit he prunes so that it will be even more fruitful. You are already clean because of the word I have spoken to you.

There are two types of Christians living today. The spiritual Christian, and the worldly Christian. When we all became converted to faith in Christ, we all started as new babes in Christ. So when it comes down to feeding on the Word of God, we needed to be already been fed the spiritual milk of the Word of God.

1 Peter 2:2–3 quote: Like newborn babies, crave pure spiritual milk, so that by it you may grow up in your salvation, now that you have tasted that the Lord is good.

If we do not discipline ourselves so that we can crave the milk of the Word of God, then we cannot expect to grow up spiritually. The Spiritual Christians are the ones that will have the opportunity to experience spiritual growth in their Christian walk. Along with the spiritual growth, they will also have become fruitful by bearing good fruit that represents good works.

Hebrews 5:14 quote: But solid food is for mature, who by constant use have trained themselves to distinguish good from evil.

When this verse of Scripture talks about solid food, this verse is referring to the Word of God. In order for you to move on to the very next level in the Christian faith, you have to be matured in the Word of God. What will you be doing? *Carrying out God's good work inside of you.*

Ephesians 2:10 quote: For we are God's workmanship, created in Christ Jesus to do good works, which God prepared in advance for us to do.

On the other hand, those who are still babes in Christ, they will remain worldly Christians. All they want to receive is the spiritual milk of the Word of God. And while they are still receiving the spiritual milk of the Word of God, they still are not ready to move on to the very next level of their faith.

1 Corinthians 3:1–2 quote: Brothers, I could not address you as spiritual but as worldly-mere infants in Christ. I gave you milk, not solid food, for you were not yet ready for it. Indeed, you are still not ready.

When God our Heavenly Father created us in Christ Jesus to do good work, we were all labeled as someone very special. Church, we are to be considered as a work of art, or a masterpiece.

2 Corinthians 5:17 quote: Therefore, if anyone is in Christ, he is a new creation; the old has gone, the new has come!

As we continue to allow ourselves to grow in the Christian faith, your Heavenly Father is going to allow gifted things to take place in your life, like they have never happened before. One of the gifts that I have already received, which helps me to quote the Word of God so well, is the ability to memorize biblical Scriptures. As a Bible-believing pastor, I'm able to implement the Word of God in my preaching and in my teachings. This is the very reason why we have the Word of God with us today.

2 Timothy 3:16–17 quote: All Scripture is God-breathed and is useful for teaching, rebuking, correcting and training in righteousness, so that the man of God may be thoroughly equipped for every good work.

Church, if you hear and see your pastor preaching and teaching to you the Word of God, don't get jealous of him, and do not get offended by him. But learn all that you can from him. This is where you will have the opportunity to benefit from his ministry.

Luke 6:40 quote: A student is not above his teacher, but everyone who is fully trained will be like his teacher.

Every pastor is so unique and gifted in his own way. This is why you do not see them copying each other. They all have been given and fully equipped with their God-given abilities when it comes down to their style of preaching and teaching God's Word. When are you learning from your pastor's sound biblical teachings, you are going to come up with your very own style, to be able to present the Word of God to others as well. What will you be doing? *Carrying out God's good work that's inside of you.*

Ephesians 2:10 quote: For we are God's workmanship, created in Christ Jesus to do good works, which God prepared in advance for us to do.

We all have been programmed to do good work. It doesn't matter how young you are. Or how old you are. How unlearn you are, or how smart you are.

Listen to what was said about Peter and John in Acts 4:13: quote: When they saw the courage of Peter and John and realized that they were unschooled, ordinary men, they were astonished and they took note that these men had been with Jesus.

As you get into the reading and the studying and applying of the Word of God, no one will be able to equip you as well as God's Word can. Whenever we get into the Word of God, we are not going to read it and put on a shelf. But we are going to become doers of the Word of God.

James 1:22–24 quote: Do not merely listen to the word, and so deceive yourselves. Do what it says. Anyone who listens to the word but does not do what it says is like man who looks at his face in a mirror and, after looking at himself, goes away and immediately forgets what he looks like.

Why is it that we have to become doers of the Word of God? It is so that every believer can learn how to bear spiritual fruit in their lives. Whenever you are bearing good fruit, others are going to see it.

John 15:5 quote: "I am the vine; you are the branches. If a man remains in me and I in him, he will bear much fruit; apart from me you can do nothing.

In order for you to remain in Christ as the true vine, you have to stay in the Word of God. Where did John 15:5 come from? It came from the Gospel of John that represents the Word of God. If you do not know where to look when it comes to understanding John 15:5, how are you going to know the Word of God?

Luke 11:28 quote: He replied, "Blessed rather are those who hear the word of God and obey it."

Hearing and obeying the Word of God is going to allow us to bear good fruit and to do good work that God has prepare for us in advance to do. Do not be misled Church, the good work that we are doing comes after salvation, and not before salvation.

This is why we are told in Ephesians 2:8–9 quote: For it is by grace you have been saved, through faith-and this not from yourselves, it is the gift of God-not by works, so that no one can boast.

Salvation has been given to us as a gift. And it was given to us by grace. Grace is God giving us what we do not deserve. If we can understand grace, then we can understand what the gift of salvation in Christ Jesus is all about.

For this reason we are told in Philippians 2:12–13 quote: Therefore, my dear friends, as you have always obeyed-not only in my presence, but now much more in my absence- continue to work out your salvation with fear and trembling, for it is

God who works in you to will and to act according to his good purpose.

Our Heavenly Father has a purpose for each and every one of us. This is providing we do exactly what we all have been called to do. If you are not bearing any good fruit in your life, you cannot expect your Heavenly Father to carry out His purpose for your life.

John 15:16 quote: You did not choose me, but I chose you and appointed you to go and bear fruit-fruit that will last. Then the Father will give you whatever you ask in my name.

The very reason why so many Christians today are not getting their prayers answered is because they are not bearing any good fruit. Our Heavenly Father wants our fruit to last, and not dry up and rot away. Just because you gave your life to Jesus, doesn't mean that the Christian life is going to be peaches and cream. We have to take the bitterness with the sweet.

James 1:2–4 quote: Consider it pure joy, my brothers, whenever you face trials of many kinds, because you know that testing of your faith develop perseverance. Perseverance must finish its work so that you may be mature and complete, not lacking anything.

This is how we must endure as believers, reaching maturity.

Psalm 1:1–3 quote: Blessed is the man who does not walk in the counsel of the wicked or stand in the way of sinners or sit in the seat of mockers. But his delight is in the law of the LORD, and on his law he meditates day and night. He is like a tree planted by streams of waters, which yields it fruit in season and whose leaf does not wither. Whatever he does prospers.

In order for you to become prosperous in everything that you do, you have to bear fruit, especially when it comes down to doing good work in the Kingdom of God. The very reason why every believer has been prepare to do good works, is so that we could enter into the Kingdom of God. And it is because of the one who dwells inside of us. The third Person of the Godhead who is the very one that is at work in our everyday lives.

1 Corinthians 6:19–20 quote: Do you not know that your body is the temple of the Holy Spirit, who is in you, whom you have received from God? You are not your own; you were bought at a price. Therefore honor God with your body.

CONCLUSION

We are God's workmanship (work of art, masterpiece). Our salvation is something that only God can do. It is His powerful, creative work in us. If God considers us His work of art, we dare not treat ourselves or others with disrespect or inferior work.

This is why we are told in Galatians 6:10 quote: Therefore, as we have opportunity, let us do good to all people, especially to those who belong to the family of believers.

If an individual tells you that they are a Christian, until you know anything further, you are to take them at their word. Just like God is working in you, the Lord is also working in them.

Philippians 1:6 quote: Being confidence of this, that he who began a good work in you will carry it on to completion until the day of Christ Jesus.

Just like the Lord isn't finished with you yet, God is not finished with them yet either. Because you still need to be *carrying out God's good work that's inside of you.*

Ephesians 2:10 quote: For we are God's workmanship, created in Christ Jesus to do good works, which God prepared in advance for us to do.

Amen!

19

Celebrate the Divine Royalty that Almost Was

Luke 19:35–40. They brought it to Jesus, threw their cloaks on the colt and put Jesus on it. As he went along, people spread their cloaks on the road. When he came near the place where the road goes down the Mount of Olive, the whole crowd of disciples began joyfully to praise God in loud voices for all the miracles they had seen: "Blessed is the king who comes in the name of the Lord! "Peace in heaven glory in the highest! Some of the Pharisees in the crowd said to Jesus, "Teacher rebuke your disciples!" " I tell you," he replied, "if they keep quiet, the stones will cry out."

Palm Sunday Sermon

SERMON MESSAGE:

Has this ever happened to you? You were invited to a very special program, or an event, such as a wedding or a special performance, where everything was orchestrated and well planned. But all of a sudden, right at the very last minute, this special program was cancelled. How did it make you feel? You probably felt disappointed.

Because you had set aside some time to make some preparations to be able to participate in this invitation. You might be saying to yourself, if they only knew what I had to go through. Such was the case for the Lord Jesus Christ. Jesus was sent here for a very important reason, and a very important purpose. The Lord Jesus Christ was considered as royalty at birth. He was a born a King. When the Magi was led by the star as they traveled from the east, they asked King Herod a question, as stated in Matthew 2:2: "Where is the one who has been born King of the Jews? We saw His star in the east and have come to worship Him."

Jesus was born a king to be worshipped. Other than what has been requested here, nowhere in scripture are we told to worship a king. We are to pay tribute to a king, but never are we told to worship a king. During the time that the Prophet Daniel was in exile, and was promoted as one of the three administrators; the other administrators along with the satraps in Daniel's day, tried to set Daniel up by using King Darius against him. No one was allowed to pray to any god or man, unless it was the king for thirty days. Punishment for this offense was being thrown into the lion's den. This edict was put into writing and it couldn't be altered. What happened in the end?

Galatians 6:7–8 quote: Do not be deceived: God cannot be mocked. A man reaps what he sows. The one who sows to please his sinful nature, from that nature will reap destruction; the one who sows to please the Spirit, from the Spirit will reap eternal life.

Every one of these political leaders that took part in this evil plot was thrown into the lion's den, with their entire family. But the Prophet Daniel's life was spared because of his innocence. King

Darius knew that Daniel had done nothing wrong, and all this had to do with directing worship in the wrong place. As Jesus was born as a king, the Book of Matthew was written for this purpose, to show Jesus as King. Though Jesus would come as Israel's king, the day would come when Jesus would be rejected as Israel's king. Scripture prophesied beforehand that the Lord Jesus Christ, the anointed one, would be rejected as king. Listen to what is says in Daniel 9:26, concerning the prophecy of Jesus Christ: "After sixty-two 'sevens,' the anointed will be cut off and will have nothing." Church, this passage of Scripture predicted and prophesied what led up to Jesus being rejected by the Jews. This was Palm Sunday. This was supposed to be a day of celebration and jubilee.

This is a portion of Genesis 3:15 coming into place. Quote: And I will put enmity between you and the woman, and between your offspring and hers; he will crush your head, and you will strike his heel."

It was the opposition of the offspring of the serpent that led to the rejection of Jesus as King of the Jews. Remember the statement that Jesus gave to Pilate? In John 18:36, Jesus said, "My Kingdom is not of this world. If it were, my servants would fight to prevent my arrest by the Jews. But now my Kingdom is from another place." What did Jesus mean by saying, "But now my Kingdom is from another place"? Jesus was about to be given the opportunity to establish His Kingdom here on earth. But instead, He was cut off and rejected. Jesus already had His divine plan to be carried out. What divine plan was that?

In Matthew 16:18 quote: And on this rock I will be build my church, and the gates of Hades will not overcome it.

But in order for Jesus' plan to be accomplished, He had to be betrayed in the hands of the elders, chief priests, and teachers of the law, and He had to be killed and, on the third day, raised to life.

This is why we are told in John 10:17–18 quote: The reason that my Father loves me is that I lay down my life-only to take it up again. No one takes it from me, but I lay it down on my own accord. I have the authority to lay it down and the authority to take it up again. This command I receive from my Father.

The elders and the chief priest did not take Jesus' life. They were just playing right into Jesus' hands. And they fell for it, hook, line, and sinker. The triumphal entry of Jesus, riding through Jerusalem on a donkey, would bring all this celebration to a standstill. For some of us in high school, the teachers would always give us homework assignments. Some of us did not prepare ourselves for the assignment, by not doing our homework at all, and when we were given the test, we were not ready for it. When it came down to the religious leaders, they found themselves in a similar position. They didn't really do their homework.

This is why Jesus told them in Matthew 22:29 quote: Jesus replied, " You are in error because you do not know the Scriptures or the power of God.

When you really look at it, the elders, and the chief priest, and the teachers of the law all wanted to become wannabes. Jesus had a name for them He called them hypocrites. Many pastors want to be pastors, but the problem is this: they haven't really taken the serious quiet time to study the Word of God.

2 Timothy 2:15 quote: Do your best to present yourself to God as one approved, a workman who does not need to be ashamed and who correctly handles the word of truth.

Church, anybody can learn how to study the Word of God for themselves. If you are a Bible-believing pastor, or biblical teacher, you should know it. There is no excuse.

This is why we are told in 1 Timothy 3:2 quote: Now a overseer must be above reproach, the husband of but one wife, temperate, self-control, respectable, hospitable, able to teach.

This was the problem that Jesus had with all the religious leaders of His day. They were in ignorance. If they had really known the biblical Scriptures like they were supposed to, then they would have recognized the coming of Jesus Christ as king. Because of their ignorance, this moment is labeled as *the celebration of divine royalty that almost was.* Luke 19:35 says, "They brought it to Jesus, threw their cloaks on the colt, and put Jesus on it." During the three and a half years of Jesus' ministry on earth, He made Himself known through the miracles, the healings, the preaching, and the teaching about His Father in heaven. The healing was designed for Jesus to get His foot in the door, so that He could point the people to Himself. The only way that the people can know the Father is through Him.

John 14:6 quote: Jesus answered, "I am the way and the truth and the life. No one comes to the Father except through me.

Everywhere Jesus went during His earthly ministry, He always drew a crowd. Jesus always got the people's attention. Even when Jesus is speaking today, His Words still bring about attention; Hebrew 1:1–3 quote: In the past God spoke to our forefathers through the prophets at many times and various ways, but in these last days he has spoken to us by his Son, whom he appointed heir of all things, and through whom he made the universe. The Son is the radiance of God's glory and the exact representation of his being, sustaining all things by his powerful word. After he had provided purification for sins, he sat down at the right hand of the Majesty in heaven.

Jesus is still speaking to us today through His Word. For this reason we are told in Colossians 3:16 quote: "Let the Word of Christ dwell in you richly as you teach and admonish one another with all wisdom, and as you sing psalms, hymns, and spiritual songs with gratitude in your heart to God." As Jesus would continue to minister to the people in His day, it would have an everlasting impact from generation to generation. The Jewish people, and the Gentile people, living in Jesus' day during the time He spent ministering on earth, were without excuse, especially the Jewish leaders.

Proverbs 16:25 quote: There is a way that seems right to a man, but in the end it leads to death.

They had failed to do their homework. In Matthew 15:22-28, when a Canaanite woman came to Jesus asking Him to heal her daughter who was suffering from demon possession, Jesus told her that He was only sent to the lost sheep of Israel. But it was because of her faith that Jesus was able to heal her daughter. Not only the Jews, but people from all over the region put their trust in Jesus. Over the three years that Jesus had spent during His ministry, He had made Himself known. By this time Jesus had become a threat to the elders, the chief priest, and the teachers of the law. This is what the leaders said about Jesus in John 11:48: "If we let Him go on like this, everyone will believe in Him, and then the Romans will come and take away both our place and our nation." This was the main key to the very reason Jesus came, so that everyone could put their trust in the Lord.

John 3:16–17 quote: "For God so loved the world that he gave his one and only Son, that whoever believes in him shall not perish but have eternal life. For God did not send his Son into the world to condemn the world, but to save the world through him.

Not only the Jews were to be given the opportunity to place their complete trust in Jesus, but the whole entire Gentile race as well. Jesus had made Himself known. You cannot appear on the scene, and do nothing, expecting to make yourself known. If you truly want to make yourself known, this is how you do it.

Proverbs 3:3–6 quote: Let love and faithfulness never leave you; bind them around your neck, write them on the tablet of your heart. Then you will receive favor and a good name in the sight of God and man. Trust in the Lord with all your heart and lean not on your own understanding; in all your ways acknowledge him, and he will make your paths straight.

While Jesus continued to minister on earth, His trust was in His Father, because it was Jesus' Father that sent Him. Despite the three years of ministry that Jesus spent on earth, the triumphal entry should have been the time of Jesus' recognition. But instead, it had become *the celebration of divine royalty that almost was*. Look what happened in Luke 19:36–37: "As he went along, people spread their cloaks on the road. When he came near the place where the road goes down the Mount of Olives, the whole crowd of disciples began joyfully to praise God in loud voices for all the miracles they had seen." Church, these Jewish people were not kept in the dark about the miracles and the healings that they had seen Jesus perform; they were happening right before their very eyes. They had become the eyewitnesses. The miracles and the healings that Jesus was doing had never been done before.

Nicodemus said to Jesus in John 3:2 quote: "Rabbi, we know you are teacher who has come from God. For no one could perform the miraculous signs you are doing if God were not with him."

Nicodemus wasn't the only Pharisee who wanted to know about Jesus. There were others who had become secret followers of Christ. They had all become eyewitnesses to what they saw Jesus do, but in the midst of the Pharisees and the teachers of the Law, they had skeptics who criticized everything that Jesus did. This is why Jesus exposed them.

Matthew 23:2–3 quote: "The teachers of the law and the Pharisees sit in Moses' seat. So you must obey them and do everything they tell you. But do not do what they do, for they do not practice what they preach.

Jesus referred to these religious leaders as hypocrites. Jesus called a "spade a spade." If you know for certain that someone is doing something wrong, you have to take the time to correct them. And if they do not listen to you, knock the dust off your feet and keep on walking, because you have done your part. This is why the Word of God is very valuable to us today.

2 Timothy 3:16–17 quote: All Scripture is God-breathed and is useful for teaching, rebuking, correcting and training in righteousness, so that the man of God may be thoroughly equipped for every good work.

If I am doing something wrong in my Christian walk, it is the Word of God that's going to hold me accountable and place me in check. Every time you study and read the Word of God, you have the opportunity to be taught, to be rebuked, to be corrected, and to be trained in the area of righteousness. Why is this very important to every believer? This is very important because we are being held accountable to the Word of God.

Hebrews 4:12–13 quote: For the Word of God is living and active. Sharper than any double-edged sword, it penetrates even to dividing soul and spirit, joints and marrow; it judges the thoughts and attitudes of the heart. Nothing in all creation is hidden from God's sight. Everything is uncovered and laid bare before the eyes of him to whom we must give account.

Do not fault the pastors, because all they are really doing is speaking and preaching God's Word; 1 Peter 4:11 quote: If anyone speaks, he should do it as one speaking the very words of God. If anyone serves, he should do it with the strength God provides, so that in all things God may be praised through Jesus Christ.

The reason why the disciples didn't have to attend Rabbinic schools was because there was no need to. They were already spiritually equipped three years ahead of time. This all had to do with those three years that they all spent with Jesus, while being under Jesus' anointing.

After Jesus' Ascension, and the disciples were empowered from on high with the Holy Spirit, look what had happened in Acts 4:13 quote: When they saw the courage of Peter and John and realized that they were unschooled, ordinary men, they were astonished and they took note that these men had been with Jesus.

If the religious leaders had done their homework in the first place, they would have never rejected the Lord Jesus Christ while He appeared as Israel's King in the triumphal entry. This was *the celebration of divine royalty that almost was.* Luke 19:38–40 says, "Blessed is the King who comes in the name of the Lord! Peace in heaven and glory in the highest!" Some of the Pharisees in the crowd said to Jesus, "Teacher, rebuke your disciples!" "I tell you," He replied, "if they keep quiet, the stones will cry out." The people who had come out to worship and to praise Jesus had their own ideas. They were thinking that Jesus coming as King of the Jews would liberate Israel and overthrow the Roman government. This was not the case. But Jesus came to establish God's Eternal Kingdom. This has to do with all the nations and races coming together. But instead, the Lord Jesus Christ was rejected as King.

This is why we are told in John 1:11–13 quote: He came to that which was his own, but his own did not receive him. Yet to all who received him, to those who believed in his name, he gave the right to become children of God-children born not of natural descent, nor of human decision or a husband's will, but born of God.

Now when the Pharisees saw what the crowd was doing, these religious leaders wanted Jesus to rebuke them by ordering them to keep quiet. Have you ever known someone who hated you because they didn't like the way you looked? Nothing that you did satisfied them. These are the people who create problems that you just can't sweep under a rug and walk away from. These are the people you have to deal with all the time. This is where you have to learn how to hold your tongue and keep the peace.

1 Corinthians 15:58 quote: Therefore, my dear brothers, stand firm. Let nothing move you. Always give yourselves fully to the work of the Lord, because you know that your labor in the Lord is not in vain.

Even though you do not attend your place of worship every day, you are still laboring in the Lord, and your labor is not in vain. As it says in Philippians 1:6 quote: Being confidence of this, that he who begins a good work in you will carry it on to completion until the day of Christ Jesus. "When the crowd laid down their cloaks, and their palm branches, the praises and the Worship that Jesus was receiving from among them, was not in vain." This is why Jesus said, "If they keep quiet the stones will cry out." Church, the Lord Jesus Christ Himself had a right to receive this worship and this praise. The stones that Jesus was referring to were only there for a backup. How many of you know that the Lord Jesus is still being praised and worshiped today? All throughout God's creation, God is constantly being praised.

Psalm 148:7–14 read: Praise the Lord from the earth, you great sea creatures and all ocean depths, lightning and hail, snow and clouds, stormy winds that do his bidding, you mountains and all hills, fruit trees and all cedars, wild animals and all cattle, small creatures and flying birds, kings of the earth and all nations, you princes and all rulers on earth, young men and maidens, old men and children. Let them praise the name of the Lord, for his name alone is exalted; his splendor is above the earth and heavens. He has raised up for his people a horn, the praise of all his saints, of Israel, the people close to his heart. Praise the Lord.

For this reason, the Jewish leaders of Jesus' day failed to recognize Jesus' coming.

This is why Jesus told them in John 5:43 quote: I have come in my Father's name, and you do not accept me; but if someone else comes in his own name, you will except him.

This verse of Scripture opens up the door to the Tribulation Period, when the Antichrist is revealed after the Rapture of the Church. The Jewish Leaders living in that generation will openly accept the Antichrist. They make a seven-year treaty with him, but the treaty is only going to last for three and a half years. The sixty-ninth week is when Jesus was rejected as the King and Messiah. The seventh week starts at the very beginning of the Tribulation Period.

These are the words that Jesus gave to Church of Philadelphia in Revelation 3:10 quote: Since you have kept my command to endure patiently, I will keep you from the hour of trial that is going to come upon the whole world to test those who live on the earth.

CONCLUSION

The Jewish leaders had rejected their King. They had gone too far.

They had refused God's offer of salvation in Jesus Christ, when they were visited by God Himself, Acts 4:12 quote: Salvation is found in no one else, for there is no other name under heaven given to men by which we must be saved."

In AD 70, their nation would suffer, and the Jewish race was killed and dispersed. God did not turn away from the Jewish people who obeyed Him. However, God has continued to offer salvation to the people He loves, both Jews and Gentiles. Eternal life is within your reach, accept it while the opportunity is still offered.

Romans 10:9–10, 13 quote: That if you confess with your mouth, "Jesus is Lord," and believe in your heart that God raised him from the dead, you will be saved. For it is with your heart that you believe and are justified, and it is with your mouth that you confess and are saved. For, "Everyone who calls on the name of the Lord will be saved."

The celebration of divine royalty that almost was has now been put on hold. This opportunity will come again in the Millennium Kingdom when Jesus Christ shall reign as King of all kings, and Lord of all lords. Amen!

20

Allow the Kingdom of God to Work on Your Behalf

Mark 4:26–29. He also said, "This is what the kingdom of God is like. A man scatters seed on the ground. Night and day whether he sleeps or gets up, the seed sprouts and grows, though he does not know how. All by itself the soil produces grain-first the stalk, then the head, then the full kernel in the head. As soon as the grain is ripe, he puts the sickle to it, because the harvest has come."

SERMON MESSAGE:

In a world in which we all live, there are two different types of systems that the people of the world can have the opportunity to live in. We have the world's system, and we have the Kingdom of God's system. There are also two types of people who live in the world. You have those who are saved, and those who are not saved. To begin with, everyone who is born into the world automatically enters the world's system. The world's system came about by the fall of man. When Adam disobeyed God, it automatically changed the world's system. It all had to do with what God had given to Adam. Adam was given dominion and rule. It wasn't taking away from him, he lost it, and Satan has it now. This is why the world is in the shape that it is in today.

For this reason, we are told in Ephesians 5:15–16 quote: Be very careful, then, how you live-not as unwise but as wise, making the most of every opportunity because the days are evil.

The days became evil the very moment that Adam sinned and Satan took over. The world has been in a very big mess ever since. The Good News is that the Lord God sprung forth His plan the very moment that sin came into existence. It comes right out of Genesis 3:15: "And I will put enmity between you and the women, and between your offspring and hers; He will crush your head, and you will strike His heel." The offspring of the woman is the Lord Jesus Christ. This is where the Virgin birth comes into play. The offspring here refers to her seed. Jesus Christ is the only person who has come from a seed of a woman but not the seed of a man. If Jesus had come from a seed of a man, then He would have also inherited Adam's sinful nature, just like the rest of us. Jesus' coming was to fulfill the law and the prophets.

Matthew 5:17 quote:"Do not think I have come to abolish the Law or the Prophets; I have not come to abolish them but to fulfill them. Jesus came to save the whole human race.

John 3:16–17 quote: "For God so loved the world that he gave his one and only Son, that whoever believes in him shall not perish but have eternal life. For God did not send his Son into the world to condemn the world, but to save the world through him. And Jesus came also to take back dominion and rule over the earth.

Matthew 28:18 quote: Then Jesus came to them and said, "All authority in heaven and on earth has been given to me.

Because every human being living today has descended from Adam, it is a must that we all become saved through the blood of Jesus Christ. We are told in 1 Corinthians 15:22, "For as in Adam all die, so in Christ all will be made alive." What this means is this, if an unsaved person remains in Adam, they will die in their sins. But on the other hand, if an unsaved person receives the Lord Jesus Christ as their Savior, they will live.

2 Peter 3:9 quote: The Lord is not slow in keeping his promise, as some understand slowness. He is patient with you, not wanting anyone to perish, but everyone to come to repentance.

An unsaved person will always remain in this world's system until they are converted to faith in Christ.

1 Corinthians 2:14 quote: The man without the Spirit does not accept the things that comes from the Spirit of God, for they are foolishness to him, and he cannot understand them, because they are spiritually discerned.

But when it comes to the believer in Christ, they will have the opportunity to enter into the Kingdom of God's system.

Matthew 6:32–33 quote: For the pagans run after all these things, and your heavenly Father knows that you need them. But seek first his kingdom and his righteousness, and all these things will be given to you as well.

When we as believers begin to worry about ourselves with what we need, it can only mean one thing. We are not seeking first the Kingdom of God and His righteousness for our lives, but instead, we are doing the very same thing that the pagans of the world's system are doing. Jesus tells us as believers not to worry about our life; what will we eat or drink? Not to worry about our body; what will we wear? Church, Jesus could have gone on and on and talked about the other things that we need. Jesus was making a point about meeting our everyday needs. If we, as believers, begin to seek first the Kingdom of God and His righteousness, then our Heavenly Father will begin to meet our needs.

Philippians 4:19 quote: And my God will meet all your needs according to his glorious riches in Christ Jesus.

What does God's Word mean to seek first the Kingdom of God? It means to stop what you are doing and drop everything. From that very moment on, begin to seek first the Kingdom of God and His righteousness in everything that you do. Colossians 3:17 says, "And whatever you do, whether in word or deed, do it all in the name of the Lord Jesus, giving thanks to God the Father through Him." In a nutshell, this is what seeking first the Kingdom of God and His righteousness is all about. As we continue seeking first the Kingdom of God and His righteousness, this will take us right into eternity. The things we do for Christ will be the only things that matter when we get to heaven.

2 Corinthians 5:10 quote: For we must all appear before the judgment seat of Christ, that each one may receive what is do him for the things done while in the body, whether good or bad.

If we are not seeking first the Kingdom of God and His righteousness, it will wind up interfering with our heavenly rewards. As believers, we have to discern between what is of the

Kingdom of God's system, and what is of the world's system. If you have been saved for a long period of time, you should know this by now.

1 John 2:15–17 tells us, quote: Do not love the world or anything in the world. If anyone loves the world, the love of the Father is not in him. For everything in the world-the cravings of sinful man, the lust of his eyes and the boasting of what he has and does-come not from the Father but from the world. The world and its desires pass away, but the man who does the will of God lives forever.

Christians today are too busy looking for what this world has to offer. Is fifteen minutes of fame really worth it?

What should profit a Christian; to gain the whole world and lose their heavenly rewards? Every believer needs to be constantly seeking to do the will of God. It is the will of God that every believer not get involved in the system of the world.

This is why Apostle Paul tells us in Romans 12:2 quote: Do not conform any longer to the pattern of this world, but be transformed by the renewing of your mind. Then you will be able to test and approve what God's will is-his good, pleasing and perfect will.

Church, Apostle Paul doesn't leave the believer hanging, but he gives an alternative. If you were on drugs and you wanted to quit, you would look for a way to wean yourself off of drugs by entering into a rehabilitation program. The same is true of a person who wants to quit drinking. They would enter a twelve-step AA program. For the believer in Christ, it is the same way. So what do we do once we refuse to allow ourselves not to be conformed to the patterns of the world's system? We get into reading and studying the Word of God.

2 Timothy 3:16–17 quote: All Scripture is God-breathed and useful for teaching, rebuking, correcting and training in righteousness, so that the man of God may be thoroughly equipped for every good work.

Why should we read the Word of God? This is where we can have the opportunity to *allow the kingdom of God to work on your behalf.* In Mark 4:26, Jesus said, "This is what the Kingdom of God is like. A man scatters his seed on the ground." Jesus spoke to His disciples in parables; He told them that the seed that the farmer sowed was considered as the Word of God. In order for believers to experience the Kingdom of God, they have to get the seed of the Word of God sown into their hearts. The Word of God can be considered as biblical knowledge. Once we get the biblical knowledge of the Word of God inside of our hearts, it becomes biblical wisdom. The very reason why I am able to quote Scripture is because the seed of Word of God has been planted inside of me.

James 1:5 quote: If any of you lacks wisdom, he should ask God, who gives generously to all without finding fault, and it will be given to him.

The question is this: how serious do you want the Word of God placed inside of you? Because the more we get the Word of God in us, the more we are going to become transformed by the renewing of our minds. Every one of us has the opportunity to have our minds transformed by getting into the Word of God. Why do we need to be transformed by the Word of God? Because there is no other book on the market that can change us like the Word of God can!

In fact, we are told in Hebrews 4:12–13 quote: For the Word of God is living and active. Sharper than any double-edged sword, it penetrates even to the dividing soul and spirit, joints and marrow; it judges the thoughts and attitudes of the heart. Nothing in all creation is hidden from God's sight. Everything is uncovered and laid bare before the eyes of him to whom we must all give account.

After Jesus' Resurrection, He talked to two people who were walking down the road to Emmaus. Jesus spoke to them by giving them the Scriptures of the Word of God; He let them know that the Christ had to suffer and enter His glory. After that, Jesus broke bread with them and gave thanks. Their eyes were both opened and they recognized Him. Jesus then disappeared from their sight. Their statement was this: "Were not our hearts burning within us while He talked with us on the road and opened the Scriptures to us?" Church, the Word of God is to have an impact on our everyday lives while we are reading, studying, and applying it to ourselves.

This is why James 1:22–24 is so very important to us; quote: Do not merely listen to the word, and so deceive yourselves. Do what it says. Anyone who listens to the word but does not do what it says is like a man who looks at his face in a mirror and, after looking at himself, goes away and immediately forgets what he looks like.

The very reason why so many Christians are missing out on the Word of God is because they have not become doers of the Word.

Matthew 23:2–3 quote: "The teachers of the law and the Pharisees sit in Moses' seat. So you must obey them and do everything they tell you. But do not do what they do for they do not practice what they preach.

You cannot expect the Kingdom of God to work for you when you are reading the Word of God, but you are not practicing what you preach. Whenever you are reading, studying, and applying the Word of God to your everyday life, the Kingdom of God is going to work automatically for you on your behalf. What are you doing? *Allowing the kingdom of God to work on your behalf.* Mark 4:27 says, "Night and day, whether he sleeps or gets up, the seed sprouts and grows, though he does not know how." While the Kingdom of God is working for you on your behalf, you will have the opportunity to experience spiritual growth.

1 Peter 2:2–3 quote: Like newborn babies, crave pure spiritual milk, so that by it you may grow up in your salvation, now that you have tasted that the Lord is good.

From the very moment we receive the Lord Jesus Christ, we train ourselves to receive the spiritual milk of the Word of God to build us up to move on from spiritual infancy to spiritual maturity. The writer of the Book of Hebrews wanted to move his readers forward on to spiritual maturity, but they were slow to learn.

Hebrews 5:11–14 quote: We have much to say about this, but it is hard to explain because you are slow to learn. In fact, though by this time you ought to be teachers, you need someone to teach you the elementary truths of God's word all over again. You need milk, not solid food! Anyone who lives on milk, being still an infant, is not acquainted with the teaching about righteousness. But solid food is for the mature, who by constant use have trained themselves to distinguish good from evil.

In the same way, Church, we need to move on. As we move on in the course of time, we, along with others, are going to see results in our lives. As we continue to grow up in the Christian faith, people are going to see spiritual good fruit developed in our lives.

John 15:1–3 quote: "I am the true vine, and my Father is the gardener. He cuts off every branch in me that bears no fruit, while every branch that does bear fruit he prunes so that it will be even more fruitful. You are already clean because of the word I have spoken to you.

If you choose not to bear fruit, expect to be cut off. So many Christians today are running to the small local churches. Instead of being a help to those small churches, they have become draining leaches to them. The Lord will meet your every need, providing that you do whatever it is that you are supposed to do.

Philippians 2:12–13 quote: Therefore, my dear friends, as you have always obeyed-not only in my presence, but now much more in my absence-continue to work out your salvation with fear and trembling, for it is God who works in you to will and to act according to his good purpose.

Notice what these verses of Scripture did not say? They say, work it out; ask God to help us do His will for our lives. While we are doing the will of God for our lives, the seed of the Word of God sprouts and grows up inside of us. We can't explain why this takes place or how this takes place. We just know that it works. There are a lot of things in our world today that we can operate. If we were asked to explain how some of these things work, we just couldn't explain it. We usually start up an automobile with a car key; some cars do not need an ignition key to start. We may not know how these things and other things work, we just know that they do.

Hebrews 11:6 quote: And without faith it is impossible to please God, because anyone who comes to him must believe that he exists and that he rewards those who earnestly seek him.

The Kingdom of God also operates in the faith realm. Whenever we step out of faith, things don't always appear as they seem.

2 Corinthians 5:7 quote: We live by faith, not by sight.

When we are constantly living in sin, it can hinder our inheritance to the Kingdom of God. This is why we need to live by the Holy Spirit leading our lives. This is why believers are able to feel the Spirit's leading. They say, "I can feel the Spirit leading me to do this, or I can feel the Spirit leading me to do that." What is the very reason why we know that this is true? Because it is being lined up with the Word of God. This is when you are *allowing the kingdom of God to work on your behalf.* Mark 4:28 says, "All by itself, the soil produces the grain: first the stalk, then the head, the full kernel in the head." As the believer grows up in the Christian faith, they are going through a process of Spiritual growth. This is where the fruit comes in for the believer in Christ.

John 15:16 quote: You did not choose me, but I chose you and appointed you to go and bear fruit-fruit that will last. Then the Father will give you whatever you ask in my name.

This is a picture of a believer who's already experiencing the Kingdom of God in their lives. They are going to expect to see their prayers answered. Their prayer life is no longer centered in self, but in the will of God. When the Lord had Moses to lead the Israelites into the Promised Land, the Israelite community refused to move forward. Because of this, the Israelites had to wander in the wilderness for a period of forty years. The Old Testament saints had the opportunity to enter into the Promised Land, and the New Testament saints had the opportunity to enter into the Kingdom of God.

Romans 15:4 quote: For everything that was written in the past was written to teach us, so that through endurance and encouragement of the Scriptures we might have hope.

Discipline plays a very important role in the Kingdom of God. To be a Christian is going to cost you. During Apostle Paul's ministry, he made this statement to the disciples in Acts 14:21–22: "Then they returned to Lystra, Iconium, and Antioch, strengthening the disciples and encouraging them to remain true to the faith." We must go through many hardships to enter the Kingdom of God. When we are living the Christian life, not everything is going to be "peaches and cream."

Luke 9:23 quote: Then he said to them all: "If anyone would come after me, he must deny himself and take up his cross daily and follow me.

As long as we are operating in the flesh, it would be very difficult for us to become followers of Christ. One of the major key elements to becoming a follower of Christ is to say "no" to our flesh.

Galatians 5:16–21 quote: So I say, live by the Spirit, and you will not gratify the desires of the sinful nature. For the sinful nature desires what is contrary to the Spirit, and the Spirit what is contrary to the sinful nature. They are in conflict with each other, so that you do not do what you want. But if you are led by the Spirit, you are not under law. The acts of the sinful nature are obvious: Sexual immorality, impurity and debauchery; idolatry and witchcraft; hatred, discord, jealousy, fits of rage, selfish ambition, dissensions, factions and envy; drunkenness, orgies, and the like. I warn you, as I did before, that those who live like this will not inherit the kingdom of God.

Church, Apostle Paul is not talking to all the people of the world, but he is speaking to every believer. If you truly want to be *allowing the kingdom of God to work on your behalf,* you must abstain from the acts of the sinful nature. Mark 4:29 says, "As soon as the grain is ripe, he puts the sickle to it, because the harvest has come." As we stay committed to the very things of God, we need not to lose sight of what we are doing in the Body of Christ. We are not to quit or to give up.

In fact, we are told in Philippians 1:6 quote: Being confident of this, that he who began a good work in you will carry it on to completion until the day of Christ Jesus.

As long as we live on this earth, we will never meet perfection. We can be able to reach spiritual maturity as we are growing in the Christian faith. As this happens, expect to receive a spiritual harvest.

Galatians 6:9 quote: Let us not become weary in doing good, for at the proper time we will reap a harvest if we do not give up.

Jesus tells us that we are in the world, but we are not of it. As believers, we must continue to keep our complete trust in the Lord and stop looking to man for solutions. Our Heavenly Father has all of the answers.

Psalm 37:4–5 quote: Delight yourself in the Lord and he will give you the desires of your heart. Commit your way to the Lord; trust in him and he will do this.

We delight ourselves in the Lord, because we have lined ourselves up with the Word of God.

CONCLUSION

When it comes to seeking first the Kingdom of God and His righteousness, humility needs to play a very important role in our lives. What does this mean?

1 Peter 5:6 quote: Humble yourselves, therefore, under God's mighty hand, that he may lift you up in due time.

You might be wondering why New Bedford Heights Baptist Church still has empty pews during Sunday school and the Sunday worship service. As pastor, I can't answer that question, but I truly believe that my Heavenly Father can and will. I have been committed here from the very first day I became the pastor of this church, and I will remain committed until my Heavenly Father calls me home. I'm *allowing the kingdom of God to work on my behalf,* and so can you.

Philippians 3:13–14 quote: Brothers, I do not consider myself yet to have taken hold of it. But one thing I do: Forgetting what is behind and straining toward what is ahead, I press on toward the goal to win the prize for which God has called me heavenward in Christ Jesus.

Amen!

21

You Cannot Please Everybody, So Why Not Please God?

2 Timothy 4:2–5. Preach the Word; be prepare in season and out of season; correct, rebuke and encourage-with great patience and careful instruction. For a time will come when men will not put up with sound doctrine. Instead, to suit their own desires, they will gather around them a great number of teachers to say what their itching ears want to hear. They will turn their ears away from the truth and turn aside to myths. But you, keep your head in all situations, do the work of an evangelist, discharge all the duties of your ministry.

SERMON MESSAGE:

During Jesus' ministry on earth, He went up against the Pharisees, the Sadducees, and the teachers of the law. The very reason why Jesus took them on was because they were filled with all kinds of hypocrisy and deceptions. They did not practice what they had preached.

Matthew 23:2–3 quote: "The teachers of the law and the Pharisees sit in Moses' seat. So you must obey them and do everything they tell you. But do not do what they do, for they do not practice what they preach.

As believers in Christ, we have to set the better examples by the very lives that we live. Do not expect to expose someone if you are also caught up in the act of doing the very same thing. To do so would be like "the pot calling the kettle black." Your ability to witness and share your faith with others has got to line up with the very life that you live.

Matthew 5:16 quote: In the same way, let your light shine before men, that they may see your good deeds and praise your Father in heaven.

If we are not living the Christian life around those who are not saved, then we need to keep our mouths shut. Because all we will be doing is hindering people from getting saved. The very lives that we live as believers will allow us to get our foot in the door to witness effectively. An unsaved person can tell whether or not there is something different about your walk and if you are really living the Christian life. They may not be able to put their finger on it, but they will certainly be able see that there has been a change in the way you live as a believer in Christ.

1 Peter 2:12 quote: Live such good lives among the pagans that, though they accuse you of doing wrong, they may see your good deeds and glorify God on the day he visits us.

Church, if we put our lives out there in the open as believers, the unsaved people of the world are going to want the very same thing that we have.

This is why we are told in 1 Peter 3:15 quote: But in your heart set apart Christ as Lord. Always be prepared to give an answer to everyone who asks you to give the reason for the hope that you have. But do this with gentleness and respect.

As we set apart Christ as Lord in our hearts, we are also going to set apart Christ as Lord in the very lives that we live. In Matthew 11:4-6, John the Baptist was locked up in prison, he sent his disciples to Jesus with this question: "Are you the One who was to come, or should we expect someone else?" Jesus replied, "Go back and report to John what you hear and see: The blind receive sight, the lame walk, those who have leprosy are cured, the deaf hear, the dead are raised, and the Good News is preached to the poor. Blessed is the man who does not fall away on account of me." The purpose of all the miracles that Jesus was doing was for Him to get the people's attention, so that they could hear the message of the Good News of Jesus Christ. Once they would hear the Good News, then they would have the opportunity to respond and receive Jesus as Savior and Lord.

Listen to what Apostle John wrote in John 20:30-31 quote: Jesus did many other miraculous signs in the presence of his disciples, which are not recorded in this book. But these are written that you may believe that Jesus is the Christ, the Son of God, and that by believing you may have life in his name.

Another way that we can ask what John the Baptist's disciples asked Jesus is this: Are you worth dying for, or should we expect someone else? The very reason why John the Baptist was in prison was because he spoke out against King Herod and Herodias, his current wife. Herod had taken his brother Philip's wife as his very own wife, while Philip was still alive. John the Baptist took a stand for what was right, and we should take a stand as well.

1 Corinthians 15:58 quote: Therefore, my dear brothers, stand firm. Let nothing move you. Always give yourselves fully to the work of the Lord, because you know that labor in the Lord is not in vain.

As serious Christians, we must take a stand when it comes down to living the Christian life. You may have to take a stand on your job when it comes down to doing what's right. Your employer may force you to tell a lie in order to keep your job. You may have to take a stand in your community when it comes down to drugs, violent crimes, gangs, violence, and thieves in your neighborhoods. Regardless of what you are up against, you should allow the Gospel of Jesus Christ to surface in your life. Jesus said in Matthew 10:26–28, "So do not be afraid of them. There is nothing concealed that will not be disclosed, or hidden that will not be made known. What I tell you in the dark, speak in the daylight; what is whispered in your ear, proclaim from the roofs. Do not be afraid of those who can kill the body, but cannot kill the soul. Rather, be afraid of the one who can destroy both body and soul in hell." Many of us as believers have experienced the spiritual change that has taken place in our lives.

2 Corinthians 5:17 quote: Therefore, if anyone is in Christ, he is a new creation; the old has gone, the new has come!

To continue to live a sinful lifestyle is going to cause you to feel very uncomfortable with the very things that you are doing. You are not going to receive any peace until you have fully surrendered your life completely to the Lord Jesus Christ.

Romans 13:14 quote: Rather, clothe yourselves with the Lord Jesus Christ, and do not think about how to gratify the desires of the sinful nature.

Once we as believers in Christ begin to live a changed lifestyle, then we can take a stand against the very things that we are totally against. People try to get me to do things, to go places, and to say things that I am totally against, because of my Christian belief. I have to refuse to give in to them. Church, you have to place yourselves out there in the open, so that the unsaved can see the real you. Matthew 5:14–15 says, "You are a light of the world, a city on a hill that cannot be hidden. Neither do people light a lamp and put it under a bowl. Instead, they put it on a stand, and it gives light to everyone in the house." We are the only Jesus that the people in our world will ever see. Seeing that this is the case, we need to raise the bar for who we are representing. When Jesus walked this earth during His earthly ministry, who do you think that He represented? Jesus represented His Heavenly Father.

John 5:19 quote: Jesus gave them this answer: "I tell you the truth, the Son can do nothing by himself; he can do only what he sees his Father doing, because whatever the Father does the Son also does.

Church, the same is true with every believer living today.

Jesus said in John 8:12 quote: When Jesus spoke again to the people, he said, "I am the light of the world. Whoever follows me will never walk in darkness, but will have the light of life."

Do you recall a time when you were younger, when your parents or your teachers sent you somewhere? Or, it might have been a teacher, or babysitter, or a person taking you to a concert. The person sending you there told you to be on your very best behavior. We are representing the Lord Jesus Christ as our own true light. We need to be on our very best behavior everywhere we go.

2 Corinthians 5:20 quote: We are therefore Christ's ambassadors, as though God were making his appeal through us. We implore you on Christ's behalf: Be reconciled to God.

While you are representing the Lord Jesus Christ, there are always going to be people who are not going to like you because of who you are representing. *You cannot please everybody, so why not please God?*

2 Timothy 4:2–5 quote: Preach the Word; be prepared in season and out of season; correct, rebuke, and encourage-with great patience and careful instruction. For the time will come when men will not put up with sound doctrine. Instead, to suit their own desires, they will gather around them a great number of teachers to say what their itching ears want to hear. They will turn their ears away from the truth and turn aside to myths. But you, keep your head in all situations, endure hardship, do the work of an evangelist, discharge all the duties of your ministry.

Just imagine if all believers in Christ were to preach the Word of God, all the local churches in America would be full to capacity. Many of you are going to disagree with me, but I just want you to know that I am pleasing God. When you are told to stand to show reverence in the reading of the Word of God, you are not showing reverence to your pastor, but you are standing in reverence to the Lord. Whenever you are representing the Lord in everything you do, you need to glorify and honor God.

Colossians 3:17 quote: And whatever you do, whether in word or deed, do it all in the name of the Lord Jesus, giving thanks to God the Father through him.

The same is true when it comes down to preaching the Word of God. There should be no shortcuts when it comes down to preaching the Word of God. Either you know it, or you don't. This is how you are going to know the Word of God.

2 Timothy 2:15 quote: Do your best to present yourself to God as one approved, a workman who does not need to be ashamed and who correctly handles the word of truth.

If you do not know the Word of God, then you need to come out of the pulpit until you do. When Apostle Paul wrote to Timothy and Titus, he was writing pastoral letters to them. These letters were not only written to these two men, but they were also written for every Bible-believing pastor, as well. As pastors, we need to do exactly what the Word of God says.

2 Timothy 4:2 quote: Preach the Word; be prepared in season and out of season; correct, rebuke and encourage-with great patience and careful instruction.

As you are preaching the Word of God, the Holy Spirit is going to do the rest. Many times pastors like to help the Holy Spirit out, by putting their two cents in the message and not being prepared. So, they begin to make up the message as they go along. In order to preach the Word of God, you have to know the Word of God.

This is why 2 Timothy 3:16–17 says quote: All Scripture is God-breathed and is useful for teaching, rebuking, correcting and training in righteousness, so that the man of God may be thoroughly equipped for every good work.

Every pastor who knows the Word of God has also been taught the Word of God. If your pastor does not know the Word of God, chances are, you are not going to know the Word of God either. Your pastor is just going through the motions.

Luke 6:40 quote: A student is not above his teacher, but everyone is fully trained will be like his teacher.

There are no two pastors who are alike. They have their very own styles of preaching and teaching. This is why you have to examine your pastor, instead of criticizing him. Just because the pews in your local church aren't yet filled up, doesn't mean that your pastor is not preaching the Word of God. *You cannot please everybody, so why not please God?*

2 Timothy 4:2–5 quote: Preach the Word; be prepared in season and out of season; correct, rebuke and encourage-with great patience and careful instruction. For the time will come when men will not put up with sound doctrine. Instead, to suit their own desires, they will gather around them a great number of teachers to say what their itching ears want to hear. They will turn their ears away from the truth and turn aside to myths. But you, keep your head in all situations, endure hardship, do the work of an evangelist, discharge all the duties of your ministry.

The reason why so many Christians are flocking to very large churches today is so that they can hide in them and go through the motions. They want to make up their own rules while they are attending these churches. But notice what Jesus said in Matthew 15:8–9: "These people honor me with their lips, but their hearts are far from me. They worship me in vain; their teachings are rules taught by men." You take the prosperity messages or sermons, for example. The prosperity message doesn't speak that well of God, but instead, there are only short passages of Scripture given to motivate the people. Rules that are taught by men are not lined up with the Word of God.

2 Timothy 4:3 quote: For the time will come when men will not put up with sound doctrine. Instead, to suit their own desires, they will gather around them a great number of teachers to say what their itching ears want to hear.

Church, that time has come today. Preachers are not really presenting to you the Word of God, but instead, they are motivating and pumping you up around their "feel good" and prosperity sermons. They are giving the people exactly what they want to hear. Church, when was the last time that you examined your pastor?

Acts 17:11 quote: Now the Bereans were of more noble character than the Thessalonians, for they received the message with great eagerness and examined the Scriptures every day to see if what Paul said was true.

Church, you have to do that with your pastor each time you hear him preach and teach. When is the best time that you examine your pastor? Whenever you attend a Bible study. A Bible study allows you to ask questions. The pastor's teachings and preaching are going to line up with each other. And the reason why they are going to line up together is because they are going to come from the Word of God.

And here is the reason why the teaching and preaching needs to come from the Word of God: Hebrews 4:12–13 quote: For the Word of God is living and active. Sharper than any double-edged sword, it penetrates even to dividing soul and spirit, joints and marrow; it judges the thoughts and attitudes of the heart. Nothing in all creation is hidden from God's sight. Everything is uncovered and laid bare before the eyes of him to whom we must give account.

As long as the pastor is preaching the Word of God to you, while you are paying close attention, something in his message is going to touch your heart. It is not the pastor that's touching you, it is the Holy Spirit. The Holy Spirit is going to teach you. The Holy Spirit is going to rebuke you. The Holy Spirit is going to correct you. The Holy Spirit will also bring about training in righteousness. So don't get offended each time the pastor is preaching the Word of God; it may not be for you, but for someone else who really needs to hear it the most.

We are told in 1 Peter 4:11 quote: If anyone speaks, he should do it as one speaking the very words of God. If anyone serves, he should do it with the strength God provides, so that in all things God may be praised through Jesus Christ. To him be the glory and the power forever and ever. Amen.

Question: What was Paul doing when he was led by the Spirit to write each epistle? Apostle Paul was speaking the very Words of

God. Every time we read every one of these epistles that Paul was inspired to write, we are reading the Word of God. Whenever you are quoting from the Scriptures, you are speaking the very Words of God.

2 Peter 1:20–21 quote: Above all, you must understand that no prophecy of Scripture came about by the prophet's own interpretation. For prophecy never had its origin in the will of man, but men spoke from God as they were carried along by the Holy Spirit.

This is what the preachers are supposed to be doing today, but they are not. They are trying to please men instead of God. *You cannot please everybody, so why not please God?*

2 Timothy 4:2–5 quote: Preach the Word; be prepared in season and out of season; correct, rebuke and encourage-with great patience and careful instruction. For a time will come when men will not put up with sound doctrine. Instead, to suit their own desires, they will gather around them a great number of teachers to say what their itching ears want to hear. They will turn their ears away from the truth and turn aside to myths. But you, keep your head in all situations, endure hardship, do the work of an evangelist, discharge all the duties of your ministry.

If a pastor really wants to please men, all that he has to do is compromise, water down the Gospel, and give the people what they want and not what they really need to hear. Christians today are looking to have itchy ears. They are not interested in the biblical sound doctrine of the Word of God, and yet, it is a must that they hear it. If you are going through a storm and a trial, you need to hear what the Word of God has to say.

James 1:2–4 quote: Consider it pure joy, my brothers, whenever you face trials of many kinds, because you know that the testing of your faith develops perseverance. Perseverance must finish its work so that you may be mature and complete, not lacking anything.

If you are dealing with being tempted to give in to temptation, when it comes to overcoming a sinful habit, we are told in 1 Corinthians 10:13 quote: No temptation has seized you accept what is common to man. And God is faithful; he will not let you be tempted beyond what you can bear. But when you are tempted, he will also provide a way out so that you can stand under it.

As long as you stay fully committed to studying God's Word, you can expect to receive victory every time. What about when you are struggling with your finances? Never put yourself in a position where you are unable to tithe.

Proverbs 3:9–10 quote: Honor the Lord with your wealth, with the firstfruits of all your crops; then your barns will be filled to overflowing, and your vats will brim over with new wine.

The New Testament's reference to giving is the same as the Old Testament's reference to giving: Romans 15:4 quote: For everything that was written in the past was written to teach us, so that through endurance and the encouragement of the Scriptures we might have hope. Luke 6:38 quote: Give, and it will be given to you. A good measure, pressed down, shaken together and running over, will be poured into your lap. For with the measure you use, it will be measured to you."

As a believer in Christ, if we do exactly what we are supposed to do, then our Heavenly Father will do what Jesus said that His Father promised to do.

Matthew 6:32–33 quote: For the pagans run after all these things, and your heavenly Father knows that you need them. But seek first his kingdom and his righteousness, and all these things will be given to you as well.

Jesus talked about food and clothing. Jesus could have talked about other needed things as well. The pagans are chasing after all these things, and there is no guarantee that they are going to get what they are chasing. When it comes down to seeking first the Kingdom of God and His righteousness, Our Heavenly Father has promised it to us as His children. Every believer has to give up something in order to have the Kingdom of God to operate for them.

Jesus said in Luke 9:23 quote: Then he said to them all: "If anyone would come after me, he must deny himself and take up his cross daily and follow me.

One of the sound biblical doctrines in the Word of God is giving up a sinful lifestyle. Because as long as we continue living in it, it's going to hinder our blessing to receive what our Heavenly Father has in store for His children.

Listen to how we need to be living: Galatians 5:16–18 quote: So I say, live by the Spirit, and you will not gratify the desires of the sinful nature. For the sinful nature desires what is contrary to the Spirit, and the Spirit what is contrary to the sinful nature. They are in conflict with each other, so that you do not do what you want. But if you are led by the Spirit, you are not under law.

Church, this is sound biblical information that Christians are running from today, and they don't want to hear this. All these so-called Christians want is to eat their cake and have it too. They want to straddle the fence with one foot in the world and the other foot in the church.

1 John 2:15–17 quote: Do not love the world or anything in the world. If anyone loves the world, the love of the Father is not in him. For everything in the world-the cravings of sinful man, the lust of his eyes and the boasting of what he has and does-comes not from the Father but from the world. The world and it desires pass away, but the man that does the will of God lives forever.

You can't have it both ways. You are either pleasing God or you're not.

Romans 12:1 quote: Therefore, I urge you, brothers, in view of God's mercy, to offer your bodies as living sacrifices, holy and pleasing to God-this is your spiritual act of worship.

We are not to please men, but to please God. These Scriptures that are being used are what we call the sound doctrine that comes from the Word of God. The New Testament Scriptures are the Epistles in which every believer needs to live by.

1 Peter 2:2–3: quote: Like newborn babies, crave pure spiritual milk, so that by it you may grow up in your salvation, now that

you have tasted that the Lord is good. As you become mature in the faith, Hebrew 5:14 will also be applied to you as well, quote: But solid food is for the mature, who by constant use have trained themselves to distinguish good from evil.

CONCLUSION

If you have been called to speak, then you ought not to be quiet. People are going to give you a hard time, but you cannot back down. The Lord is not looking for wimps, but godly men and women who are ready to take a stand at a moment's notice.

Ephesians 6:10 quote: Finally, be strong in the Lord and in his mighty power.

If your pastor is standing strong in the Lord, then you can stand strong in the Lord too. *You cannot please everybody, so why not please God?*

2 Timothy 4:2–5 quote: Preach the Word; be prepare in season and out of season; correct, rebuke and encourage-with great patience and careful instruction. For the time will come when men will not put up with sound doctrine. Instead, to suit their own desires, they will gather around them a great number of teachers to say what their itching ears want to hear. They will turn their ears away from the truth and aside to myths. But you, keep your head in all situations, endure hardship, do the work of an evangelist, discharge all the duties of your ministry.

Apostle Paul told Timothy to "correct, rebuke, and encourage." It is difficult to accept correction or to be told that we have to change. But no matter how much the truth hurts, we must be willing to listen to it, so we can more fully obey God. Amen!

22

The Right to Become Children of God

John 1:12–13. Yet to all who received him, to those who believed in his name, he gave the right to become children of God-children born not of natural decent, nor of human decision or a husband's will, but born of God.

SERMON MESSAGE:

When Jesus came into the world, He came in by the Jewish race. So this means that Jesus was Jewish; He came from the tribe of Judah. Jesus came through the linage of the Kings that started with King David. When the Lord placed David on the throne, He had Jesus in mind. The promise came through King David and his son King Solomon. 2 Samuel 7:16 says, "Your house and your kingdom will endure forever before me; your throne will be established forever."

John 1:1–3 quote. In the beginning was the Word, and the Word was with God, and the Word was God. He was with God in the beginning. Through him all things were made; without nothing was made that has been made.

When we think of the name Jesus, we are reminded in the Word of God that the name Jesus is above every name that there is. Jesus is King of all kings, and Lord of all lords. In the Greek language the word *Lord* that is connected to Jesus is the name Jehovah. Whenever we say that Jesus is Lord, what we are really saying is Jesus is Jehovah, God. Many religions today would argue with us and disagree. When it comes down to the Word of God, the Word God can defend itself. All we need to do is to accept it.

Hebrews 4:12–13 quote: For the Word of God is living and active. Sharper than any doubled-edged sword, it penetrates even to dividing soul and spirit, joints and marrow; it judges the thoughts and attitudes of the heart. Nothing in all creation is hidden from God's sight. Everything is uncovered and laid bare before the eyes of him to whom we must give account.

The only way that God could redeem us is that God had to become a man, so that He could come and dwell among us.

This is why we are told in John 1:14 quote: The Word become flesh and made his dwelling among us. We have seen his glory, the glory of the One and Only, who came from the Father, full of grace and truth.

When Jesus first appeared on this earth as a man, He was 100 percent God, and He was 100 percent man. In Matthew 4:8-10, when the devil tried to tempt Jesus, to get Him to sin, the devil offered Jesus all the kingdoms of the world. The devil told Jesus that all that He needed to do was bow down and worship him. Jesus rebuked the devil by saying, "Away from me, Satan!" For it is written, "Worship the Lord your God, and serve Him only" If the church today can understand exactly what Jesus is saying here, we would take worshiping the Lord very seriously. We should not have to worship the Lord in order to get the Lord to give us something.

James 4:1–3 quote: What causes fights and quarrels among you? Don't they come from your desires that battles within you? You want something but don't get it. You kill and covet, but you cannot have what you want. You quarrel and fight. You do not have, because you do not ask God. When you ask, you do not receive, because you ask with wrong motives, that you may spend what you get on your pleasures.

We need to worship the Lord because of who God is. This is where our faith begins, and this is where it starts.

Hebrews 11:6 quote: And without faith it is impossible to please God, because anyone who comes to him must believe he exists and that he rewards those who earnestly seek him.

When I was first introduced to the Lord Jesus Christ, one of the first things that I needed to believe was, that Jesus actually existed. The first thing that I needed for the Lord to do was to forgive me of all of my sins, because I knew that I was a sinner. After I had repented, Jesus came into my heart. This was all done by faith. Today, I'm worshiping the Lord. In John 20:26-28, after the Resurrection of the Lord Jesus Christ, the Lord finally appeared to Thomas, who was one of the twelve disciples. Thomas wanted to see the nail prints in Jesus' hands, and touch His hands and His side. After the Lord Jesus had revealed Himself to Thomas, Thomas said, "My Lord and my God," then he bowed down and worshiped the Lord

Jesus Christ. What was Thomas doing? Thomas was in the act of worshiping the Lord His God. Nowhere do we read where Thomas is being rebuked by the Lord Jesus Christ.

But Jesus said to Thomas in John 20:29 quote: "Because you have seen me, you have believed; blessed are those who have not seen and yet have believed.

Church, our salvation is all wrapped up in the belief in the Lord Jesus Christ Himself.

Acts 4:12 quote: Salvation is found in no one else, for there is no other name under heaven given to men by which we must be saved.

We have so many religions in our world today, and the saddest thing about it, people all over the world are being deceived. The religions of the world have nothing to offer.

Proverbs 16:25 quote: There is a way that seems right to a man, but in the end it leads to death.

The very reason why people today are dying in their sins is because of the wrong choices and the bad decisions that they have made. The believer's faith in the Lord Jesus Christ is not considered a religion, but a relationship. This is what Christianity is all about. After we have received the Lord Jesus Christ by faith, we begin to live by faith.

Galatians 2:20 quote: I have been crucified with Christ and I no longer live, but Christ lives in me. The life I live in the body, I live by faith in the Son of God, who loved me and gave himself for me.

After we become converted to faith in Christ, we begin to operate in the faith realm, every step of the way. No longer are we operating in the sight realm because things are not always as they seem to be.

2 Corinthians 5:7 quote: We live by faith, not by sight.

So where do we go from here as believers? We begin to live as Christians. Pagans from other religions are labeling themselves as Christians. We have to take a stand and show the people of the world who we really are. So how we do this? Jesus said it this way in Matthew 5:14–16 quote: "You are the light of the world. A city on a hill cannot be hidden. Neither do people light a lamp and put it under a bowl. Instead they put it on its stand, and it gives light to everyone in the house." In the same way, let your light shine before men, that they may see your good deeds and praise your Father in heaven.

This is how it all begins with the individual. Then it spreads throughout the whole entire family. It starts with you, whether you are the man of the house or a single parent.

Jesus said of Himself in John 8:12 quote: When Jesus spoke again to the people, he said, "I am the light of the world. Whoever follows me will never walk in darkness, but will have the light of life."

Jesus has now given His light to believers. So what are we supposed to be doing with the light that we have? We have to let our light shine so that the people in our very own world can see it. You are the only Jesus that the people in our world will ever see. If the unsaved are going to see Jesus, they need to see Him in you.

1 Peter 2:12 quote: Live such good lives among the pagans that, though they accuse you of doing wrong, they may see your good deeds and glorify God on the day he visits us.

When Jesus ministered on the earth, no matter what good Jesus did, they criticized Him.

Well, you can expect the very same things to happen to you . We are considered as a new breed of people. We have been born again. We have been born of the Spirit. We have been given *the right to become children of God.*

John 1:12–13 quote: Yet to all who received him, to those who believed in his name, he gave the right to become children of God-children born not of natural decent, nor of human decision or a husband's will, but born of God.

What this means is this: God, who is your Creator, now becomes your Heavenly Father. This is because of the Spiritual Birth that connects you to your Heavenly Father through adoption. To be a member of a club, a lodge, or a sorority, you do not have to change, all you have to do is take an oath, or go through whatever rituals they have, and you are in there. To become a genuine Christian, you have to be willing to change.

Matthew 18:2-3 quote: He called a little child and had him stand among them. And he said: "I tell you the truth, unless you change and become like little children, you will never enter the kingdom of heaven.

An unsaved person cannot enter into the Kingdom of heaven as an unsaved person, or in an unsaved state of mind. Have you ever seen a caterpillar fly? The answer is no. In order for a caterpillar to be able to fly, it has got to through a transformation phase. It has to enter into a cocoon. Then, the caterpillar goes through a metamorphosis and becomes a butterfly. We become saved by the blood of Jesus Christ in the same way. I've heard people tell me many times that they are always going to be the same, that they are not ever going to change. They say, "I'm going to always cuss, that's just the way I am." Or, "You know me, man, I've got to have my drink." Or, "I'm never going to quit smoking."

John 3:3 quote: In reply Jesus declared, "I tell you the truth, no one can see the kingdom of God unless he is born again."

The people who are unsaved are missing out on the Kingdom of God. In order for an individual to enter into the Kingdom of God, they have to be Born Again. This is a place where something takes place in the life of a believer at the very moment they become Born Again.

2 Corinthians 5:17 quote: Therefore, if anyone is in Christ, he is a new creation; the old has gone, the new has come!

What this verse of Scripture means is this: Every one of us who was born into this world was born into sin. This means that we are all born spiritually dead. But the very moment that we became Born Again, our dead spirit came to life. Because we have been Born Again, the Holy Spirit is now dwelling on the inside of us.

Ephesians 1:13 quote: And you also were included in Christ when you heard the word of truth, the gospel of your salvation. Having believed, you were marked in him with a seal, the promised Holy Spirit.

We are sealed until the day of our redemption, which means that the seal cannot be broken no matter what happens to you. Our spirit that has been brought to life inside of us has not been programmed to sin, it doesn't know how. 1 John 3:9 says, "No one who has been born of God will continue to sin, because God's seed remains in him; he cannot go on sinning, because he has been born of God." Since we have been born of God, it is time to feed our spirit. So how do we feed our spirit? By getting into the Word of God. When we get hungry, we eat. And the reason why we eat is because our bodies crave physical food. If we didn't eat, our bodies would die. The same is true with our spirit, but the only difference is that our spirit doesn't die. We need to feed our spirit the spiritual nutrients that it needs.

1 Peter 2:2–3 quote: Like newborn babies, crave pure spiritual milk, so that by it you may grow up in your salvation, now that you have tasted that the Lord is good.

When babies are born, they depend on their mother's milk in order to feed them, until they are able to eat solid food on their own. The very reason why we have *the right to become children of God* is so that our Heavenly Father can care for us.

John 1:12–13 quote: Yet to all who received him, to those who believed in his name, he gave the right to become children of God-children born not of natural decent, nor of human decision or a husband's will, but born of God.

Now that we are born of God, and God has become our Heavenly Father by adopting us in His family, we are not going to continue to do the same things that the people of the world are doing. This is why reading the Bible is so very important to us. We need God's Word to feed our spirit.

Listen to what Jesus says in Matthew 4:4 when He quoted Deuteronomy 8:3 quote: "It is written: 'Man does not live on bread alone, but on every word that comes from the mouth of God.

This is what it means to live by the Spirit so that we can get the Word of God inside of us, and begin to apply it to our everyday lives. We have to feed on the Word of God. The very reason why we are still here on this earth as believers is so that we can feed on the Word of God and grow up in our salvation so that it will take us to the very next level of our faith. This is what bearing fruit is all about.

John 15:16 quote: You did not choose me, but I chose you and appointed you to go and bear fruit-fruit that will last. Then the Father will give you whatever you ask in my name.

The fruit that we are to be bearing is supposed to last. And as long as we are bearing fruit, we will have the opportunity to receive answers to our prayers. In order to do this, we have to remain in the true vine. The Lord Jesus Christ represents the true vine.

John 15:5 quote: "I am the vine; you are the branches. If a man remains in me and I in him, he will bear much fruit; apart from me you can do nothing.

329

The very reason why so many Christians are not effective today is because they haven't allowed themselves to become disciplined in the Word of God.

Hosea 4:6 quote: My people are destroyed from the lack of knowledge.

Christians today are attending their local churches for all the wrong reasons. Many are attending just to be entertained. As the Lord tarries His coming, the believers are going to get hungry for the real Word of God. These believers are the ones who have *the right to become children of God.*

John 1:12–13 quote: Yet to all who received him, to those who believed in his name, he gave the right to become children of God-children born not of natural descent, nor of human decision or a husband's will, but born of God.

Every human being who is living today has the opportunity to become a child of God. It doesn't matter what religion that they are. Religion can't save you. Our Heavenly Father wants to have a relationship with each and every one who is adopted into His family.

This is why we are told in Galatians 6:10 quote: Therefore, as we have the opportunity, let us do good to all people, especially to those who belong to the family of believers.

We are family, and since we are family, we need to have a bond with one another. We have our own siblings who we are really close to. There are things that we share with our brothers and sisters that we wouldn't share with others. This is how it needs to be among the brothers and sisters who represent the Church that the Lord Jesus Christ is still building today. We are the Body of Christ, with Jesus being the Head.

Matthew 16:18 quote: And on this rock I will build my church, and the gates of Hades will not overcome it.

Church, the Lord Jesus Christ wasn't referring to Peter, but to Himself. Jesus is the solid Rock, which the Church is still being built upon. Nebuchadnezzar dreamed about a huge statue: part gold, part silver, part bronze, part iron, and part iron mixed with clay. The Prophet Daniel was the only one who was able to interpret the king's dream. It was the Lord God who gave Daniel the interpretation of Nebuchadnezzar's dream. This dream had to do with the statue that represented all the Gentile kingdoms of the world. Daniel 2:34–35 says, "A Rock that was cut out, but not with human hands, struck the statue on its feet of iron and clay and smashed them. Then the iron, the clay, the bronze, the silver and gold were broken to pieces at the same time, and became like chaff on a threshing floor in the summer. The wind swept them away without leaving a trace, but the Rock that struck the statue became a huge mountain and filled the whole earth." Church, that Rock, which became a huge mountain, is the Lord Jesus Christ Himself. It is not about you, and it is not about me, but everything is centered in Christ. This is what it means to live a "Christ-centered life." Because the things that we do for Christ will be the only things that matter when we get to heaven.

2 Corinthians 5:10 quote: For we must all appear before the judgment seat of Christ, that each one may receive what is due him for the things done while in the body, whether good or bad.

There are going to be rewards given to the believers and not to the unsaved. This passage of Scripture that was quoted only speaks to the believers. The White Throne Judgment and the Judgment Seat of Christ are two different judgments. If you are here today, and you enter at the White Throne Judgment, it is already too late for you to be saved. Your next place of residence will be the Lake of Fires. But as long as you are living today, you still have an opportunity to escape the jaws of hell by receiving the Lord Jesus Christ as your personal Savior. Why personal? It is because the Lord Jesus Christ, Himself, wants to become personal with you. Revelation 3:20 quote: Here I am! I stand at the door and knock. If anyone hears my voice and opens the door, I will come in and eat with him, and he with me.

Only God the Father, and God the Son, and God the Holy Spirit have the exact same attributes. What does this mean? God is all knowing. God is all-powerful. God is everywhere, at the same time. And yet, there is One God.

John 1:12–13 quote: Yet to all who received him, to those who believed in his name, he gave the right to become children of God-children born not of natural decent, nor of human decision or husband's will, but born of God.

You may know someone who is Jewish; this doesn't mean that they are saved. Being born in the Jewish race cannot save you. If this was the case, then only the Jews would be the ones to enter into heaven. Salvation in the Lord Jesus Christ is a universal call.

Romans 10:9–10, 13 quote: That if you confess with your mouth, "Jesus is Lord," and believe in your heart that God raised him from the dead, you will be saved. For it is with your heart that you believe and are justified, and it is with your mouth that you confess and are saved. For, "Everyone who calls on the name of the Lord will be saved."

It doesn't matter who you are. Black, White, Hispanic, Asian, Italian, Jewish, and so on, you have the opportunity to be saved. God is not concerned with your nationality, but God is concerned with the whole human race.

2 Peter 3:9 quote: The Lord is not slow in keeping his promise, as some understand slowness. He is patient with you, not wanting anyone to perish, but everyone to come to repentance.

When individuals repent, it places them in God's family. They now become a Child of God.

CONCLUSION

John 1:12–13 quote: Yet to all who received him, to those who believed in his name, he gave the right to become children of God-children born not of natural decent, nor of a human decision or a husband's will, but born of God.

All who welcome Jesus Christ as Lord of their lives are reborn spiritually, receiving new life from God. Through faith in Christ, this new birth changes us from the inside out, rearranging our attitudes, desires, and motives. Being Born Again makes you physically alive and puts you in God's family. This all has to do with what the Lord Jesus Christ has done for us. Because of Christ, we share the same exact blessings that were given to Abraham.

Galatians 3:29 quote: If you belong to Christ, then you are Abraham's seed, and heirs according to the promise.

This gives us *the right to become children of God.* Amen!

23

Are You Sending People to Hell and the Lake of Fires?

Matthew 7:13–14. "Enter through the narrow gate. For wide is the gate and broad is the road that leads to destruction, and many enter through it. But small is the gate and narrow is the road that leads to life, and only few find it.

SERMON MESSAGE:

When the Lord God first created man in His own image and in His likeness, the Lord God had each and every one of us in mind. When God saw Adam and Eve in His creation, the Lord saw you. You are very special and so unique. As long as you live on the face of this earth, there will never be another you. When the Lord God formed you, He formed you individually. The Lord has a divine reason and a divine purpose for you. In order for you to know God's plan for your life, you first have to know Him.

Hebrews 11:6 quote: And without faith it is impossible to please God, because anyone who comes to him must believe that he exists and he rewards those who earnestly seek him.

God created you to be born, so that every one of you could become Born Again. If you are not Born Again, you cannot know God, and you cannot enter into the Kingdom of God unless you are Born Again.

John 3:3 quote: In reply Jesus declared, "I tell you the truth, no one can see the kingdom of God unless he is born again."

Why is being Born Again so important to every person? It is God's desire for every human being to be saved.

2 Peter 3:9 quote: The Lord is not slow in keeping his promise, as some understand slowness. He is patient with you, not wanting anyone to perish, but everyone to come to repentance.

God your Creator is not going to twist your arm and force you to be saved. This is why one of the greatest abilities that God has given us is the willingness to choose and to make our own decisions. God did not leave us without helping us to make the right choice. Before teachers give you a final exam or a test in high school, so that you can graduate and receive your diploma, they have already prepared you for it. They let you know what's involved in the exam, so that when you take it, you know exactly what to look for. When it comes down to salvation in Jesus Christ, the Lord also prepares you to receive eternal life. God has given us pastors, preachers, and believers to witness to us about receiving Christ. It first started out with the early Church. Jesus prepared them right after He commissioned them.

Jesus said to them in Acts 1:4–5 quote: On one occasion while he was eating with them, he gave this command: "Do not leave

Jerusalem, but wait for the gift my Father promised, which you heard me speak about. For John baptized with water, but in a few days you will be baptized with the Holy Spirit."

What is so important about this gift that the Father has promised? This gift is evidence to show the fact that you are saved. As we become saved, others, whether they are saved or unsaved, are going to see the difference in us to tell if we are saved.

Jesus said to the disciples in Acts 1:8 quote: But you will receive power when the Holy Spirit comes on you; and you will be my witnesses in Jerusalem, and in all Judea and Samaria, and to the ends of the earth.

The same power that Jesus told His disciples about, which they were to receive, is the same power that every believer will receive. That power is the power of the Holy Spirit that resides in every believer. Paul explains to the believer exactly what takes place at their conversion.

Ephesians 1:13 quote: And you also were included in Christ when you heard the word of truth, the gospel of your salvation. Having believe, you were marked in him with a seal, the promised Holy Spirit.

The Holy Spirit seals us the very moment that we are converted to faith in the Lord Jesus Christ. It is so that we cannot and we will not lose our salvation. This is why the Helmet of Salvation is so very important to every believer. We are to keep this Helmet of Salvation on at all times. So many Christians are doubting their salvation today because they are not wearing their spiritual Helmet of Salvation.

Jesus said this in John 10:27–30 quote: My sheep listen to my voice; I know them, and they follow me. I give them eternal life, and they shall never perish; no one can snatch them out of my hand. My Father, who has given them to me, is greater than all; no one can snatch them out of my Father's hand. I and my Father are one.

Just because you are not wearing your spiritual Helmet of Salvation, doesn't mean you are not saved. Having it and not wearing it and keeping it on can cause you to doubt your salvation. All this is going to do is interfere with you doing good works.

Ephesians 2:10 quote: For we are God's workmanship, created in Christ Jesus to do good works, which God prepared in advance for us to do.

This is the very reason why our Heavenly Father left us here on earth, to do the good works that we have been called to do. What are the good works that we have been called to do? Is it to witness and to share our faith with others? In order to do this, we have to be trained by getting into reading, studying, and applying the Word of God in our lives.

2 Timothy 2:15 quote: Do your best to present yourself to God as one approved, a workman who does not need to be ashamed and who correctly handles the word of truth.

Church, your Heavenly Father is the one who does the promoting in your life, and not man.

This is designed so that you can carry out the good work that you have been called to do. Philippians 1:6 quote: Being confident of this, that he who began a good work in you will carry it on to completion until the day of Christ Jesus.

How do you expect to witness to someone about Jesus when you do not know what the Word of God says?

2 Timothy 3:16–17 quote: All Scripture is God-breathed and is useful for teaching, rebuking, correcting and training in righteousness, so that the man of God may be thoroughly equipped for every good work.

If there were any other book on the market that is more important than the Word of God, it would have been revealed to us by the Lord. God's Holy Word is all that we really need to live by.

2 Peter 1:20–21 quote: Above all, you must understand that no prophecy of Scripture came about by the prophet's own interpretation. For prophecy never had its origin in the will of man, but men spoke from God as they were carried along by the Holy Spirit.

Whenever we apply God's Word to our lives, we are placing ourselves in the area of training in righteousness. Why is this so important? It is so that we can witness to those who are not saved. When Barack Obama was elected president of the United States, the majority of the country celebrated his victory. It doesn't stop there; now it is time for President Barack Obama to carry out his duties inside the Oval Office. The same is true with you. Praise the Lord that you are saved, but you have to be ready to move on to the very next level of your Christian faith. You may attend your local church, where everyone who attends the worship services is already saved, but the local pastor still needs to preach to those who are saved.

This is the pastor's duty in the local church, as in Ephesians 4:12–14 quote: To prepare God's people for works of service, so that the body of Christ may be built up until we all reach unity in the faith and in the knowledge of the Son of God and become mature, attaining to the whole measure of the fullness of Christ. Then we will no longer be infants, toss back and forth by the waves, and blown here and there by every wind of teaching and by the cunning and craftiness of men in their deceitful scheming.

Church, you need to involve yourselves in a local church ministry where no one can come in and "pull the wool over your eyes." For this reason, so many Christians are led astray and so easily deceived.

This is why Apostle Paul warned the pastors what to look out for, in Acts 20:28—31 quote: Keep watch over yourselves and all the flock of which the Holy Spirit has made you overseers. Be shepherds of the church of God, which he bought with own blood. I know that after I leave, savage wolves will come in among you and will not spare the flock. Even from your own number men will arise and distort the truth in order to draw away disciples after them. So be on your guard! Remember that for three years I never stopped warning each of you night and day with tears.

Savage wolves and so many distractions can keep us from carrying out what we've been called to do. The question that is proposed to you today is this: are you sending people to hell and the Lake of Fires?

Matthew 7:13–14 quote: "Enter through narrow gate. For wide is the gate and broad is the road that leads to destruction, and many enter through it. But small is the gate and narrow is the road that leads to life, and only a few find it.

We now know better because we are saved. So what about those who are not saved? This is where we come in as believers in Christ. This is the very reason why we are still here on this earth today: to evangelize the whole world. You are the only Jesus that the people in your world will ever see. Notice what Jesus said to His disciples before His Ascension?

Matthew 28:18–20 quote: Then Jesus came to them and said, "All authority in heaven and on earth has been given to me. Therefore go and make disciples of all nations, baptizing them in the name of the Father and of the Son and of the Holy Spirit, and teaching them to obey everything I have commanded you. And surely I am with you always, to the very end of the age."

If you notice, Jesus' disciples are not with us today. They are now in the presence of the Lord. So who is Jesus speaking to today? The Lord Jesus Christ is speaking to the Church. We are the Church. In order for you to disciple the people in your world, you must already be a disciple yourself.

Jesus tells us in Luke 9:23 quote: Then he said to them all: "If anyone would come after me, he must deny himself and take up his cross daily and follow me.

As long as your sinful flesh remains in the way, you are not going to tell anyone about Jesus. Jesus said to His disciples, "Follow me and I will make you fishers of men." (Matthew 4:19) For those three years that Jesus spent with His disciples, they were in training. As believers, each time that we attend our place of worship, we need to be in biblical training in the area of living in righteousness.

Hebrews 10:24–25 quote: And let us consider how we may spur one another on toward love and good deeds. Let us not give up meeting together, as some are in the habit of doing, but let us encourage one another-and all the more as you see the Day approaching.

Whenever we witness to others about the Lord Jesus Christ, they must be able see the change life that we are living. Anyone can say that they are a Christian, but the unsaved people need to see the evidence.

Matthew 5:16 quote: In the same way, let your light shine before men, that they may see your good deeds and praise your Father in heaven.

So many people who call themselves Christians are sending people to hell because of their sinful lifestyle. What is causing this to happen are worldly, sinful, distractions. Christians have taken their eyes off of Jesus and have placed them on the very things of this world. We have to be reminded what the Scriptures are saying to us.

1 John 2:15–17 quote: Do not love the world or anything in the world. If anyone loves the world, the love of the Father is not in him. For everything in the world-the cravings of sinful man, the

lust of his eyes and the boasting of what he has and does-comes not from the Father but from the world. The world and its desires pass away, but the man who does the will of God lives forever.

Whenever we love the things of the world, we take our aim and our focus off the very things that we are supposed to be doing: witnessing and sharing our faith with others.

1 Peter 3:15 quote: But in your hearts set apart Christ as Lord. Always be prepared to give an answer to everyone who asks you to give the reason for the hope that you have. But do this with gentleness and respect.

How can you be ready to give an answer, if you have never been taught? As believers in Christ, we are without excuse. We have the Word of God, which is holding us accountable.

Hebrews 4:12–13 quote: For the Word of God is living and active. Sharper than any double-edged sword, it penetrates even to the dividing soul and spirit, joint and marrow; it judges the thoughts and attitudes of the heart. Nothing in all creation is hidden from God's sight. Everything is uncovered and laid bare before the eyes of him to whom we must give account.

In the early Church, all that they had was the Old Testament Scriptures to rely on. This explains all the miraculous signs and the healings. Today we have the completed books of the Word of God. Every one of these sixty-six books were inspired by God, this is why we are told in 1 Peter 2:2–3 quote: Like newborn babies, crave pure spiritual milk, so that by it you may grow up in your salvation, now that you have tasted that the Lord is good.

The question that is being asked is this: *Are you sending people to hell and the Lake of Fires?* Church, if you are not reading and studying the Word of God, then you are sending lost souls to hell. When we are witnessing to unsaved people about the Lord Jesus Christ, we cannot continue to live in sin.

James 4:17 quote: Anyone, then, who knows the good he ought to do and doesn't do it, sins.

The Word of God is designed to explain to us, and to show us how we are to live among the pagan people of the world.

1 Peter 2:12 quote: Live such good lives among the pagans that, though they accuse you of doing wrong, they may see your good deeds and glorify God on the day he visits us.

The world in which we live in today is very religious. As believers in Christ, we have to show the religious people of the world that our faith in Jesus Christ is genuine and real. Saying that you are Christian and living as a Christian are two different things. Jesus had a problem with the Jewish leaders of His day, because He had exposed them as hypocrites.

Jesus told them in Matthew 23:15 quote: "Woe to you, teachers of the law and Pharisees, you hypocrites! You travel over land and sea to win a single convert, and when he becomes one, you make him twice as much a son of hell as you are.

If I am doing something wrong, and I am not aware that what I am doing is wrong, I want you to expose me, so that I can repent of it and make it right. When Apostle Paul was persecuting the

Church as he went by the name of Saul, he was in complete ignorance of what he was doing. The Lord Jesus Christ had to stop Saul dead in his tracks. Paul repented and turned his life around; from there, he gave his life to Jesus.

Paul said it this way: Galatians 2:20 quote: I have been crucified with Christ and I no longer live, but Christ lives in me. The life I live in the body, I live by faith in the Son of God, who loved me and gave himself for me.

Just like the Lord Jesus Christ gave Himself for Paul, Jesus also gave Himself for the entire human race and individually. When it comes down to death and hell, Jesus took our place on the cross. Our Heavenly Father knew that there was no way that we could endure what Jesus had to endure. In order for you to endure what Jesus had to endure, you have to be God.

2 Corinthians 5:21 quote: God made him who had no sin to be sin for us, so that in him we might become the righteousness of God.

Another way that we can look at this is this way: God made Himself to become sin for us, so that in Him, we might become the righteousness of God. Everyone who has accepted Jesus Christ as Lord has been declared as the righteousness of God. If you are the righteousness of God, then why are you sending lost souls to hell? We have to get out here and look for ways to get our foot in the door, so that we can share our faith with others. I talked to you earlier about the Helmet of Salvation. It is a must that we keep it on at all times. We need to have our feet fitted with the readiness that comes from the Gospel of Peace. What is the Gospel of Christ in a nutshell?

Romans 10:9–10 and 13, quote: That if you confess with your mouth, "Jesus is Lord," and believe in your heart that God raised him from the dead, you will be saved. For it is with your heart that you believe and are justified, and it is with your mouth that you confess and are saved. For, "Everyone who calls on the name of the Lord will be saved."

These are Scripture verses that we ought to know, and we should learn how to memorize them. The very life that we are living for Christ is going to touch others. They are going to want what you have. How are you going to give it to them if you do not know the Scriptures? *Are you sending people to hell and the Lake of Fires?*

Matthew 7:13–14 quote: "Enter through the narrow gate. For wide is the gate and broad is the road that leads to destruction, and many enter through it. But small is the gate and narrow the road that leads to life, and only a few find it.

Hell is not a laughing matter. It's not to be joked about. Hell is real. Many of us have had love ones, friends, and people, who we know, who have gone on before us. Have you ever wondered if they were saved? When death comes upon someone, there are only two places that they could go: heaven or hell. This is why your witness needs to be real. People today are making bad choices when it comes down to where they are going to spend their eternity.

Proverbs 16:25 quote: There is a way that seems right to a man, but in the end it leads to death.

Unsaved people need to know that there is nothing that they can do on their own to get to heaven.

Romans 3:23 quote: For all have sinned and fall short of the glory of God.

The very reason why we all have sin is because all of us have inherited Adam's sin. We have a sinful nature that wants us to continue to live in sin. No matter how good that we try to be on our own, we are still going to sin.

Romans 6:23 quote: For the wages of sin is death, but the gift of God is eternal life in Christ Jesus our Lord.

Whether you know it or not, someone has to pay for the penalty of sin. Jesus Christ became that someone. When Jesus paid the penalty for our sins, He paid for the sins of the whole entire human race. For this reason, there should be no one in hell. Jesus has made it easy for everyone to go heaven.

Matthew 11:28–30 quote: "Come to me, all you who weary and burdened, and I will give you rest. Take my yoke upon you and learn from me, for I am gentle and humble and heart, and you will find rest for your souls. For my yoke is easy and my burden is light."

The rest that Jesus wants every unsaved person to receive is the free gift of eternal life. If an unsaved person remains in their sins, they will experience spiritual death and separation all throughout eternity. If you are here today, and you haven't given your heart to Jesus, you need to hear this. Each time we hear that someone has died in sin, it needs to bother us. Jesus talked about hell more than anybody: the weeping and gnashing of teeth, where the worms do not die, and the fire is not quenched, in everlasting darkness.

Church, we need to have compassion for lost souls, and we can't allow ourselves to be intimidated.

1 Peter 5:8 quote: Be self-controlled and alert. Your enemy the devil prowls around like a roaring lion looking for someone to devour.

The devil isn't coming after those who are unsaved. But he is coming out to attack the genuine believers. Satan wants to destroy your witnessing to others. Notice what Jesus said in Matthew 10:28: "Do not be afraid of those who can kill the body but cannot kill the soul. Rather, be afraid of the One who can destroy both body and soul in hell." When it comes down to experiencing physical death, our Heavenly Father gives us dying grace. Death is only a shadow for those who die in the Lord.

Philippians 1:21–24 quote: For to me, to live is Christ and to die is gain. If I am to go on living in the body, this will mean fruitful labor for me. Yet what shall I choose? I do not know! I am torn between the two: I desire to depart and be with Christ, which is better by far; but it is more necessary for you that I remain in the body.

Church, our fruitful laboring is when we are sharing our faith with others whenever we let them know that they need to be saved. Adam and Eve were both clothed in the righteousness of God, but after they sinned by disobedience, they were both found naked. Unsaved people are considered as spiritually naked because of their sins. They need to be saved from their sins.

John 8:34–36 quote: Jesus replied, "I tell you the truth, everyone sins is a slave to sin. Now a slave has no permanent place in the family, but a son belongs to it forever. So if the Son sets you free, you will be free indeed.

Jesus came to set the captive free. *Are you sending people to hell and the Lake of Fires?*

CONCLUSION

We send people to hell when we choose not to love them enough the way our Heavenly Father loved us.

Romans 5:8 quote: But God demonstrates his own love for us in this: While we were still sinners, Christ died for us.

We send people to hell when we choose not to change our lifestyle as we continue to live ungodly.

James 4:4 quote: You adulterous people, don't you know that friendship with the world is hatred toward God? Anyone who chooses to be a friend of the world becomes an enemy of God.

We send people to hell when we choose not to feed on the Word of God.

Matthew 4:4 quote: "It is written: 'Man does not live on bread alone, but on every word that comes from the mouth of God.

We send people to hell when we refuse to be transformed.

Romans 12:2 quote: Do not conform any longer to the pattern of this world, but be transformed by the renewing of your mind.

Then you will be able to test and approve what God's will is-his good, pleasing and perfect will.

When was the last time that you told someone about the love of Jesus? Wherever you go, and whatever you do, and whatever you say, you are representing the Lord Jesus Christ.

Romans 13:14 quote: Rather, clothe yourselves with the Lord Jesus Christ, and do not think about how to gratify the desires of the sinful nature.

Amen!

24

The Love of Money Is Destroying God's People

1 Timothy 6: 6–10. But godliness with contentment is great gain. For we brought nothing into the world; and we can take nothing out of it. But if we have food and clothing, we will be content with that. People who want to get rich fall into temptation and a trap and into many foolish and harmful desires that plunge men into ruin and destruction. For the love of money is the root of all kinds of evil. Some people, eager for money, have wandered from the faith and pierced themselves with many griefs.

SERMON MESSAGE:

Why do so many churchgoers who refer to themselves as Christians flock to large churches to hear sermons on prosperity? It is because they are looking to have their ears tickled.

2 Timothy 4:2–4 quote: Preach the Word; be prepared in season and out of season; correct, rebuke and encourage-with great patience and careful instruction. For the time will come when men will not put up with sound doctrine. Instead, to suit their own desires, they will gather around them a great number of

teachers to say what their itching ears want to hear. They will turn their ears away from the truth and turn aside to myths.

The very reason why Christians are having their ears tickled is because they do not want to change their sinful practices. They do not want to hear the truth, but they want to listen to the half-truth. Prosperity is not the subject or message that Christians need to be listening to all the time. This sinful world that we live in is going to bring hardship, trials, and storms in our lives that we must deal with each day. God's Word gives us warning signs to what we are to be looking out for.

Ephesians 5:15–16 quote: Be very careful, then, how you live-not as unwise but as wise, making the most of every opportunity, because the days are evil.

Are you paying close attention to how you are supposed to be living as believers in Christ? Church, we need to be seeking godly wisdom for our lives. God our Heavenly Father has given us resources so that our every need can be met. This also includes the money that we have.

Deuteronomy 8:18 quote: But remember the Lord your God, for it is he who gives you the ability to produce wealth.

Our Heavenly Father gave us what we have. God gave us the ability to do exactly what we do so well. People from every walk of life have the God-given ability to accomplish something good in their lives. As believers, we need to give back to God a portion of what He has given us. This is why we use our financial resources in carrying out Kingdom work in the Kingdom of God.

We are told in Matthew 6:33 quote: But seek first his kingdom and his righteousness, and all these things will be given to you as well.

Church, we need to also seek first the Kingdom of God in our giving, when it comes down to

tithes and offerings in the local churches. Churchgoers today have a problem when it comes down to giving of their tithes and offerings. They say that tithes were required under the Old Testament Law. Abraham and Jacob were not under the Old Testament Law, and yet both of them during their lifetime gave a tenth, or a tithe, unto the Lord. Abraham did it with Melchizedek. Jacob did it when he made a vow to the Lord. Moses wasn't even thought of when these men gave a tithe to the Lord.

Romans 15:4 quote: For everything that was written in the pass was written to teach us, so that through endurance and the encouragement of the Scriptures we might have hope.

When we put God first in our lives, it should include our giving of our tithes and offerings as well. Seeking first the Kingdom of God and His righteousness also includes our money. Many Christians today want their needs met. Are they willing to do whatever it takes to have God meet their needs?

Philippians 4:19 quote: And my God will meet all your needs according to his glorious riches in Christ Jesus.

Apostle Paul commended the saints at Philippi for their giving. During Paul's missionary journey, he needed financial support from the churches in order to take the Gospel of Jesus Christ abroad to the Gentiles. The church at Philippi supported Paul's missionary journey. Their giving to Paul's ministry became a spiritual investment. The same is true with believers today. If you are supporting your local church ministries, you are investing spiritually in the Kingdom of God. You are getting spiritual dividends on your returns.

Luke 6:38 quote: Give, and it will be given to you. A good measure, pressed down, shaken together and running over, will be poured into your lap. For with the measure you use, it will be measured to you.

Today, we have so many financial charity programs available for donations, but no charity contributions can outshine the giving made in the local churches. This is when and where God will meet our every need. 2 Corinthians 9:6–8 says, "Remember this: Whoever sows sparingly will reap sparingly, and whoever sows generously will reap generously." Each man should give what he has decided in his heart to give, not reluctantly or under compulsion, for God loves a cheerful giver. And God is able to make all grace abound to you, so that in all things, at all times, having all that you need, you will abound in every good work. Under the New Testament Covenant, when it comes down to giving, giving has to do with giving from within the heart.

We are told as believers in Matthew 6:19–21 quote: Do not store up for yourselves treasures on earth, where moth and rust destroy, and where thieves break in and steal. But store up for yourselves treasures in heaven, where moth and rust do not destroy, and where thieves do not break in and steal. For where your treasure is, there your heart will be also.

This passage of Scripture is designed to change the way the believer gives. If a believer's heart is not in giving, then they are not going to be comfortable in the area of giving. Putting money in your local church is like putting money in a bank account. The only difference is this: The believer will reap a financial harvest. Man can't bless you as well as God can. This is why giving is very important to the believer.

1 Corinthians 16:1–2 quote: Now about the collection for God's people: Do what I told the Galatian churches to do. On the first day of every week, each one of you should set aside a sum of money in keeping with his income, saving it up, so that when I come no collections will have to be made.

When Apostle Paul set up this biblical mandate, Paul was setting this up for all the Bible-believing Christ-centered churches. This was the same instruction that Paul had given to the Galatia churches. Paul then passed this information on to the churches in Corinth. This is the mandate in the area of giving of our tithes and offerings unto the Lord. One of the main reasons why the local church members are to meet is so that we can give of ourselves.

Hebrews 10:25 quote: Let us not give up meeting together, as some are in habit of doing, but let us encourage one another-and all the more as you see the Day approaching.

How many of you eat every day? How many of you go to sleep at night? How many of you lock your doors after you leave for work in the morning? How many of you wear coats and jackets when you get cold? What is the point being made here? The point that is being made here is about habits. Whatever it is that we do on a daily basis, we've made it out to be a habit. The habit of attending your local church is designed so that every believer can become biblically

informed. The very reason why some Christians do not attend Sunday Worship on a regular basis is because *the love of money is destroying God's people.* 1 Timothy 6:6 says, "But

godliness with contentment is great gain." What does it mean to be content? Being content is being happy with what you have. Being content is far better than being rich. Some of my

coworkers are paid really well whenever they work overtime. As for me, I have chosen not to work any overtime. I have learned as a believer how to be content with what is given to me.

What is the purpose in working overtime when you really do not need to? The average American today is working two jobs in order to live within their means. If this is the American dream, then we should want no part of it.

When it comes down to money, Matthew 6:24 tells us, quote: "No one can serve two masters. Either he will hate the one and love the other, or he will be devoted to the one and despise the other. You cannot serve both God and Money.

If we are not careful, the love of money can easily become our God.

1 Corinthians 6:12 quote: "Everything is permissible for me"-but not everything is beneficial. "Everything is permissible for me" –but I will not be mastered by anything.

We cannot let the love of money become our master. Money is designed to be used as a monetary resource for purchasing goods and the materials that we need; this is the reason why we seek employment.

2 Thessalonians 3:10 quote: For even when we were with you, we gave you this rule: "If a man will not work, he shall not eat."

In order for us to make an honest and decent living for ourselves, if we truly want to eat, we have to have a job. Once we get a job, it gives us something to work with when it comes down to planting financial seeds in the Kingdom of God. Many Christians today are looking forward to landing that big paying job or receiving that special promotion. But yet they do not trust God.

We are told in Luke 16:10–12 quote: "Whoever can be trusted with very little can also be trusted with much, and whoever is dishonest with very little will also be dishonest with much. So if you have not been trustworthy in handling worldly wealth, who will trust you with true riches? And if you have not been trustworthy with someone else's property, who will give you property of your own?

In order for the Lord to trust you with much greater things, you first have to learn how to crawl before you can walk. If you are honest in what you are doing, expect your Heavenly Father to reward you.

1 Peter 5:6 quote: Humble yourselves, therefore, under God's mighty hand, that he may lift you up in due time.

The love of money is destroying God's people. 1 Timothy 6:7 says, "For we brought nothing into this world, and we can take nothing out of it." When we leave this world, we are even going to leave our own bodies behind. We do not even own ourselves.

Listen to what it says in 1 Corinthians 6:19–20 quote: Do you not know that your body is a temple of the Holy Spirit, who is in you, whom you have received from God? You are not your own; you were bought at a price. Therefore honor God with your body.

Church, seeing that this is the case, shouldn't we be careful with what we do with the money that our Heavenly Father allows us to have? Whenever you receive that paycheck that you have earned, you are receiving 100 percent. Whether you are being paid every week or every two weeks, you are receiving 100 percent that has been placed in your possession. Ten percent should go to your local church, because it helps to advance God's Kingdom. Malachi 3:10 says, "'Bring the whole tithe into the storehouse, that there may be food in my house. Test me in this,' says the Lord Almighty, 'and see if I will not open the floodgates of heaven and pour out so much blessing that you will not have room enough for it.'" The food that is in the Lord's house today is the Word of God.

Matthew 4:4 quote: "It is written: Man does not live on bread alone, but on every word that comes from the mouth of God.

The local shepherds are the ones who are preaching and teaching you the Word of God, which every believer should live by. Every time the Word of God is being preached and taught to you, you are being fed the Word of God.

1 Peter 4:11 quote: If anyone speaks, he should do it as one speaking the very words of God. If anyone serves, he should do it

with the strength God provides, so that in all things God may be praised through Jesus Christ. To him be the glory and the power for ever and ever. Amen.

You have Christians today who are using what belongs to the Lord on themselves. And they wonder why they are not being blessed.

James 4:1–3 quote: What causes fights and quarrels among you? Don't they come from the desires that battle within you? You want something but don't get it. You kill and covet, but you cannot have what you want. You quarrel and fight. You do not have, because you do not ask God. When you ask, you do not receive, because you ask with wrong motives, that you may spend what you get on your pleasures.

If these Scripture verses don't apply to you, then let it go in one ear and out the other. Christians today, instead of giving their tithes and offerings to the Lord, are using God's money for their own purposes. This is why *the love of money is destroying God's people*. Today's Christians do not realize that they are robbing God. Malachi 3:8–9 says, "Will a man rob God? Yet you rob me. But you ask, 'How do we rob you?' In tithes and offerings, you are under a curse—the whole nation of you—because you are robbing me." The Israelites in the Prophet Malachi's day were robbing God with their tithes and offerings. This was the reason why the Levites (the priests) had go to work taking on secular jobs so that they could make a living. By doing this, they were neglecting their God-given responsibilities. The same thing is being done in the local Bible-believing churches today. You might say, "Pastor, that is only found in the Old Testament Scriptures, but these Old Testament Scriptures don't apply to us."

Listen to what the New Testament says: 1 Corinthians 9:14 quote: In the same way, the Lord has commanded that those who preach the gospel should receive their living from the gospel.

If the pastor is pasturing the local church, then they need to be paid. The pastor has a very serious role in the local church: teaching, preaching, and building up the body of Christ. The duties are written down in the Word of God.

In Ephesians 4:12-13, the pastors are told, quote: To prepare God's people for works of service, so that the body of Christ may be built up until we all reach unity in the faith and in the knowledge of the Son of God and become mature, attaining to the whole measure of the fullness of Christ.

You are going to have local church members refusing to be built up in the Christian faith. Instead of learning or taking notes, they allow themselves to become distracted from the very things of God. They allow themselves to become deceived.

For this reason, we are told in Hosea 4:6 quote: My people are destroyed from the lack of knowledge.

Church, I wouldn't be where I am today if I didn't know the Word of God for myself. This is exactly what you have to do. A very serious pastor is here to show you, and to teach you, and to give you the understanding that you need in the Word of God.

Luke 6:40 quote: A student is not above his teacher, but everyone who is fully trained will be like his teacher.

As a pastor, I want you to become like me, when it comes down to receiving biblical godly wisdom of the Word of God. The pastors also have to set biblical examples in the local church.

1 Peter 5:2–3 quote: Be shepherds of God's flock that is under your care, serving as overseers-not because you must, but because you are willing, as God wants you to be; not greedy for money, but eager to serve; not lording it over those entrusted to you, but being examples to the flock.

We cannot be greedy for money, but eager to serve. Also as a pastor, we have to set biblical guidelines when it comes down to giving of our tithes and offerings to the Lord's work. If no one else chooses to give, the pastor has to set the example in the area of giving. *The love of money is destroying God's people.* 1 Timothy 6:8–9 says, "But if we have food and clothing, we will be content with that." People who want to get rich fall into temptation and a trap and into many foolish, harmful desires that plunge men into ruin and destruction. Church, if you had to choose between being rich or being content, you need to go with being content. Many of you would go with being rich. But when it comes down to being content, Paul passes along this statement to us in Philippians 4:11–12: "I have learned to be content whatever the circumstances. I know what it is to be in need, and I know what it is to have plenty. I have learned the secret in any and every situation, whether fed or hungry, whether living in plenty or in want."

Ephesians 4:13 quote: I can do everything through him (Christ) who gives me strength.

The rich young ruler was missing something in his life that he really needed. That was the gift of eternal life. Jesus told him to go and sell everything he had and give to the poor, then come and follow Him. With this in mind, this rich young ruler went away sad, because he had great wealth. Wealth had become this rich young ruler's master, because wealth was mastering him. As Christians, we need to learn how to be content with what we have. There are always going to be some get-rich-quick scams that Christians are going to fall into.

This is why we have to do what Hebrews 13:5 says, quote: keep your life free from the love of money and be content with what you have, because God has said, "Never will I leave you; never will I forsake you."

The love of money is nothing but a trap waiting for you to fall right into. If you are not careful, you may find yourself falling right into it. Whenever you become so assess with the love of money, back away from it.

1 Corinthians 10:13 quote: No temptation has seized you except what is common to man. And God is faithful; he will not let you be tempted beyond what you can bear. But when you are tempted, he will also provide a way out so that you can stand up under it.

When you see yourself yielding to the love of money, stop right where you are and let your Heavenly Father introduce to you what being content is all about. Contentment is to be at peace with God.

The love of money is destroying God's people. 1 Timothy 6:10 quote: For the love of money is root of all kinds of evil. Some people, eager for money, have wandered from the faith and pierced themselves with many griefs.

This is the reason why Christians today are leaving their small churches for the large mega churches. You might say, "Pastor, why do you keep coming down hard on the Christians in the large mega churches?" It is because the majority of them are not being properly fed spiritually. No pastor needs to come up with gimmicks or trickery in order to get people to give of their tithes and offerings. But they need to be shown exactly what the Word of God is saying.

For example, we are told in 1 Timothy 5:17–18 quote: The elders who direct the affairs of the church well are worthy of double honor, especially those whose work is preaching and teaching. For the Scripture says, "Do not muzzle the ox while it is treading out the grain, and "The worker deserves his wages."

If you are not willing to give your tithes and offerings unto the Lord, to help advance His Kingdom, then that is on you.

God will bless those who tithe; Proverbs 3:9–10 quote: Honor the Lord with your wealth, with the firstfruits of all your crops; then your barns will be filled to overflowing, and your vats will brim over with new wine.

CONCLUSION

Despite overwhelming evidence to the contrary, most people still believe that money brings happiness. Rich people craving greater riches can be caught in an endless cycle that only ends in ruin and destruction. How can you keep away from the love of money? Apostle Paul gives us some guidelines: 1. Realize that one day, all riches will be gone. 2. Be content with what you have. 3. Monitor what you are willing to do to get money. 4. Love people more than money. 5. Love God's work more than money. 6. Freely share what you have with others.

Luke 16:9 quote: I tell you, use worldly wealth to gain friends for yourselves, so that when it is gone, you will be welcomed into eternal dwellings.

If the love of money is destroying God's people, begin to start to turn all of this around and continue to give of your tithes and offerings to help advance the Kingdom of God.

2 Corinthians 8:9 quote: For you know the grace of our Lord Jesus Christ, that though he was rich, yet for your sakes he became poor, so that you through his poverty you might become rich.

Amen!

A PASTOR'S BIBLICAL FORMULA FOR PREACHING THE WORD OF GOD VOLUME 1

A Pastor's Biblical Formula For Preaching The Word Of God provides twenty-four completed sermons for the young pastor and the minister, and the teacher and the layman, and those pastors who are very busy; these sermons will last them for the next six months. These sermons are biblical and complete. It doesn't matter what Bible translation you use: KJV, the New KJV, The New American Standard Version, NIV, or so on. They all can be used along with this biblical formula.

Each of these twenty-four practical and easy-to-use sermons are structured in three sections. The first section shows you the Sermon Message. Next you have the body, in which the sermon title is presented in italics. The final section is the Conclusion, which allows you to wrap up your sermon in each chapter.

Here is a complete and comprehensive resource to help you preach or teach alongside the Word of God for the next six months.

KENNETH W. RUCKER is considered a people person, because he loves people and enjoys being around them. Kenneth has been in the ministry for more than twenty nine years, fourteen of which were spent pastoring New Bedford Heights Baptist Church in Bedford Heights, Ohio. Kenneth received his biblical training at the Minister Training Institute Seminary. He received his associate's degree in Biblical Studies, along with his bachelor's degree in Biblical Studies. Since 1996, he has been engaged in speaking in local churches and doing church revivals and participating in Bible church conferences. *A Pastor's Biblical Formula For Preaching The Word Of God Volume 1* is this author's very first book. You can look for other volumes to follow soon.